FREEDOM OF THE PRESS

FREEDOM OF THE PRESS

M.K. Joseph

ANMOL PUBLICATIONS PVT. LTD.
NEW DELHI - 110 002 (INDIA)

ANMOL PUBLICATIONS PVT. LTD.
4374/4B, Ansari Road, Daryaganj
New Delhi - 110 002
Ph.: 23261597, 23278000
Visit us at: www.anmolpublications.com

Freedom of the Press

First Published, 1997

Reprint, 2006

ISBN 81-7488-774-1

PRINTED IN INDIA

Published by J.L. Kumar for Anmol Publications Pvt. Ltd., New Delhi - 110 002 and Printed at Mehra Offset Press, Delhi.

Contents

Preface

'Freedom of Expression' is often treated as fundamental right. Press is the vocal organ of mass expression. In many countries freedom of Press is guaranteed by law. But in actual practice this freedom is frequently interrupted and restrained.

This volume, which is substantially based on the experiences of many renowned authors, put light on diverse aspects of the freedom of press. Major topics dealt herein are: Liberty of the Press; There is No Substitute for a Good Newspaper; Press, the Public and Foreign Policy; Commercial Outlook of Press Freedom; Press and the Policy Makers; The Utilization of News; Outward Flow of News; Libel; Free Press and Fair Trial; Review of Press and Journalism in England.

We are grateful to all the learned writers whose writings are cited or substantially made use of in the present book. Writers, journalists and students and teachers of journalism and law will find this book useful and informative.

Editor

Preface

Freedom of Expression is being treated as fundamental. The Press is the vocal organ of mass expression. In many countries freedom of Press is guaranteed by law. But in actual practice this freedom is frequently interrupted and restrained.

This volume which is substantially based on the experiences of many renowned authors, put light on diverse aspects of the freedom of press. Major topics dealt herein are: Liberty of the Press, Law is No Substitute for a Good Newspaper, Press, the Public and Foreign Policy, Commercial Outlook of Press Freedom, Press and the Policy Makers, The Ordination of News, [illegible] News, Checks upon Press and Fair Trial, Freedom of Press and Journalism in England.

We are grateful to all the learned writers whose writings are used or substantially made use of in the present book. We hope journalists and students and teachers of journalism and law will find this book useful and interesting.

Editor

1

The Liberty of the Press

In many countries the freedom of the press is nominally guaranteed by law, but this does not allow the conclusion that this liberty is really enjoyed. Sometimes the solemn declaration of the law that the printing press is open to everyone, who wants to express freely his opinions and thoughts, is followed by so many restrictions and prohibitions that this freedom remains practically on paper only.

In Great Britain no special rights are granted to newspapers; nevertheless, journalism is unfettered in the United Kingdom to an extent hardly achieved anywhere else. It is simply a matter of course; just as every Briton in his country may speak freely and independently, newspapers, too, are allowed to express their opinions, but 'the liberty of the press is no greater and no less than the liberty of every subject' [*R.*v. *Gray* (1900)].

This principle is not recognised everywhere. There are countries where the press is treated more rigorously than the citizen, because it is considered more dangerous than he, while elsewhere newspapers, owing to their mission to mould public opinion, are somewhat privileged. British courts regard journalism as an institution neither to be patronised nor to be prejudiced and, therefore, they judge journalists not better and not worse than ordinary citizens. 'The freedom of the journalist is,' according to the definition of a high judge, 'an ordinary part of the freedom of the subject, and to whatever lengths the subject in general may go, so also may the journalist, but apart from statute law his privilege is no other and no higher.... No privilege attaches to his position' (*Arnold* v. *The King-Emperor of India* (1914)).

For this reason a legal establishment of the freedom of the press seemed to be superfluous in Great Britain. It crystallised organically from the right of the citizen to the free expression of his personal opinion and went through all stages of the development to full political liberty. However, this freedom creates an obligation to the citizen as well as to the press. A person who violates a law is, as a rule, punished in Great Britain more severely than elsewhere. Also a British newspaper which misuses its liberty may often atone for it more heavily than journals abroad, although they may be subjected to various restrictions unknown in this country. The right of the press to speak its mind was for the first time embodied in the Constitutions of France and of the United States. These two important events took place almost simultaneously.

The French National Assembly in the meeting of the 24th August, 1789, passed the famous definition of press liberty: 'The free communication of thoughts and opinions is one of the most precious rights of mankind. Therefore, every citizen may express his views by words, writings, and printed matter, but he will be held responsible for any misuse of this liberty in the cases fixed by the law.' However, the United States of America had already incorporated the declaration of press liberty in the Constitution (The First Amendment of the Bill of Rights, 1791), and thus had become the first state to lay down this right in a law. According to it, the Congress shall pass no law restricting the liberty of the press and other rights such as freedom of religion, speech and meetings. In the same year of 1791 the definition of press liberty mentioned above was added as Article 11 to the French Constitution. Here, too, the provision stated that henceforth no regulation shall be passed which would restrict the liberty of the press. Such actions should even be liable to penalties.

These two proclamations of the liberty of the press had a far-reaching influence. In the Old and New World regulations following the French and American model were taken up partly by the constitutions, partly by the press laws of many countries where political liberty was achieved. The freedom of the press had become a symbol of the modern state. The Belgian Constitution pronounced with pride, after the victorious Revolution in 1830, that there would be no more censorship or regulations which would suppress the free speech. Other constitutions made similar promises. It sounded like a vow.

Freedom of the Press 'Forever'

Such assurances for the future are to be found in the constitution of many states of the American Union. They even outstrip the model of the Federal Constitution. 'The liberty of the press shall for ever remain inviolate.' 'The freedom of the press is one of the great bulwarks of liberty and, therefore, ought never to be restrained.' Also the Constitution of Virginia calls the liberty of the press 'one of the great bulwarks of liberty' and draws from it the conclusion that it 'can never be restrained but by despotic government.' In this way every government which ventures to restrict the liberty of the press is stigmatised in advance. According to other constitutions, e.g. to that of Mississippi, the freedom of the press 'shall be held sacred.' The French definition of the press liberty from 1789 recurs in the Constitutions of the States of Pennsylvania (art. 1, par. 7) and Tennessee (art. 1, par. 19).

Short-lived Press Liberty

The solemn declarations of the American Constitutions that the liberty of the press must be preserved for ever have been honoured. But in some European countries the good intentions of the legislators had been frustrated by sudden reactions. France is certainly the most marked example of it. Following the ups and downs of the political development of the country, the French press experienced time and again the various phases of liberty and restrictions. During the Great Revolution as well as in the years of 1830 and 1848, when reactionary governments were overthrown, newspapers in France enjoyed unfettered freedom based upon the most generous press laws, while during the intervals the press lost step by step all its rights, until it was completely muzzled, e.g. after the return of the Bourbons (1814-1830) and in the reactionary era of Napoleon III (1852-1870). But with the great revision of the French press laws in 1881, a period undisturbed by political reverses started, which finally brought the French press the blessings of a long spell of liberty.

Limits of the Freedom of the Press

The first French and American Constitutions already made provision against the misuse of the right of newspapers to express their opinion freely. The individual is to be protected from defamatory publications and the society from crimes against public order and morals in the widest sense. In real democracies the safeguard of the citizens' reputation is one of the main concerns of the press laws and no encroachment of newspapers upon the rights of persons can be justified by the liberty of the press.

In countries, however, where democratic institutions are not deeply rooted, it is more the protection of the authorities which governs the press than that of the individual. This difference becomes particularly obvious as far as the right of the press to comment on acts of the government, of the authorities, and of public officials is concerned. Press regulations do not always deal with this question and sometimes leave it to the ordinary criminal law. According to it, in the semi-democracies mentioned above, a defamation of a civil servant or of an administrative authority, to which every strong criticism may amount, is prohibited under all circumstances, and punishment is always imposed upon the critic or the responsible newspaperman. Consequently, this kind of criticism is silenced and freedom of the press is essentially curtailed, although the press laws concerned pronounce in the first Article that the printing press is open to everyone.

In no other country is this right to free criticism on acts of the authorities and their organs by the press more strongly emphasised than in the United States of America, where in actions for libel, particularly of criminal nature, the defamed newspaper-man is expressly allowed to plead justification. This provision goes back as far as 1734, when the editor of the weekly periodical *New York Weekly Journal*, John Peter Zenger, after having been remanded for 10 months, was tried for a harsh comment on the English governor, William Cosby. Although at that time the plea of justification was impossible, Zenger's counsel succeeded in satisfying the jury that the accused editor had, by his criticism, exercised a basic right due to every citizen. Zenger was acquitted and public opinion insisted later in the demand that in such cases the defendant newspaper-men should be allowed to plead justification. Finally, this right was introduced in the Constitution.

The natural limits of the freedom of the press, provided for the protection of the people, are chiefly laid down in the ordinary criminal law and concern, among others, publications of blasphemous or obscene character, further, instigations to commit crimes, and so on. In some press laws, however, the wording of these restrictions is open to interpretations and may be used by reactionary governments as a back door to censorship.

If, for example, contributions are regarded as unlawful, which might 'injure the national honour or dignity' (Portugal, Hungary), or which are intended to provoke harmful thoughts 'in intellectually weak persons' (Spain), and no details are given about the intention of the legislators or the meaning of these provisions, their application will depend upon the policy of the government.

Many press laws passed in the 1930s used such an obscure wording which could only be understood as a veiled attempt to deprive the press of its most valuable rights; for instance, if newspapers were ordered to have regard in their contributions to 'recommendations of the government based on the requirements of the Home and Foreign Policy' (Estonia). Sometimes such intentions were not even laid down in the laws. When the Fascists in Italy and the Nazis in Germany came to power and wiped out the independence of the press, they did not take the trouble to repeal the press laws which guaranteed the liberty of newspapers. They simply put their followers into the editorial chairs and achieved, without changing the law, that no free opinion could be expressed any longer in those countries.

Another method of restricting the liberty of the press in those years between the two World Wars was the so-called Press Agreements, by which the states concluding the treaty undertook to abstain from attacks in the mutual press. Such obligations could be, of course, only fulfilled if the authorities of the states concerned had the power to give their newspapers directions regarding their writings. An agreement of this kind was concluded between Germany and Austria in July, 1936, providing that the newspapers of both countries should not comment unfavourably on the policy of the partner, and a similar treaty, significantly called 'Press-Non-Attack-Pact,' was agreed upon by Poland and Lithuania in November, 1938, the purpose of which was also the omission of a propaganda unfriendly towards each other.

Prosecution of Press Offences

In the countries of the British Empire and in the United States of America, and also in large parts of Latin America (Mexico, Argentine, Paraguay, Venezuela, and others) no special press regulations exist. Even in France, the classic country of press laws, attempts have repeatedly been made to abstain from the introduction of such laws. As early as in 1819 the commission, charged with the preparation of the French press law, in its report, made the suggestion to embody the offences committed by the press in the penal law and to provide for them the proper penalties. The commission stated that, as there are still other means of publication than the newspaper, the press cannot be the subject of special legislation. But the Chamber rejected this point of view and created the notion of particular press offences, such as newspaper attacks on the Constitution, religion, and morals (1819). Moreover, they introduced at the same time the caution which is a special and exceptional measure against newspapers.

Still, in 1881, during the deliberations on the great French press law, the deputy Floquet proposed to return to the ordinary criminal law as far as the press was concerned. 'There are no special press offences,' he said. 'He who misuses periodical or other publications must be made responsible according to the criminal law. His Bill was rejected on the grounds that it was impracticable, since there were offences which could be committed by newspapers only and thus require laws which deal with the press. If the penal law were applied to newspapers, press offences would be tried either more leniently or more strictly than they deserve.

But even in countries where a proper press law does not exist, certain offences committed by newspapers, e.g. libels, are tried according to special regulations. Also the provisions concerning the formal requirements, to which newspapers are subjected, constitute a kind of special law.

2

There is no Substitute for a Good Newspaper

Two problems of the newspaper press have attracted the attention both of its management and of observers of the journalistic scene in the postwar period, which is the period of *Nieman Reports.* The two problems are related. One is the competition from the newer, more dramatic medium of broadcasting, with its more immediate reports. The other is to obtain and hold the talent to sustain the newspaper's role against the excitement of careers in television, and also against the ever-widening area of communication in government, public relations, and allied fields—all of them seeking the same talents as the city news rooms and willing to pay a premium to get them.

The competition with broadcasting in news has forced the newspaper to seek new ways to hold its readers. The most definite result of this has been the increased emphasis on interpretive reporting, to put more depth in the story.

Interpretive reporting began with much headshaking over the dangers of departure from the tradition of objective reporting. For a long time the *New York Times* was meticulous in labeling as "news analysis" any story that ventured into more explanation and background exploration than the surface facts. The debate continues, though obviously the broader and deeper report has added a permanent dimension to the press.

The other problem, attracting and holding a necessary share of journalistic talent, has very slowly pushed newspapers into recruiting and in-training programs for which they felt no need before television had stolen so much of the glamour of the newspaper job.

The self-examination of the newspaper induced by these two problems of the newer competition exposed also other factors that have lessened the appeal of journalism to many ably qualified young people. Questions have been raised as to the opportunity the newspaper affords to the idealistic reporter to uncover evils and campaign for reforms. How much has the business office restricted editorial freedom? How much has its merchandising role cramped the newspaper as crusader? Has it joined the ranks of big business as a bulwark of conservatism? Urgent discussion of all these aspects of the changing journalistic scene has occupied extensive space in *Nieman Reports,* some of it represented here.

As for television itself, the long-deferred hope to see television journalism free itself from its commercial blinders and realize its graphic potential has been reflected in the *Reports* from the first year. The complaint of the dominant control of the advertiser found classic utterance by television's great journalist.

Three years ago I was called into the office of the publisher of the *St. Louis Star-Times* and told that the next day's editions would be the last. I do not intend to conduct here a public post-mortem. I raise the subject because I think you are entitled to a sort of backdrop for what I am about to say. The main point is that for five and a half months I was an unemployed managing editor. They may well have been the most important months in my whole life because for the first time—literally, the first—I had to think.

All of us use the word "think" very loosely. We "think" this and we "think" that. We do nothing of the kind. We operate by a kind of mental prearrangement. Rarely do we sit down and really think—to reason things out, to weigh, to balance and arrive at conclusions.

I grew up in newspaper offices. There was nothing else I had ever wanted to do. Like everyone else, I learned a thousand and one what *nots* to do. I also picked up bad habits. From assorted bosses, I picked up some good attitudes, discarded some bad. Mainly, I operated on instinct. My politics had been partly formulated by boyhood exposure to a valuable and partisan father; by debate around newspaper offices; by some personal experience. My newspaper attitudes—fortunately, I think—had been fashioned principally by a youthful exposure to some great crusading editors—men who had both ideas and ideals.

Like every other managing editor, I had had my battles with the business offices. Perhaps some of them had been more intense than others had experienced. But even these arguments were instinctive on my part. I cannot truthfully say that they were every thought out and when I looked back I could see that many of my positions were arrogant and pig-headed.

My friends were wonderful. They tried to rustle up many jobs for me. Some flattering nonjournalism business offers were made. But did I want to leave newspapering? If I did stay in it, did I insist on being a managing editor? Did it matter what kind of newspaper I want to work for—providing, of course, they would give me a job? What about newspapering anyway? Was it worth the effort? Wouldn't I be better off in some cushy spot in business or industry? What was it I really wanted to do?

Well, I preferred newspapering. But not at the expense of my convictions. That, it seemed to me, was an empty life. What good would money be if you had to walk down alleys to avoid the people you knew? I would like to go to work for a newspaper that rather reflected my own attitudes—an honest newspaper; a clean one; a decent one—a *responsible* one.

I must be candid and tell you that I had all but given up hope of such a connection when the unanticipated telephone call came from Louisville. And I am quite aware that I am probably the one in a thousand who got the lucky break at a decisive moment. If I never have good luck tap me again, I am still ahead.

This is the backdrop. If it were not such a painful and unsettling process, I wish all of you could have the same opportunity to sit back and really think it through—not only to think backward, but forward as well.

If all of you had that opportunity, I am convinced that the field of newspaper promotion would move forward in seven-league boots.

For newspaper promotion, gentlemen, shares greatly in the indignities which are frequently heaped on good newspapermen and on potentially good newspapers. I have had my share of those indignities. In my time, I have had to promote old automobile contests, baby picture contests, bathing beauty contests, marathon dances, moving picture tie-in events, personal sketch artists, handwriting analysts, comic strip contests. You name it; I probably have had to promote it at some time or another.

Yet what did all these promote? The newspaper? No sir, not by a long shot. They degraded the newspaper. These events either made the advertising department think they were making some client delighted—which wasn't true—or the promotion manager had talked himself into believing that if he just promoted something, he was helping keep the newspaper's name before the public.

I shudder when I speculate on how many hundreds of thousands of dollars have gone down the drains in this type of inane, inept, unworthy, and useless promotion.

The conclusion is inescapable that there is no substitute for a good newspaper—honestly published, honestly sold, and honestly promoted. Check for yourself the list of America's top newspapers and you will find very little of the cheap and tawdry in either their production methods or their promotion activities.

Sure, you can buy circulation. And you can buy yourself broke, too. I do not have to defend that statement. The record also will bear that out.

Yet to this day there are publishers who will buy—on the recommendation of their circulation managers and promotion managers—contests, stunts, and assorted gimmicks designed to buy circulation. So the newspaper will add a few thousand papers. All the while, everyone knows that holding that circulation means paying a higher price on the next go-round. And still higher and higher. Nonetheless, this same type of publisher will have no hesitancy about sitting down to write a biting editorial about the insanity of a government permitting an ever-spiraling inflation.

I am one who has had my fill of newspapers which have to exist by peddling cheap insurance. Or by promoting newsboys' bands. Or by any other kind of expensive side-promotion to cover up the fact that what they are selling isn't really worth buying.

Some newspapers still believe that one way to get advertising clients and influence them is to give expensive parties and to buy expensive blocks of tickets for important events—charging the whole bill to promotion and then hammering down on all other expenses on the grounds that business conditions do not justify any leeway. These are the newspapers—the "Lucky Buck" promoters, the insurance peddlers, the sponsors of newsboys' bands, the party givers and the ticket buyers—which fail to understand Mark Ethridge's profound observation that the best newspaper dollar ever spent is the editorial dollar.

Men who who choose not to understand can easily misinterpret that statement. It takes some thinking to understand it fully and I repeat again that too many have not had the opportunity to get sufficient time to sit down and think.

Looking back, I have become more deeply convinced than ever that the newspaper advertiser can never be bought by any phony promotional methods. He may listen because someone has been nice to him; but he will not buy space for that reason. There is only one justification for his advertising: To bring results.

My first experience with this came a long time ago. It made a tremendous impression on me and embittered me for some years because I didn't understand.

I was about 19 at the time, a kid sports writer. Boyd Gurley was editor of the *Indianapolis Times* and in the process of winning the Pulitzer prize for breaking up the Ku Klux Klan in Indiana. The Klan—in retaliation for the steady drumfire of exposure—called for a circulation boycott and later an advertising boycott. The Klan was strong and circulation did drop. You can understand my consternation when advertisers also dropped out with alacrity—even those advertisers whom one would judge to be so emotionally involved in the crusade that you would almost take it for granted that they would see it through to the bitter end.

No thanks to them, of course, the crusade persisted and was successful. The Klan was destroyed as an organisation in Indiana. Circulation came back—then climbed. And the advertisers came back.

For years after that, I had only contempt for them. I looked upon them as moral cowards. Years later, I came to understand it more clearly and more tolerantly.

The advertiser has no morals. He is utterly and completely selfish—and undoubtedly has to be in order to survive. He may hate everything for which a newspaper stands—and yet be its greatest space-buyer. He may read a newspaper avidly because he likes its editorial viewpoint; yet the moment he is solicited for advertising he becomes a cold, calculating businessman.

Nothing in the way of phony promotion can change this single overriding factor. And yet so many newspapers waste the talents and time of promotion men trying to build solicitations and campaigns that deal in fantastic extravagance and overstatement.

I am proud to work for a company that undersells itself ever so neatly. I consider this phrasing a masterpiece of sound judgment: "We publish two good newspapers. They are read by everybody in and around Louisville. We sell advertising space at reasonable rates. It produces sales."

Four sentences. An intelligent, proud statement. And it has stood up for years.

Don't you think, too, that the same approach goes for the reader? It does. Down to the last detail. Given a good newspaper and good service, you have a reader who is constant, dependable, and loyal.

Isn't it a dreadful admission of weakness to buy billboards shrieking about "the best" comic strips? Or to run full-page office ads promoting a contest of some type or another?

Wouldn't the dollars be better spent improving the newspaper as a product?

If newspapering is to move ahead, we have to quit kidding ourselves about the media we are working with. That is one of the big troubles with it. We haven't understood it well enough. For too many years, we've had too many charlatans running around, making fancy speeches—and almost all of them covering up, attacking anyone who dares to criticize us, wailing about the dangers to freedom of the press, and about the designs of a big, bad government against us—and almost all of them heavy with the dreadful economic perils that beset us on all sides.

Once radio was listed as one of the dragons in the list. Lately, television has taken its place. Such nonsense.

It is time we ourselves—we who work with newspapers—took stock. We need no St. Georges come to slay the dragons. We need an understanding approach to our work. We need a proper assessment of the role the newspaper plays in society.

The newspaper is a curious anomaly in a free-enterprise society. It is, on the one hand, a business enterprise—unregulated and uncontrolled by the state; yet given certain privileges of expression by the constitution; a business yet a public utility, serving the needs of the people. If it is to succeed in its multiple roles, it must have an appreciation of its position—a humility of its role as a public servant—it must have assurance of its power—and, most of all, it must have a deep integrity, going all the way from owner to apprentice. Every single one who works with the paper must have a pride in his calling and in his product. And everyone must *want* to keep the freedoms which are so precious to all of us.

I recall vividly the calumny heaped by so many newspaper owners and editors upon the Commission on Freedom of the Press—the Hutchins Commission—back in 1947 when the report was issued. Get a copy of the book, *A free and Responsible Press,* read it and see for yourself the pathetic shortsightedness of so many newspaper executives. When you read it, you will readily see that the commission was serving nobly the best, long-range interests of the press.

It pointed out many of our weaknesses and it called for voluntary, internal reform in order to forestall any encroachment by government. The wiser and saner publishers and editors praised the report, but they were all but drowned out in the cacophony of those who to this day think almost every critic of the press is a violently dangerous enemy. These are the men themselves who are the most dangerous enemies to a free press. It is they who bring discredit on the whole profession by their money-grubbing, by their selfishness, and by their arrogance.

Let us look at the picture in its total form.

Newspapers have been, are, and probably will remain the most vital part of the nation's vast communications machinery. The total national circulation is tremendous. And it covers everything from the biggest cities to the smallest.

The news and picture magazines are popular, but they are a supplemental medium—no more than that. Where a newspaper in a city may have 100,000 circulation, a news magazine with more than 10,000 would be amazingly successful. I would estimate the figure to be half that.

Radio, I believe, has more news impact than the news and picture magazines. Television is still a lesser form of news competition. At this stage it is purely supplemental—but it has some great natural advantages and over a long period it may prove to have more adaptability than we presently believe.

Rather than being menaces, these competing media have had a salutary effect on newspapers. We have been forced to change emphasis; we have been compelled, by competition, to do many things better.

Let me hark back for the moment to the almost-forgotten day of the newspaper extra. Some of the older gentlemen here will recall with ease the day of the baseball extra. No week day afternoon was complete without it—home delivery routes and all. I wonder how many extras are put out now in the United States. Not very many. I'd guess, in a year's time.

What killed the extra? Radio. That simple. We couldn't compete with instantaneous transmission. But while it may have killed the extra edition, it didn't damage newspapers in the slightest. Circulations dipped, recovered and climbed. We found that sports interest had increased. And where once we were able to get by with perhaps ten columns of sports news, we had to go up to twelve and fourteen and sixteen and beyond. We found that radio wasn't such a terrible villain after all.

I remember when I was told that the introduction of the weekly picture magazines, on slick paper, was the beginning of the end. This we could not possibly compete with. Today, our newspapers are equipped with wire transmission photo equipment and it is the rare big-city newspaper which cannot within an hour reproduce a photograph taken in Washington or San Francisco, or even on a battle front five thousand miles away. We publish more pictures in a week than even the flossiest picture magazines—and we not only give the top national and international pictures, but the one field the national magazines can't possibly touch—the local pictures, the meat and potatoes of our daily existence.

We do so many things better than we once did. We have newspapers today which if they are not great newspapers, at least are very, very good newspapers. To me, it is no accident that these good newspapers are also successful newspapers financially.

To me, it also seems no accident that these are the newspapers which are carefully promoted—and by carefully, I mean prudently, sensibly, cleanly. The whole import of their promotions is to emphasize the quality of their products, the quality of their editorial content.

Which brings me back, full-cycle, to some of our weaknesses. I suspect that our greatest weakness as a group is stubbornness.

Let me take it first from the news and editorial side. News and editorial men have fallen down in their jobs these past several years in quite a few respects. One of them has been in failing to keep pace with the changing quality of our readers. Another has been in clinging to outworn and outmoded techniques of writing, editing, and producing newspapers. And still another has been a sort of ivory-tower attitude toward all other departments on the newspaper—as if we in the news and editorial deparments possessed all the brains available. Too many news and editorial men are contemptuous of the mechanical departments; supercilious toward the advertising and circulation departments; and blind as bats toward the usefulness of proper promotion.

I think almost the same things, in slightly different proportions, can be said of the failures of those in the promotion field. Promotion too, has failed to keep pace with the changing attitudes of the readers. It has clung to outworn stunts, presentations and assorted gimmicks. Promotion has seemed to be blind toward the possibilities of learning what the newspaper actually has to offer the customer.

Because some of us were trained in a certain way does not necessarily make that way the right one. I know of one publisher—now no longer a publisher—whose stubbornness was a thing of wonder. Once, many months ago, his newspaper had a big package deal with one of the major syndicates. He had all his comic strips in one basket. His major competitor made a backdoor deal, buying the whole package at double the price. You can imagine the publisher's consternation when the syndicate notified him that on the contract's expiration date there would be no renewal.

The publisher was in a panic. His plight was described to me in detail by the managing editor. The publisher tried desperately to talk the syndicate out of the cancellation. No soap. So—helter-skelter—he slapped together a whole new collection of comic strips and then waited fearfully for his day of doom.

What happened? Nothing. A few squawks here and there. A few stops and switches to the rival paper. But no catastrophe. You would think from this experience that the publisher would have learned that comic strips were not the answer; that good ones, bad ones, or indifferent ones, his newspaper's livelihood did not depend on them so urgently.

But, no. This gentleman proceeded then to enter into the most rigid deals for comic strips—long-term, ironclad contracts at fabulous prices—and some which never even appeared in his newspaper. And he called himself an astute business man. He was one of those who believed in billboards advertising comic strips as his paper's best offer and he continued these practices to the day he went out of business.

The cold truth of the matter is that all of our newspapers could dispose of comic strips today with no earth-shaking consequences. I have no particular desire to eliminate them. I think some of them are amusing. And I think the youngsters are particularly attached to them. My point is only that we are kidding ourselves if we insist they are essential. Any editor who has dropped a comic strip in recent years can testify that it makes practically no difference. I dropped one recently and as far as I know no one even knows it is gone.

Try dropping the vital statistics and see what happens.

The way to stay on top is to do the basic newspaper job—the printing of news—in clean and decent and complete fashion. Let's make our own advertising—the advertising of newspapers—a model for all other advertisers. Let us state the facts of the case honestly and with integrity.

—Norman E. Isaacs

3

The Press, The Public and Foreign Policy

Let us review the role of press, in this chapter and the part played by the public and framing of foreign policy based on press.

The belief among newspapermen that the citizen's requirement for more and more information about public affairs must be met by wider and wider distribution of news and opinion has its source as much in the historical development of the newspaper as in the independent elaboration of a democratic political ideology. In the first half of the nineteenth century, the conditions of newspaper publishing favoured journals of limited circulation, which were aimed at small and specialized communities of interest. It was only in the latter half of the century that a developing technology and an increasing urbanization made possible the larger journal that "synthesized the newspaper-reading audience by appealing in a single paper to a wide range of interests. Once the process was under way, competitive pressures sustained it; the increasing investment that newspapers represented in plant and in news-gathering facilities necessitated increased advertising revenues, which in turn meant that newspapers had to appeal to larger and larger publics by including in one inexpensive paper all the subjects and features that separate audiences had hitherto found in specialized publications. The big city newspaper had acquired much of its present form by the last quarter of the nineteenth century, and set the model for the papers in the rest of the country.

One result of this homogenization of the newspaper was the homogenization of the concept of the newspaper reader; the special interests of special readers were substantially lost in the adaptation of the newspaper to the interests, standards, and pastimes of a mass public that was lightly educated and in the market for diversion and amusement. Foreign affairs, a special subject that would have been easy to handle in the era of special-audience newspapers, came to pubic attention just at the time when the newspaper had successfully absorbed all areas and all subjects. The means of giving it wide public distribution were thus at hand when the movement for more democratic control of foreign policy spread in the early twentieth century. The juncture of these two phenomena further strengthened the image held by journalists (and others) of an undifferentiated mass audience for foreign affairs who should be and could be reached by foreign affairs coverage in the newspapers and, once reached, would be an unparalleled force, by virtue of its informed opinions, for wisdom and peace in the conduct of foreign policy.

In its capacity to withstand the direct and indirect assaults that have been made on this image in the years since it took clear shape, the American press has demonstrated not only its resilience but also its insensitivity to insight and knowledge. One of the earliest and most enduring attacks came from a young journalist; Walter Lippmann brilliantly dissected the theoretical premises underlying the role of the press in the public life of the American democracy, arguing that "It is not possible to assume that a world carried on by division of labor and distribution of authority, can be governed by universal opinions in the whole population.... Acting upon everybody for thirty minutes in twenty-four hours, the press is asked to create a mystical force called Public Opinion that will take up the slack in public institutions." The burden of Lippmann's criticism has been supported in recent years by the main lines of social science research in the field of mass communications, and also in the specific area of public opinion and foreign policy. This research has pointed to the differentiation in exposure and receptivity of individuals to communications on various subjects, and has stressed the connections between this communications behavior and political, social, and psychological variables. This line of inquiry in the communications field, focusing also on the different political and social roles of various audiences, has invaded modern schools of journalism and their affiliated research institutions as well as their professional journals; yet has not made much of a dent in the public philosophy of practicing journalists in the foreign affairs field, who seem to possess only the vaguest and most fragmentary notions of whom they are writing for, and the uses that this audience makes of their work. But what are the essential facts of the situation, and what do they suggest by way of alternative possibilities on the part of the press? How much is read, and by whom?

We noted earlier that the volume of international news was a small proportion of total news space in most newspapers, and that it was small in absolute terms as well. And we indicated then that if little foreign affairs news was published, even less was read, on the average (a most important qualification). The extent of such leadership is suggested in the American Institute of Public Opinion's readership survey of 51 newspapers, conducted for the International Press Institute; of the daily average of 106 column inches of international news from home and abroad that was published, the average number of column inches actually read by adult readers came to 12, or about a half a column. It was further estimated that only two and one-third minutes were devoted to reading this material. Other studies suggest the same general pattern of over-all readership of foreign affairs news.

These figures are likely to dismay anyone who is intensely interested in international affairs and who shares a philosophic concern for extensive public participation in foreign policy-making. They are also confusing to newspaper people, who often overlook the fact that these data represent an *average* of very different levels of interest in and exposure to foreign affairs news. The reactions of the press, in the face of this kind of evidence, are manifested in a continuing "debate" over who is to blame for the situation: the public, the newspapers, or both. One point of view claims that the reader sets the pace, that popular demand will not support greater coverage or more analytical content, and that the comparatively low volume of foreign affairs news in American newspapers represents the editors' normal response to lack of reader interest. A United Nations reporter, for example, said, "....I don't absolve reporters, editors and publishers and networks entirely of blame in this matter, but they cannot go beyond what the public demands." And a columnist explained why foreign correspondents write material that does not get into the papers: "It goes back to exactly the same thing we've been talking about—the American people are too distracted, too busy, too indifferent. They don't want it." This side of the debate has been able to introduce, as evidence to support its claim, the results of public opinion polls showing that the public is substantially satisfied with the existing amount of foreign affairs coverage in its newspapers, and is unwilling to see local or national news reduced in order to give more space to foreign news.

In view of the strength of their conviction that the reader determines the character and amount of foreign affairs news that is published, it is interesting that so few newspaper people acknowledge the inconsistencies that it gives rise to: in particular, the common situation wherein the newspaper gives the reader only a minimal dose of foreign affairs news, on the ground that he is not interested in the subject and will not take any more of it, and then puts that small dose on the front page and in lead positions, where it presumably responds to what editors refer to as "the public's news values." This circumstance points to the role of the press in forcing foreign policy material to the forefront of policy attention even though the large majority of the population would be as happy to see it sink into oblivion—and indeed immediately consigns it there. It is in this sense that the press should be seen as a significant part of the public audience for foreign policy, a creator of a structure of policy attention that has a very limited additional public audience and may never even be recorded in the mind of the *average* newspaper reader.

The contrary position in this argument is that the state of foreign affairs coverage, and therefore of readership, reflects editorial choices, and hence that editors and publishers rather than readers are responsible for the current conditions of coverage. News provides a situation in which the blame for the lack of material in the press is assigned, explicitly or implicitly, to the editors. Earl J. Johnson said: "After more than 20 years of pushing Latin American news on the wires, I've concluded that very few editors are really interested. Much is said at inter-American press meetings about the importance of printing more news from Latin American countries. But not much is done about it when the North American delegates return to their desks. An Associated Press house organ recently raised the question, "Is there a gap between what managing editors tell us they want and what their papers actually print?

Leo Rosten candidly put the responsibility on the editors, with the argument that "giving the public what it wants" is another way of saying "what we [i.e., the editors] *say* the public wants." Another important and familiar claim on this side of the debate is that the average reader is actually a lot more interested in foreign affairs than he is given credit for, and that his disinclination to read foreign affairs material in the press is due to the complexity of the material that is presented to him. The burden of altering this situation is thus transferred to reporters and editors, who are challenged, to present foreign news in terms that are correct, concise and, above all, clear."

Finally, there are others who are frankly puzzled over the location of responsibility, or who regard it as a "vicious circle," with both parties equally at fault. Thus, "Newspapers do not emphasize foreign affairs because the people are not interested, because they do not find much foreign news in their papers." This position is no doubt closest to the truth in the sense that the pattern of coverage is a response to perceived interests and priorities at both ends of the line. When the editor fails to draw attention to a subject because the prevailing news judgments give priority to other topics, then the majority of readers who are only marginally interested are not persuaded that it is important enough to read; and the editor in turn looks at the readership figures and draws justifiable conclusions about what people are reading. But the vulnerable part of this chain of reasoning, and of the whole argument, is the failure of the vast majority of reporters and editors to differentiate among their readers—to understand that some of the public *will* read more foreign affairs news if it is offered to them, even though there may be no new recruits to the over-all readership ranks of foreign affairs news. What patterns of readership are involved here?

Readership of foreign affairs news is a poorly understood subject despite the attention that has been paid to the problem of audience analysis in communications research. One reason for this is that efforts to delineate the audience structure of the media of mass communication have rarely focused explicitly on foreign affairs news as a classification of newspaper content. Another reason for the uncertainties is that the available data are apparently misleading, in the sense that they appear to overstate both the extent and the depth of newspaper reading in the foreign affairs field. To ask a sample of respondents where they get their information about foreign news events, and to learn that between 44 and 50 per cent of the respondents get most of their foreign affairs information from newspapers and a similar proportion from the electronic media, implies a level of exposure and information-seeking that exaggerates the true state of affairs. Similarly, to learn that "For their news on foreign affairs, more than 90 per cent of the population depends principally on ... the radio and the daily newspaper," or even that about 90 per cent of the population reads a daily newspaper, is also suggestive of a much higher state of exposure to the news in it that is actually the case. Studies of communities deprived of newspapers in the course of strikes make the point that newspapers fulfill social and psychological functions more often than intellectual or intelligence functions, even when readers express their loss in terms of missing "what is going on in the world." A more accurate impression of the extent of readership of international news is suggested by data from a survey in Albany, New York, in 1949. Forty-seven per cent of the respondents read "just the headlines" of the national and international news, 4 per cent did not read even that much, and another 4 per cent read "not much more than headlines." At the other end of the spectrum, 6 per cent claimed to read both kinds of news "very carefully," and another 1 per cent read international news carefully, but not national news. In the middle, 33 per cent picked and chose among items, and "sometimes read carefully, sometimes not."

Who are these few careful readers? They seem to be the same few people who show up as well-informed on repeated surveys of information on international affairs, the people whom Gabriel Almond called the "elites" and the "attentive public." Readership of foreign affairs news increases with age, education, and economic status; with an increase in these variables, the newspaper is used increasingly for information and decreasingly for entertainment; more men than women read such news; the larger the community (counting suburbs as part of metropolitan areas), the higher the interest in and readership of international events. Basically, however, it is educational level and socio-economic status that seem to be the best predictors of newspaper readership of foreign affairs.

The significance of all this is generally missed by newspapermen, many of whom tend to think that the market for foreign affairs news can be—and should be—enlarged by techniques of simplifying the news and making it more attractive, or even by providing more of it. But an individual's exposure to foreign policy communication and his interest in international affairs that directs that exposure are concomitants of attitudes that have deep roots in his psychological orientations and his social setting. And so long as this is the case, the important variables in determining interest and participation in foreign affairs and exposure to information on the subject will be found chiefly in the life patterns of individuals, in the things that are relevant to their perceptions of and orientations to the political universe, and only marginally in such ephemeral things as the way foreign affairs stories are written for the newspapers, the amount of pictorial or human-interest content in them, and so forth. These relevant variables change slowly, and they are not readily amenable to modification by the stream of information the very exposure to which they in fact regulate. Consequently, the hope that the audience can be expanded significantly by a greatly simplified discussion of foreign affairs is illusory. It is no doubt true that most newspaper readers find foreign affairs news rather complicated and difficult to understand, but it does not necessarily follow that their interest would be stimulated if the material were presented in more simplified ways or more abundantly. It is equally likely that their basic disinterest in the material contributes to their impression of its difficulty. Furthermore, even if the hope were not illusory, even if one could succeed in attracting substantially larger numbers of readers to a discussion of foreign affairs that has been simplified by the use of pictures and one-syllable words, leavened with human interest, and related to everyday life on Main Street, the degree of simplification involved would be so great as to cause some doubt whether there would be any net increase in the capacity of the American people to understand and think through the undeniably complex issues of international relations. In other words, simplications might succeed in drawing, a new audience, but to material that is so far from reflecting difficult international political realities as they confront responsible statesmen that it has no politically relevant public opinion uses.

Since the available evidence suggests that the chief market for foreign affairs coverage in the American press is a small policy and opinion elite, and a somewhat larger attentive public whose personal characteristics and interests are much the same as those of the policy and opinion elite, though their roles are not so specialized, it is important to think about foreign affairs coverage in terms of its relevance and usefulness for the professional and personal interests and needs of this audience. This argues for a quantitative and qualitative improvement, an up-grading, of foreign policy news and comment, rather than the down-grading that is implicit in the attempt to attract new people into the audience. But two problems immediately arise in connection with such a suggestion, and should be disposed of first: the philosophical problem wrapped up in "the people's right to know," and the practical problem of ensuring the survival of newspapers and even cultivating their prosperity through mass circulation.

Let us consider the latter first. The present endeavors of reporters and editors represent a compromise between the foreign policy interests of a few and the news values or tastes of a mass audience that "ought" to be interested in foreign affairs but presumably has to be seduced into reading about them. The practical effect is that the specialists and the attentive few are thus drawing and depending heavily on material written for a mass market that is relatively indifferent to the effort made on its behalf. This compromise is clearly not to the taste of any of the parties involved. Those who are steady consumers of foreign affairs news are dissatisfied from the running criticism of the press in intellectual circles. The large majority that rarely or never looks at foreign affairs news is most likely neutral towards its presence, in the sense that it is merely something these people walk around; but their non-readership is itself a good measure of their preference for other kinds of newspaper content.

It is possible to conceive of ways to satisfy the needs or preferences of a small audience for a higher order of foreign policy intelligence without raising the costs of publication, and without changing the character of a newspaper in ways that might alienate the larger number of non-readers—granting, however, that we do not even know what kind or proportions of material would give offense to people who do not read it. The important obstacle, it would seem, has been thinking about this problem in the context of the customary shape and format of the daily newspaper. But there is no reason why larger amounts and different kinds of foreign affairs content, whatever its sources, need take up more front-page space than at present, or be reflected more often in the dominant headlines. Since it would be meant to serve a specialized audience, it could be handled like other material that have few customers, like financial news or shipping news (or even materials like comics and sports that have many customers!): whatever was not deemed important by conventional standards could be put in an unobtrusive place without much regard for format, headlines, and the other trappings of "news." It is possible in this way to think of substantially increasing the amount of foreign affairs information in the average newspaper without changing the over-all identity of the newspaper and with only a very marginal increase in the costs of production.

Since such an endeavour would take nothing away from the present exposure of the general public to foreign affairs news, there could be no complaint about it on philosophical grounds that cannot already be leveled at the mass media. Despite the low level of attentiveness to problems of foreign policy and the low priority given them by the public at large, one can justify the general order of importance that the press attaches to a few foreign policy questions on the ground that it is important to pretend that everybody is listening—that acting as *if* foreign affairs were of widespread public interest has important consequences in the realm of public confidence in the basic actions of government. This particular function, however, can no doubt continue to be served by the present (comparatively small) allocation of front-page foreign affairs news, thus permitting us to think about additional coverage more in terms of the particular needs of particular audiences. In any case, since there is considerable evidence that much of the information on world affairs currently at the disposal of the general public comes to it not directly from the media but at one remove or more, via people who have a greater interest in the subject and expose themselves to mass media discussions of it, any alternative that increases the flow of information and analysis to these primary consumers should result in a subsequent larger flow to *their* secondary audience. Thus the broad political-philosophical purposes of press coverage of foreign affairs can be served by additional news that is directed primarily towards its few direct and heavy readers than to its many marginal scanners.

Further support for this argument stems from the point, made earlier, that the press is itself one of the most important components in the public audience for foreign affairs. From this point of view, greater press responsiveness to foreign policy developments and problems of foreign affairs, even in the form of specialized inside-page coverage of them, would inherently enlarge the scope of interaction between the government and its foreign policy public. Hence, increased coverage and more substantial analysis of more specialized problems as well as of issues already "in the news" would be an important contribution to democratic foreign policy-making even if this material were read only by foreign policy officials and a small group of attentive citizens. At its best, it might narrow the range within which major miscalculations in policy might be made as a consequence of insufficient exploration of alternatives and their implications within the confines of a bureaucratic structure, and as a consequence of insufficient interchange of value premises and preferences among policy officials and articulate people on the outside.

4

Commercial Outlook of Press Freedom

It is useless to criticise the press without relation to its trading position. But terms of trade are not all. The freedom of the press does not exist in order that newspaper owners should grow rich. It is not a possession of newspapers or their proprietors or editors but of the community, won by many who were not journalists, as well as many who were, during that long struggle for freedom of religion, opinion and association and for the independence of Parliament, judiciary and press on which our democratic society rests. Those responsible for a newspaper are in a different position from those responsible for a business who may properly govern their activities by what is commercially advantageous to themselves, their employees and their shareholders: they have inherited other calls on their fidelity. A newspaper must sell to live, but it cannot claim that what sells most is by that fact alone justified. It has other obligations: obligations to the past, for newspapers would never have known independence if earlier men had not been ready to sacrifice themselves for principle; obligations to the present and the future, for the press is as much a custodian of national freedom and the qualities of civilisation as Parliament or the courts. It cannot turn its back on these obligations without reducing its stature, for it is on them that its stature depends.

Those who control or write for newspapers have no more

right to claim immunity from the historical responsibilities of their office on the excuse that these responsibilities come between them and commercial advantage than have Members of Parliament or judges: the positions of all three in our society are analogous, just as the independence of the press was won in the same struggle as that for a free Parliament and an independent judiciary. The journalist is not buttressed as they are by constitutional safeguards; his status and the principles which must govern him in the exercise of his duties are less firmly rooted in acknowledged tradition and less clearly defined. Unlike them he is a hybrid, a Janus with two faces, a two-purpose beast. He has commercial obligations they do not have. But he has obligations to society not less important than theirs. It is by the manner and degree in which these dual demands are reconciled that the press is properly to be judged. The nature of the reconciliation is not the same for every age, nor is it the same for all newspapers. But its compulsion exists for all and at all times.

Recognising this special relationship of a newspaper to its readers the owners of some have voluntarily made over their property to non-profit-making trusts, others have deliberately imposed restraints upon themselves or their heirs in the matter of a sale.

The control of three national newspapers, the *New Chronicle* (with its companion evening paper, the *Star*), the *Manchester Guardian* (with its evening companion, the *Manchester Evening News*) and the *Observer*, is vested in non-commercial, non-profit-making trusts, the *Daily News* Trust, the Scott Trust and the *Observer* Trust. These trusts are required to devote their income firstly to development and secondly to charitable and educational purposes so that there shall be no question of their newspaper properties being run purely for the profit of individual share-holders or proprietors, now or in the future.

The Times is under ordinary commercial ownership but its future is similarly safeguarded by articles of association which require that any transfer or ordinary shares shall be subject to the approval of a committee which was truly formidable and diverse body. In giving or withholding approval this committee is required to have regard to the importance (a) of maintaining the best traditions and political independence of *The Times* and national rather than personal interests and (b) of eliminating as far as reasonably possible questions of personal ambition or commercial profit. The sale of shares to a Corporation is prohibited.

Safeguards of similar effect are contained in the articles of association of both the *Economist* and the *Spectator*. Restrictions on the transfer of shares to prevent any basic change in the character of the paper also operate in the case of a number of important provincial journals, among them the *Yorkshire Post*, the *Liverpool Daily Post* and the *Birmingham Post;* indeed the present owners of the latter paper and its evening companion, the *Birmingham Mail*, are required by a trust deed established when they bought the property in 1944 and effective until 1965 to conduct the two papers on substantially the same lines and with substantially the same policies as under the previous owner, the late Sir Charles Hyde. In particular they are required under this trust (1) to provide a full and impartial news service with only such comment as is fair and free from bias and (2) to preserve the independent and local character of the newspapers and their freedom from control by any political party or trade association or any London newspapers or any combine or syndicate of newspapers.

Although very far indeed from being universally accepted, the principle that commercial consideration wholly proper in the general conduct of business are not so in the conduct of newspapers is thus formally recognised by several newspapers to whom the influence the press can exert seems more important than profit.

What is the extent of this influence? Contrary to some expectation there is no evidence that it has been diminished by broadcasting or is likely to be much affected by television. The difference between the two mediums is too great. This difference was well set out by the editor of *The Times* and former director-general of the B.B.C., in his Clayton Memorial Lecture to the Manchester Literary and Philosophical Society on 'The Public Influence of Broadcasting and the Press' three years ago. I am grateful to him for his permission to quote from it. Comparing the influence of press and broadcasting he asked his listeners to bear in mind the limitations of broadcasting before coming to any judgment. The first of these limitations he suggested was its inaccessibility.

Broadcasting Vs. Newspaper

'This may,' he went on, 'seem surprising, but ubiquity and accessibility are not the same thing. Broadcasting is geographically the most pervasive means of communication yet devised. Simultaneously it can enter millions of homes: be available to everyone in the land. But that simultaneity is also one of its greatest drawbacks. If you are not available to hear the broadcast then you cannot recapture it. A newspaper can be read during any hour of the twenty-four, a broadcast (I am not speaking primarily of news bulletins, which are repeated) must be heard when it is made.... The effect is made all the worse by the vast area of interests that broadcasting has to cover. A day's broadcasting, even in the spoken word alone, ranges far more widely than any newspaper (or indeed than all newspapers combined). But again whereas in a newspaper the reader can turn from one column to another, or from one page to another instantaneously—and read whatever he chooses at whatever pace he wishes—the listener can only go from subject to subject as they are offered over long stretches of time, and then cannot take any broadcast faster than it is delivered. Only the complete leisured, bedridden, or fanatically single-minded listener can get from his wireless set as comprehensive a service as he gets from his newspaper....

'Further there is the limitation—and this applies above all

to the news bulletins—of the space factor. (In broadcasting space is time). The fifteen-minute news bulletin contains under 2,000 words—that is less than two columns of the *Manchester Guardian*. In that compass everything from world events to Parliament and sport has to be compressed. It is good discipline in concentrating on essentials but it has its drawbacks.'

Broadcasting has it is true some strengths that newspapers do not have. The first, as Sir William Haley pointed out, is immediacy, not merely in time but in contact: the ability, particularly where television adds vision to sound, to bring events to the listener or viewer in the home when they are actually taking place. When it comes to great occasions, historic events, or even sporting encounters then broadcasting comes into its own. The heart can be lifted or depressed, the profoundest emotions can be stirred. Some broadcasts live in the memory for ever, as no newspaper report can hope to do.

Yet this being said the balance is still heavily on the side of the press. 'Newspaper production, is an infinitely simpler and more flexible operation. It is therefore capable of far greater adaptability. On a matter such as the Budget, or devaluation, or some scientific revolution, the press can at once provide a wealth of information, opinion, discussion, illustration that would take days to assemble at the microphone (and then be physically unmanageable on the same scale when it got there). In political matters the press is far freer and less inhibited. This has nothing to do with the B.B.C. monopoly; similar limitations affect American broadcasting. Because its output can be comprehended—I am using the word in the sense of being all-embraced and not merely of being understood—by each individual reader, a newspaper can have an impact which no broadcasting station can have.'

Sir William Haley's paper was read before Commercial Television had come into operation in Britain, but I doubt whether he would feel it necessary to alter much of what he had to say on that account. This is not to discount the impact of television. No one who has appeared regularly on the television screen and found himself hailed as an old friend by strangers in bars and restaurants, on buses and trains and in the street, and precipitated into scores of discussions on the various subjects dealt with in his programme is likely to do that. Television and sound broadcasting clearly have an immense and pervasive influence on social attitudes and social values.

So far as the most popular programmes of entertainment and family interest are concerned this influence tends to be directed to sustaining mediocrity as the most acceptable social value. But it can hardly be doubted that in their more serious documentary and discussion programmes broadcasting and television open windows on the world for many people and stimulate a good deal of interest in public affairs that would otherwise remain dormant. Yet for the reasons given by Sir William Haley this influence, although often more direct and sometimes more profound than that of the press, cannot compete with it in total extent.

Scope of Television & the News

Nor is television likely to rival the press in the field of news itself for the truth is, as Sir william Haley pointed out, that 'a great deal of news, particularly the most significant and important news, has no visual quality'. In most instances the nature of the medium is bound to be at war with the real values of the news. This is not, of course, true in every case. The impact made by a television reporter who brings to the microphone in front of a television camera Jews and Arabs in the Middle East, there to express in bitter broken English their hatred to each other and of Britain and their longing for war as a means of salvation, is likely to be much greater on those who see it than a dozen newspaper dispatches warning of crisis. But over the whole range of news the television camera cannot compete with the newspaper.

On the premise that he who pays the piper calls the tune it is the newspaper owner who is now generally regarded as possessing this great influence. It would not have been thought so in earlier times. It was Barnes, not John Walter II, whom Lord Lyndhurst dubbed, 'the most powerful man in the country,' and J.A. Spender, as recorded earlier, felt it incumbent upon him as editor to disabuse his chief proprietor, Sir Alfred Mond, of the idea that a proprietor had any right to use his paper for the expression of his own opinions—even in its letter columns. Lord Northcliffe is frequently thought to have altered all this. But in fact he did so only as regards a part of the press—and that the least politically influential.

The influence that C.P. Scott of the *Manchester Guardian* exercised—and it was infinitely greater than that of Northcliffe—was exercised as an editor, not as a proprietor, although the fact that he inherited his uncle's financial control of the paper naturally helped him immeasurably in making it what he wanted it to be, as many another editor struggling against proprietorial caprice has woefully reminded himself. *Geoffrey Dawson* was a master of publicity whose ability as such 'enables him to associate himself, and to be associated by others, with political movements and events with which in nine cases out of ten he has hardly the remotest connection.'

He indeed had a genius for identifying himself so completely with the *fait accompli* in politics that in the eyes of the uninformed he became the person responsible for it. In fact in most instances his part was small; absurdly so compared with that of Dawson. This was due in part, no doubt, to the fact that Dawson had an infinitely greater understanding of the real nature of political power and a much more subtle comprehension of the springs of political action than Northcliffe had. But it was also due to the very nature of their functions as proprietor and editor.

The influence exercised by a newspaper derives from the nature of the medium—from the fact that it arrives daily before its readers as an ambassador from the outside world conveying to them news of events as seen through the eyes of its staff, docketed and assessed in importance and interest by men working daily at high speed, interpreted and commented on by men required by the nature of their task to make immediate judgments.

The Character of a Newspaper

The character of a newspaper may be set in a certain mould by its proprietor. But even with such a newspaper the selection of news and features, the twist and turn given to the reporting of events, the total flavour of the daily dish put before the public, reflect, and cannot help but reflect to a very large degree, the personality and judgment of the man who does the daily job of producing it—the editor. The proprietor may inspire the big political campaigns. They seldom, experience indicates, have much influence anyway. It is the editor who makes each daily issue what it is.

It is curiously the case indeed—although some newspaper proprietors and managers do not even yet appear to have got around to the fact—that the commercialisation and popularising of the press so far from diminishing the importance of the editor has in many ways enhanced it—even by the standards of commercial success themselves. That great newspapers are made by great editors the whole of newspaper history shows. But it is also the case that popular papers depend for their success upon their editors to a degree not always sufficiently appreciated for their own good by those who profit from them.

Editor's Role in a Successful Newspaper

There is indeed nothing like a good editor for a newspaper. Whatever may be the level of journalistic success to which they aspire, only those newspapers that hold their editors seem to succeed. The correlation between stability of tenure in the editor's room and a newspaper's success, whether in prestige or circulation, is so close, in fact, as almost to provide the basis for a mathematical formula for the guidance of ambitious newspaper proprietors.

This is obviously so in the case of the more serious

newspapers: no one has ever disputed the importance of its editor to *The Times* or the *Manchester Guardian*. Similarly the *Observer* has been made by two editors, the first that great journalist J.L. Garvin who created serious Sunday journalism, the second David Astor who, coming to the editor's chair young and with little political experience, so that many regarded him as no more than his father's—and mother's—son, has shown himself an editor of great courage and ability, giving to the paper new life and vigour.

The *Sunday Times* has been equally sparing in its use of editors. It has had two only in the period of its great modern revival. So also has the *Telegraph*, which owes its amazing progress over the last twenty years to the fact that the first Lord Camrose disposed of all other daily newspaper interests when he acquired it, and became not, as its previous proprietor had been, its manager, but its editor-in-chief, attending daily at the office to conduct its journalistic affairs, even to the reading of all proofs.

It is, however, when one turns to popular journalism where the unimportance of the editor compared with the proprietor is now sometimes accepted as a proven fact that the principle demonstrates itself in the most surprising way. There are no doubt a number of reasons for the success of the *Daily Express*, the biggest of all being Beaverbrook. But one of the most important is that it has had only three editors in its more than fifty-five years life and that its present editor, Mr. Arthur Christiansen, has now been in undisturbed possession for close on a quarter of a century.

In fact although the industrialisation, commercialisation and popularisation of the press have done a good deal to alter the face of journalism they have done nothing to impair the basic journalistic fact that newspapers are made by journalists. This was first demonstrated a century and three-quarters ago when the *Morning Chronicle* fell in circulation by two-thirds as soon as Perry, whose editorship had raised it to greatness, left. It is the daily impress of an editor's personality that gives a newspaper character whether the character be grave or gay, austere or scandalous.

Moreover, the importance of the editor which seemed at one stage in the commercialisation of the press to be in so much danger of being diminished seems likely to become not smaller but larger as time passes. The age of the strongly individualist newspaper proprietor who himself impressed as editorial personality on his paper is almost over: we are moving into the era of the administrators. Only Lord Beaverbrook remains of the old breed. And even he although he has no difficulty in controlling his newspapers by telephone—or telepathy—wherever he happens to be is growing old. The first Lord Camrose is dead, Lord Kemsley's empire shrinks around him. The second Lord Rothermere shows (fortunately for his properties) none of his father's passion for using newspapers as platforms for personal publicity.

Large circulations and greater costs have increased the capitalisation of newspaper companies, making it more difficult, especially in an age of heavy taxation and high death duties, for one man to own a newspaper and virtually impossible for even the richest to dream of starting one. The characteristic pattern of newspaper ownership in the national press, although less so in the provincial morning press where family ownership still persists, is now becoming that of the large public corporation in which many commercial interests have to be taken into account.

The ownership of the *Daily Mirror* with a readership greater than any other on earth so far from being in the personal possession of one single proprietor, or even of a small group of proprietors, is so widely spread over so many shareholders, many of them small shareholders, that it is quite impossible to give any specific answer to the often repeated question 'Who owns it?' The largest single block of shares, some 22%, is held by the *Sunday Pictorial* Limited. As, however, the *Mirror* is in its turn the only large shareholder—and at that a minority holder—

in the *Sunday Pictorial*, and as the rest of the *Pictorial* shares are spread as widely among the ordinary investing public as those of *Mirror*, this does nothing to concentrate ownership in one group of hands.

Only three national newspapers still remain in private ownership in any complete sense: *The Times* in which Lord Astor of Hever holds 90% of the shares and Mr. John Walter 10%; the *Daily Telegraph* in which the Berry family hold all the ordinary shares; and the *Daily Express* of which Lord Beaverbrook's absolute mastery has never been in any doubt—even although he did announce in 1929 that he had given his controlling interest to his eldest son, the Hon. William Maxwell Aitken, and in 1954 that he had given the same controlling interest to the Beaverbrook Foundation, a British Empire Educational Trust.

The age of the press lord moves into history to be replaced by that of the big business administrator.

The substitution of ownership by public corporations for ownership by individuals does not of course mean, any more than it does in other industries, that effective managerial control is not in fact vested in the hands of a very few people. In this industry, as in others, the control over very large capital enterprises can be exercised with masterful ease through voting control over minority blocks of shares—at any rate so long as things are going well. But it does make it less likely now than in the past that newspapers will become the personal vehicles of dynamic personalities and more likely that their commercial control will pass increasingly into the hands of high-grade salaried executives. The managerial revolution came to Fleet Street somewhat later than most other places but it is by now firmly entrenched there.

As for the consequences, they may turn out both good and bad. The vast conglomerations of press power in a few individual hands which seemed likely to become the most characteristic feature of newspaper development in the twenties and thirties obviously had greater potentialities of public mischief, although the danger, like the political influence of the press lords, tended to be over-exaggerated by the nervous. To that extent the extension of ownership by public corporations is to be welcomed.

But although there may be risks in a newspaper becoming the personal mouthpiece of one man there are dangers of a different kind in its becoming simply a business. The great press lords made fortunes out of journalism, but all of them—even the first Lord Rothermere although to a lesser extent than the others—were prepared at times to put both profit and circulation second to the advocacy of what seemed to them important. Lord North-cliffe's attack on Kitchener in the First World War may, as Geoffrey Dawson for instance claimed, have come long after Kitchener had been entirely discredited in governing circles and may have had the effect of making it not more but less easy to get rid of him. But it was conducted by Northcliffe in a spirit of patriotism that did not count the effect of public reaction on the *Mail's* circulation. The *Daily Express* is as brilliantly entertaining and unpredictable a newspaper as it is because Lord Beaverbrook has always been ready to use its profits to make it a better one, spending large sums to give real news more promptly and sometimes more fully than its competitors and following a policy of ploughing money back into development at a rate that his successors may find both difficult and unattractive.

The real danger facing a good deal of journalism today, in fact, is not, as it seemed to be a generation or two ago, that much of its historic duty of public information may be twisted to serve the propaganda purposes of powerful individuals but that it will be pressed into a pattern that denies it all purposes other than the purely commercial one of attracting the largest number of paying customers by whatever means comes most readily to hand.

The responsibility of journalists, and especially of those in editorial authority, will become especially great if this should prove to be the case. The defence of journalism as more than a trade and greater than an entertainment technique—although a trade it is and entertaining it must be—is properly the journalists' and no one else's. It is they who are the legatees of history in this respect. They have both a professional and a public duty to look after their inheritance.

Relationship between the Editor and the Publisher

This is not, of course, to suggest that the interests of editor and publisher are necessarily antagonistic. They are far from having proved so in many famous partnerships of the past: they are very far from being so in many instances today, indeed it is difficult to see how any newspaper can succeed at the highest level except when they are identical. Nor is it to suggest that the proprietor and publisher is necessarily likely to be less concerned with the truest interests of the press than is the journalist; this has certainly not proved so on many occasions since the days when Henry Sampson Woodfull, the owner of the *Public Advertiser*, gladly risked prison in order that "Junius" should have a platform for his views. Nevertheless the guardianship of journalistic values rests primarily with the journalist: *c'est son metier*. He cannot disassociate himself from this responsibility without ceasing, in a fundamental sense, to be a journalist. Nor is there any final excuse for him in the claim that he is, after all, simply a hired man who must do as he is bid. He must be ready, as much all men when issues of principle arise, to stand up and be counted.

The relationship between editor and publisher can never be simple—unless indeed it is so simple as to make the editor no more than a paid servant. The Royal Commission on the Press was content on the whole to accept this simple version as the correct one—especially in relation to popular newspapers. But to do so is, in fact, to set aside a good deal of what is most important in the history of the press and to overlook the fact that the freedom of the journalist—freedom not only from censorship or intimation by the State but from censorship or intimidation by anyone including his own employer—is an essential part of press freedom.

This freedom involves the right of individual reporters to report facts honestly even if they prove inconvenient to the fancies or prejudices of editors or news editors, it involves the freedom of foreign and political correspondents to report and interpret the evidence before them according to their independent judgments and journalistic conscience, even if to do so is awkward for the policy of the paper that employs them, and it most certainly involves the degree of independence possessed by an editor in his relations with his publisher. Such independence clearly cannot be absolute. Whether a newspaper is owned by an individual, a joint stock company or a trust the right to decide the kind of newspaper it is to be, the sort of public it is to aim for, and the policies it will in general support must rest mainly with those who own it.

Mainly but not entirely, for a newspaper is more than a piece of property, it is a living personality with a character and tradition deriving not only from those who own or edit it but from its readers, from the interests it has historically served, and from the community of which it is a part, a fact, as earlier shown, recognised by some proprietors through the formal instrument of trust deeds and articles of association. This double responsibility is especially true of those newspapers that serve a specific local community, nourished, as C.P. Scott said of them, 'by its resources, reflecting in a thousand ways its spirit and its interests,' so that they 'in a real sense belong to it.' To alter the character of such a paper for reasons solely of increased profit, or to buy and sell it as though it were no more than a piece of merchandise without regard to the purposes and policies that have won for it its special place in the community, is an abrogation of the true responsibilities of newspaper ownership, although one which some of those who have made large profits out of newspapers have found by no means uncongenial.

Free enterprise is a valuable bulwark of a free press. But the freedom of the press differs from, and ought always to be recognised as greater than, the simple freedom of an entrepreneur to do what he pleases with his own property. A journalist has commitments to the commercial interests of those who employ him. But he has other loyalties also and these embrace the whole relationship of a newspaper to its public.

This is equally so whether the character of a paper derives from the authoritative discussion of public affairs or from its power to interest and entertain a wide variety of readers whose concern with public affairs is limited and intermittent. The influence of a newspaper on its readers derives not only from its expressed opinions but from its daily selection of news, the honesty of its reporting, the weight of its headlines, the values it emphasises in its features, the whole picture of the world and what is important in it that it daily presents to those who read it. By the very nature of daily newspaper production these depend more upon the editor and his staff than on anyone else. The editor is legally responsible for all that appears in the paper he edits; his moral responsibility is not less. He ought not to be allowed to escape it. But he ought also to be put in a position to sustain it in the public interest no less than his own.

The correct working relationship between a newspaper editor and his proprietor or publisher is not easy to define. It has been much discussed, although less so in Britain that in some other countries. In Norway the leading journalists' associations have defined the correct relationship as one that, within the broad framework of policy laid down for a paper by its owners and mandatory on it by reason of its traditions, gives the editor 'complete freedom to maintain his own opinions even though they may not in some cases be shared by the publisher or management,' and that places upon him 'the entire responsibility for the editorial content of the paper.' 'He must not,' according to this definition, 'allow himself to be influenced to uphold opinions which are contrary to his conscience and conviction.

He directs and accepts the responsibility for the activity of his editorial staff.' This definition has been largely accepted by influential Norwegian public opinion and has been reflected in the constitution of the leading newspapers.

Much the same is true in Sweden. Thus although the editor of the leading Swedish Liberal paper, the *Dagens Nyheter*,is required under the terms of his appointment to consult with the chairman of the board on major political matters it is also stipulated in the paper's constitution that it is the view of the editor and not of the chairman that shall be decisive in such matters and that political questions shall not be discussed at board meetings but shall determined by the political staff of the paper. Approximately the same procedure rules in the chief Swedish Conservative paper, *Svenska Dagbladet*. A number of Dutch papers have similar provisions in their company-statutes requiring that so long as he holds office the editor shall have absolute independence in his decisions on the editorial contents of the paper.

In Britain independence in the control of editorial policy is similarly guaranteed to the editor of the *Manchester Guardian* under the Scott Trust and also to the editor of the *Manchester Evening News*. Although formally the articles of association of *The Times* vest control of policy in the chief proprietors in practice the independence and authority of the editor is virtually absolute. That of the editor of the *Observer* is specifically safeguarded in its articles of association.

Such independence is far from belonging to the editors of most great commercial newspaper enterprises. Nor, since their purpose and the relations they have with their readers are so different, would it be wholly appropriate. Yet although the relationship between editor and publisher necessarily differs on a popular mass-circulation newspaper from that on a journal of opinion the diminution in the status of the editor to no more than a paid servant of proprietorial interests, the mere tool of other men's whims and financial appetites, that has accompanied a good deal of the commercialisation of the last half century or so runs dangerously counter to the public interest and is contrary to the traditional role of journalism in public life.

The journalist is at once freer and more vulnerable than the barrister, the solicitor, the doctor. Freer because he belongs to a more open profession that recruits men and women of diverse experience through many different doors and must be able to do so if it is maintain its true character; more vulnerable because he is a wage-earner dependent for the most part on one employer. Yet his professional responsibilities to the public are not less than theirs. The obligations imposed upon them in their relations with the public and supported by the powers vested in their governing professional bodies, the Bar Council, the Law Society, the General Medical Council, are not applicable to him in the same form. Yet the preservation of the strictest ethical and professional standards in the press is no less important to society than in their case. And because he is dependent, to an extent they are not, upon the goodwill of a single employer, the journalist may find himself less able than they to resist pressures that would reduce them.

The journalist ought to accept and ought to be required to accept standards of professional integrity morally not less mandatory than those of the barrister, the solicitor or the doctor. But what is required in their case to safeguard the public against professional malpractice is required in his case not only for this reason, important though it is, but also to provide the journalist himself with a safeguard against those pressures to which one who is dependent upon a single master may find himself vulnerable: a professional power to set against, and if necessary act as a counter-balance to, the immense and growing power of financial control in the newspaper industry.

It is possible that the Press Council will provide such a counter-power: indeed there are already some signs that it is beginning to do so. At the time of its foundation I took the view, as did several members of the Royal Commission out of whose recommendation it was born, that there would have been great advantage in establishing the Council as a statutory body with powers analogous to, although not identical with, those of the General Medical Council. Such a statutory body would from the beginning have entered the field able to provide a valuable counter-balance to the massive power of commercial interest, which ought not to be left to decide alone the standards by which popular journalism is to live. Yet it is possible that a voluntary Press Council may in the end succeed in doing this no less effectively. The moral pressures it can bring to bear, both on proprietors and journalists, are considerable. Its specific judgments may be overridden, but they can serve to create a general climate of public and professional opinion that cannot be ignored so easily and whose effects may be pervasive and far reaching. To create such a climate is the most important of all the responsibilities that rest upon the Council. It is a responsibility to which it is applying itself with considerable courage and in which it needs all the public and professional support it can get.

Yet whatever the Press Council may do it is upon the individual journalist that the ultimate responsibility rests. He is the legatee of a great tradition. He cannot abdicate. He has loyalties greater than to his pay packet and they should be paramount.

5

The Press and the Policy Makers

Role of Press and Foreign Policy Makers

An inquiry into the role of the press in foreign policy-making that examined only the 'behavior of the press would be one-sided, for it would miss the range of interactions that complete the circuit between press and policy maker. The "mirror" that the press holds up "by which its readers can see the world" is not fashioned exclusively by the initiatives of the press, nor is it the product solely of the criteria of judgment that mark the news-gathering and editorial processes. Foreign affairs news comes out of an interplay between the correspondents and the men of responsibility whose thoughts and actions are the objects of the correspondents' interest. The figure of the mirror, indeed, is rather inappropriate on a number of accounts; the glass that the press holds up is refractive rather than reflective, and the beams that come out of it strike the policy makers as well as a larger public. The readers, in particular, include both the members of the press itself and those who dwell in the policy-making structure—that is to say, those who manage the prism are also managed by it. And so in our search for an understanding of the significance of the press in the foreign policy process, we must look at the uses to which the press is put by foreign policy officials, and the patterns of thought that shape those uses. The policy maker both contributes to and extracts from the fund, or the flow, of foreign policy news; and both the putting in and the taking out help to define the nature of the press's participation in the process of foreign policy making.

A GUIDE TO "THE PRESS"

The newspapers in the United States are all part of the ill defined, amorphous institution known as "the press." Equally apparent, however, is the fact that no one, not even a large extractive industry like the United States government, can assimilate or even be exposed to more than a small part of the institution. What does the foreign policy press look like to the officials in the Executive and Legislative branches of the government who have foreign policy responsibilities? There are several layers in the foreign policy makers' image of the press.

The "Prestige Papers"

It should occasion no great surprise to discover that foreign policy officials recognize that there is a small and specialised foreign affairs press in the United States; and that the single most important newspaper, by general admission, is the *New York Times* should also be a familiar datum. The *Times,* which regards itself as a newspaper of record, a daily contribution to history, is read by virtually everyone in the government who has an interest or a responsibility in foreign affairs.

The importance attached to the *Times* may be seen in some examples of its use. A freshman Congressman wanted to reach the State Department, the White House, and his fellow members of Congress with his foreign policy ideas, but he felt that his junior status in itself gave him no platform in Washington from which to reach this audience. So he chose to communicate to the foreign policy-making community by writing letters to the editor of the *New York Times,* for publication, hoping to make a substantive contribution to foreign policy that way. In another circumstance Senator Monroney, Democrat of Oklahoma, worked closely with the *New York Times,* seeking coverage of his proposal for an International Development Association-favorable or unfavorable—as an essential ingredient in his efforts to organize public support. His reasons for wanting *New York Times* coverage were these: "First, he believes *The Times,* especially the Sunday edition, is read by some of the most influential individuals throughout the nation and indeed the world. Second, he knows that often what appears initially in *The Times* will be picked up by other newspapers. And third, he likes to circulate reprints of such articles and editorials which he thinks will, because of their source, carry great weight.

The *Times* has long been regarded as *the* American "prestige paper": "In each major power, one newspaper stands out as an organ of elite opinion. Usually semi-official, always intimate with the government, these prestige papers are read by public officials, journalists, scholars, and business leaders. They seldom have large circulations, yet they have enormous influence.... We find, then, that despite local and individual variations, the prestige paper has come to be an important and respected institution. Governments, politicians, and businessmen depend upon it. One might ask what would happen in Washington if the *New York Times* stopped publication and no other paper took its place. There would certainly be a deterioration in American political intelligence. But if a prestige paper is defined by its importance to the political and governmental elite, then the notion of a single prestige paper has to yield, in the foreign policy field at least, to a plural concept.

There can be no question that the *New York Times* is of prime importance; but it has distinguished company on the desks of foreign policy-making officials, very few of whom limit their consumption to one or even two newspapers: the *Washington Post*, the *New York Herald Tribune*, the *Wall Street Journal*, the *Christian Science Monitor*, the *Baltimore Sun*, the *Washington Evening Star*. Collectively these papers, with extensive foreign affairs coverage and in many cases independent sources of news via their own staffs of foreign correspondents and foreign affairs reporters and analysts, form the prestige press in the foreign policy field. Their relative importance varies, obviously, from individual to individual; but one can hardly avoid recognizing the significance, in Washington, of the *Washington Post* and to a slightly lesser extent (perhaps because it is an evening paper) the *Star*. The following comments are typical. A

Senator: "I read the *Post*, of course, and the *Star*, and the *New York Times*"; a State Department official: "I read the *New York Times*, of course, and the *Post*, and the *Star*"; a former State Department official: "Everyone in the State Department reads the *New York Times* and the *Washington Post*." Running behind these papers in the number of daily official readers, yet carefully scrutinised within the policy-making institutions themselves, are the other newspapers on the above list.

If one hypothesizes that the order in which newspapers are read has some impact on the relative attention paid to each—on the plausible assumption that the major items will be read most thoroughly in the first newspaper one takes up, and even that, under the pressure of work, only one newspaper will be read on a number of days—then there is additional reason to upgrade the *Washington Post*. For the *New York Times* is often the second newspaper to reach the foreign policy specialist in Washington, the *Post* usually being the first. In fact, for many of these people, the *Post* is the doorstep newspaper, and it is read over the breakfast table. They will then pick up the *Times* on the way to the office, or it will be on their desks when they arrive. The *Times* is uniformly regarded as the authoritative paper in the foreign policy field. But our judgments must be based on the practices of these men as well as on their expressed attitudes, and their practices put the *New York Times* in the position of *primus inter pares*.

The prestige press, then, does not consist simply of *one* newspaper whose publisher and editors have determined to make it quantitatively, if not qualitatively, distinctive in the foreign affairs field; rather, it is an amalgam of the eastern metropolitan newspapers of higher quality and better coverage that are available to the policy makers on the day of issue. There are others, too, not yet mentioned, which perhaps belong on this list; these are the better newspapers whose regional circulation does not include Washington in any substantial way, such as the *St. Louis Post-Dispatch*, the *Louisville Courier-Journal*, the *Milwaukee Journal*, the *Minneapolis Tribune*, to mention just a few.

These papers *do* get to Washington, and they *are* read, but because of their regional interest and their time of arrival they are not serious competitors for the early and daily attention of foreign policy makers; they are more likely to be scrutinised as the best examples of the flow of foreign policy intelligence to the "provinces."

To sum up, then, the prestige press is not a unique newspaper that policy makers depend on for their political intelligence; rather, it is a larger network of communication that helps to define for the policy maker the current political universe. Washington survives when, from time to time, the *New York Times* is not published; it may be sorely missed, but there are a half-dozen other papers that collectively fill the gap. (There may even be secret relief when the pressure to read, and respond to, the *New York Times* is temporarily lifted). The larger network of communication is marginally, not centrally, affected.

This general description of the foreign affairs communication environment among decision makers in Washington needs to be qualified slightly in one respect. As some of the above quotations indicate, the member of Congress from a non-eastern constituency has a more compelling reason to read newspapers published in his state or district than has any particular official in the Executive branch (although the job of some persons in the State Department is to keep track of what a range of newspapers from all over the country are saying).

The News Agencies

For most newspapers in the country, as we noted earlier, the flow of national and international news from the wire service tickers represents the well into which they must dip for their coverage of national and international affairs. Thus wire service coverage may be regarded as a vast, continuous, unedited newspaper—much more extensive in its coverage of foreign affairs than virtually all newspapers in the country, since no paper that relies on this source publishes all the information it produces. Moreover, not only do the wire service teletype machines define the outer limits of foreign affairs coverage for most newspapers and for many policy makers; they also may be regarded as "tomorrow's paper today," or "this afternoon's paper this morning." They give the news a number of hours before it can be obtained from ordinary newspaper sources.

For both of these reasons, the news tickers occupy a prominent place in the foreign policy makers' world. The State Department's News Office maintains Associated Press, United Press International, and Reuters news tickers; the *Agence France Presse* ticker in the State Department is located, for language reasons, in the Bureau of European Affairs. The machines in the News Office are monitored constantly; eight copies come off each ticker, and additional copies are often duplicated in order to distribute the news items to all the relevant areas in the Department. The News Office rates the tickers as very important; "in fast-breaking situations, the tickers beat [State Department] cables by four or five hours—and in some cases by up to twenty-four hours." And the fact that the Secretariat has its own teletype machines may be taken as circumstantial evidence that the steady flow of news over the tickers is regarded as too important to be slowed down by the human processes of getting the clippings delivered from the News Office. The tickers are used and appreciated in the geographical bureaus of the Department, too. It was said, for example, that "the NEA people [Bureau of near Eastern and South Asian Affairs] get their information from the tickers, not from newspapers or from correspondents per se." An official in the Bureau of European Affairs said that the tickers were "a faster medium" than reports from the posts abroad. In the Bureau of African Affairs: "We follow the Congo on the ticker and in the press, and you get a quicker report of what is going on than you do through official reports." This same theme is repeated in other Bureaus, in an acknowledgment of the importance of the private news agencies in the communications network that sustains the foreign policy makers.

Considering the attention that men of top political and governmental rank pay to the wire services, one must include these services as part of the larger "prestige press." Each of them has its own staff of correspondents all over the world. Thus, each news agency represents an independent source of news about world affairs, more extensive in coverage and more rapid in impact than the best of the "prestige" newspapers, which maintain their own staffs of correspondents abroad and in Washington. The political importance of wire service news is additionally—though indirectly—heightened by the Washington newspapers, which rely very heavily on the news agencies for their international news.

The "Press" as People

Foreign policy-making officials also see "the press" as the output of particular reporters and columnists whom they respect or whom they believe to be influential in the political community even if they themselves do not think very highly of them. There is very widespread agreement on who these able and influential individuals are: Walter Lippmann, Joseph Alsop, Marquis Childs, James Reston, C.L. Sulzberger, Hanson Baldwin, Chalmers Roberts, and John Hightower are mentioned most frequently. And all of them, it might be noted, appear in the newspapers that make up the foreign policy "prestige press." These men are put in a somewhat special class; their columns or stories are a kind of personal communication rather than the output of an impersonal communication system. One person with experience in both the Executive and Legislative branches remarked, "I look for by-lines as well as subject matter." The following comments are illustrative of the predominant attitudes towards these men as representatives of the press. A Senate staff man: "A man like Reston must be considered as a statesman." There are, to be sure, less exalted expressions of respect toward these same men, and even some strong dissents from the very attitude expressed here; some people in the State Department, for example, pointed out that Lippmann does not make the correspondent's customary rounds in the Department and remarked that, if he did, he would not make so many "silly statements" in his columns. One went so far as to say, "Generally all columnists are pretty terrible." But on the whole this "inner circle" of foreign affairs reporters and columnists is esteemed for the excellence of its contacts, and for its intelligent, insightful, and responsible use of information delicately and privately given. In a spiral of cause and effect, the doors of high-level policy officials open more easily for them; and when the policy makers evaluate a columnist as responsible and intelligent in their *own* dealings with him, they will more readily respect the rest of his writings as similarly authoritative, intelligent, and responsible.

Foreign policy makers see the press in a personal way in still another respect: the press also enters the world of foreign policy-making through the personal relationships among policy makers and correspondents who gather and comment on foreign affairs news in Washington. Personal friendships between government officials and newsmen are common, extending right up to the Presidential level, and more-than-causal acquaintanceships are even more numerous, owing to the constant contact between officials and the reporters on a steady "beat," and to the fact that the foreign affairs reporters, who have high status among the Washington press corps, move in many of the same social circles as the government officials.

Informal interplay, where it does occur, is valued by both sides—by the reporter who must establish good contacts to do his job well; and by the official who wants to see the press do a good job of presenting the issues and who also knows that a good reporter has more ideas and information than he ordinarily uses in his columns in any one day. For the correspondent, like a traveling salesman, gets around a great deal, and hears a lot of things that may not rate as publishable news but that are nonetheless relevant and of interest to policy-making officials. The correspondent learns, too, that his relationships with officials develop best when he can trade bits of information—when he can give as well as get, and thus be useful to his sources instead of being, from their point of view, an endlessly prying nuisance. In this way the correspondents become direct personal communications links among the participants in the foreign policy-making process, over and above the intermediary function they may serve through the stories they write; they make their rounds carrying the germs of policy thought from one interested party to another. One State Department official, for example, who remarked that he was not in direct contact with reporters because he sat in a "protected position," nevertheless named about ten leading foreign affairs correspondents as personal friends: "I'm lunching today with a correspondent..... I do it often, with a number of them. I get ideas from—, and he gets them from me. He knows all the top people here. We have a public duty to the press, to help them cover foreign affairs adequately." Another officer in the Department said that "about 80 per cent of my contacts with reporters are on a personal basis—reporters whom I know personally, some of them since we were in the 'field' together." A staff assistant to a Senator, both of them active in the foreign policy field, reported that "Sometimes reporters call you to give you information. Almost always this requires a friendly relationship and a sympathetic issue-orientation. A reporter will interview a Cabinet officer, and then he will call me and tell me what he said—and he may ask me what I think of it, too. Reporters are human, and they get swept up in issues." Personal contact of this kind between reporters and officials is much more specialised, intermittent, and unevenly distributed than are their other points and varieties of contact; its qualitative importance would be very difficult to measure, to be sure, but it is too prominent a form in which the policy world experiences "the press" to be overlooked.

PATTERNS OF ATTITUDES TOWARD THE PRESS

Not all foreign policy-making officials by far, have close personal relations with correspondents; indeed, the mutuality of trust that characterizes such a relationship is narrowly circumscribed, in the sense that many officials do not come into direct contact with foreign affairs reporters at all, and those who do are far from indiscriminate with their favors. Because the attitudes toward the press that circulate at any time among the policy makers are more or less related to the behavior of these individuals toward the press, it is relevant here to inquire into the nature of those attitudes and the particular patterns that may be found among them. It has been claimed, for example, that the attitudes of career officers in the State Department are more favorably disposed to the public affairs function within the Department, and to the press, than are the attitudes of men who come to the Department from the business world; this is too simple a formulation to stand for very long, but it does at least suggest what a "pattern of attitudes" might look like.

At one level, it might be true to say that among those officials who have any contact with correspondents there is only one orientation toward the press that has any meaning—and that is ambivalence. The "love-hate relationship between us and the press," pervades the remarks of many thoughtful persons in the Executive branch, and even of some of the foreign policy people in the Congress. Sometimes this comes out in the form of remarks that the press as whole is both good and bad in its impact—as in the general comment from a former sub-Cabinet official that 20 per cent of what the press had to say on foreign policy was constructive and 80 per cent destructive. Sometimes the love and the hate are explicitly attached to different constituent parts of the press. It may be a case of some reporters being regarded as "responsible" and others not; for example, "You have to learn what reporters you can trust, and which you can't"; or, "You have to be careful with the press—you need to *know* the guy." Or it may be put as a reporter-editor problem, where the foreign affairs reporters do a good job but the editors do not use the good material. Sometimes it may come out in the form of a direct relation between the esteem in which a reporter is held and the nervousness he causes—the abler the correspondent, the harder it is to keep his nose out of what the officials feel are especially sensitive policy areas. As a general proposition, it might be said that the most favorable factors in the ambivalence tend to be the product of successful personal relations with particular newsmen over periods of time, whereas the unfavorable elements are a response more to the headaches that the press may have caused an official without his having been personally involved with the correspondent, than to direct instances of rough handling by the press. In any event, considering the large amount of negative feeling toward the press, a considerable number of respondents insisted that their own personal relations with the press had invariably been good.

Another way of looking at the ambivalent attitude toward the press—although officials themselves do not express it this way—is to see it as a reflection of the fact that the press performs a number of different roles in the foreign policy area, some of which are favorable or neutral to the policy maker's cause, while others are adverse. The press is thus a useful instrument to the policy maker in some of its manifestations, and an annoyance in others. The role of the press as critic, for example, may not unnaturally induce a considerable amount of hostility on the part of the official, even while he acknowledges the function of criticism in a democratic society, and even as he responds very favorably to the opportunities that the same or other correspondents present, via their neutral roles, to the advancement of his interests.

Since the press manifests its roles in different and particular guises, it is not surprising that ambivalent attitudes are found almost everywhere, even among those who profess to have uniformly favourable or unfavorable images. There are some officials, for instance, who emphatically repeat that the press and diplomacy are fundamentally *antithetical*—that the press must proceed on the principle of openness while diplomacy can only develop in a protected place; but significantly even these people have learned how to live on good terms with the press, and how to use it to further their own policy purposes. One often hears officials say that the press is helpful where it is responsible, and harmful where it is irresponsible. But the context just as often suggests that the true order is the reverse: where the press is thought to have been helpful, it is then regarded as responsible, and where it is judged to have been harmful, it is then viewed as irresponsible. But what is helpful and what is harmful in any circumstance depend on how particular individuals define their interests. Ambivalence, in other words, is compounded from a range of negative and positive attitudes that are partly ideological and partly instrumental in character, and that are a response to the various roles the press performs.

Let us, then, look separatively at the constituents of love and hate in the policy makers' image of the press. Perhaps, in the process, we can shed a little more light on the things that cause both this hate and this love, and thereby contribute to the development of better "understanding" on both sides. Although the question of how to "improve" the relations between the foreign policy agencies and the press is not a central focus of our inquiry, one cannot be totally indifferent to this problem in the democratic management of foreign affairs.

Favorable Attitudes

Far and away the most frequently expressed comments in defense of the press concerned the characteristics and qualities of the correspondents themselves, and their helpfulness in the processes of foreign policy-making. The fact that favorable attitudes cluster around these two points is not accidental. The personal qualities of newsmen, and their helpfulness from the viewpoint of the policy maker, are different aspects of a larger instrumental attitude toward the press on the part of the foreign policy officials.

Foreign affairs reporters and columnists in Washington are commonly (though by no means universally) well-regarded, even by foreign policy officials who are highly critical of the press on other scores. These correspondents, specializing in foreign policy, are able to talk to policy makers in a language they understand, and they are sufficiently familiar with the issues of policy so that they can ask relevant questions that the policy officials find difficult to answer openly. In the course of the daily encounter between the two, which generally revolves around substantive policy matters, the official develops a respect, sometimes freely acknowledged, sometimes grudgingly given, for the correspondent: "They're a pretty savy group of guys." "A fact of life in a free society is a corps of very intelligent, shrewd, indefatigable newspapermen. Some are tremendous... and can hold their own in any college political science department." "Reporters are clever, adept, well informed, responsible; I have great respect for them." "Good reporters are remarkably astute.... They are agreeable, interesting, knowledgeable people. They read a lot." "There are many qualified newsmen who are respected by government officials."

One of the characteristics most frequently cited by officials in favor of these correspondents is their trustworthiness, as attested by favorable experiences with them in the past. The reporter in an institution like the State Department, it should be noted, can function effectively only if his lines of communication through the institution are in good working order. He therefore feels obvious pressures to *be* trustworthy, for he knows that the reporters who violate confidences, or who undermine the policy positions of their sources by their revelations, or who cause their sources trouble as a by-product of their search for a front-page angle, will soon find themselves with no sources other than the handouts, or releases. Trust worthiness is thus a prerequisite to tenure in this "elite" group of reporters. A top-level career officer said, "I've never been *badly* let down by any of them; I've had good experiences.... You can take the senior and responsible correspondents into your confidence." a desk officer: "This is something that strikes the officers—press officers and desk officers alike—the freedom with which they can speak. The press is responsible and is able to distinguish between what it can publish and what it cannot." A former political official in the mutual security program: "Most policy people have their pet newsmen.... They are people with whom they can consult and whose judgment and discretion they respect." Not all correspondents are trusted equally by everyone, of course; certain correspondents and columnists do have nearly universal reputations for reliability, but they circulate chiefly at the upper levels in the foreign policy establishment. Below them the situation is more segmented; networks of trust are more limited in size and scope, and the over-all pattern is made up of these limited but overlapping areas of profitable experience.

The "helpfulness" of foreign affairs correspondents, which is perhaps the key to all the other favorable attitudes, is not wholly separable from the latter, since being helpful is a product of both personal qualifications and characteristics of performance as seen by the policy makers. This component of favorable images of the press reveals more clearly than any other how the foreign policy officials tend to judge people and performances by an instrumental criterion. If the reporters and analysts side with the Administration in its general foreign policy orientation, and if that basic predisposition is translated from time to time into articles or stories that help rather than hinder the officials in their pursuit of their vision of policy, and if, in the times in between, the reporters are governed generally as much by conceptions of desirable foreign relations as by conceptions of how to make the front page, then they are deemed to be helpful—that is to say, responsible—reporters. A White House aide during the Truman years remarked, "Most of the newsmen are liberal, and they gave the Administration a good break." A sub-Cabinet official in the same Administration said, "I think the press did a good job. Explaining to the people is really their best role.... In such instances as the Greek-Turkish aid program, the Marshall Plan, and so on, they made a real contribution." It should be made clear that the requirement is general enough so that a reporter does not have to become a spokesman for a man or an institution in order to be regarded as helpful; but at a minimum he cannot contravene the larger assumptions governing both means and aspirations in the prevailing foreign policy.

This is, of course, a familiar subject to the careful reader, for it involves the neutral roles of the press and the potentialities that those roles contain for exploiting or "using" the reporter for policy purposes—only here we are looking at it from the standpoint of the official rather than the newspaperman. It would be too strong to say that the *really* helpful correspondent, in the official's eyes, is one who lets himself be used by the policy makers for goals that may or may not be shared by both of them, but this is surely an important element in the instrumental syndrome. For reporters to share the policy makers' image of desirable foreign policy is not necessarily difficult, nor does it necessarily or even often involve toadying; the typical foreign affairs reporter himself, remember, is strongly in favour of liberal international commitments. This personal orientation is part of his motivation in foreign affairs reporting, and so long as American Administrations stay on this path in their foreign relations, the correspondents, may even welcome a chance to be "used" on particular occasions. A State Department official described the situation this way: "We have no press in this country that is an available tool for creating understanding, domestically or abroad, of foreign policy. We use it from the point of view of 'news'... where you give them the straight dope, to set them straight or to impress upon the reporters the seriousness of a matter.... You count on your Lippmanns, your Childs, your Restons, etc., your better columnists, to carry the straight story, without attribution. That is as near as you can come to using the press to convey policy, to directing the press as to what to say."

A reporter may sometimes be helpful, in the same sense of serving the policy maker's purposes, even when he is ostensibly critical of policies or relationships with which the foreign policy makers are identified; this is the case, for example, when the reporter expresses some criticism that the policy maker would like to express but is not free to do so in his official capacity. But since it is not clear to what extent these critical newspaper accounts are initiated by policy officials—"we can reap the benefits, but it is hard to organize such pieces to begin with"—we cannot be sure whether "helpfulness" of this kind is an accidental by-product of the reporter's critical function, or an example of the press's lending itself to the policy maker's purposes. In either case, however, the officials look benignly on the reporters so long as their points of view converge. Clearly, though, "helpful" can only be defined with reference to a particular set of personal or policy interests or preferences, and what is helpful to those who share these interests may be regarded rather differently by those who have other interests or purposes.

A corollary to the fact that instrumental considerations are foremost as a basis for policy makers' favorable attitudes toward the press is that ideologically based reasons for being favorably disposed toward the press are much less in evidence, and where they are expressed they are generally rather weak and unconvincing. One might have expected, on a *priori* grounds, that men who give some years of their lives to public service might have an ideological super structure that justifies their own effort and relates it to a philosophy of democratic government and public participation. If ideologies or rationalisations of this kind do exist, however, they are not often articulated. Only a handful of foreign policy officials couched their approval of press activities in the foreign policy field in terms of the requirements of an informed public. For example, "The more news you can give out, the better.... The more people know, the better." "You have to have an informed public. You have to tell them what the problem is, what they are in for." "I am convinced that the people do not go wrong if properly informed. This is the real contribution made by the columnist to foreign policy—to create understanding, to educate." The ideological component may be even further diminished by the fact that a few of these officials had some public relations responsibilities; at least this makes it a little difficult to separate ideological from instrumental factors in their defense of the press.

There are, finally, some institutional and some personality factors that appear to be associated with favorable images of the press. There seem, for instance, to be certain personality types, certain kinds of people, who manifest a sense of self-confidence and of control over their environment that enables them to look on the press, on balance, more as a structure of opportunities than as a natural antagonist, an enemy. Instead of timidity or fear in the face of the press, they display a mastery, an instrumental competence (even though they may also have some negative feelings about the press). A high State Department official noted that government officials tended to favor caution and secrecy as ways of dealing with the press, adding, "But if you know what *not* to tell and *what* to tell, you can establish a confidential relationship and help to get across the favorable side of what you are doing, rather than the nit-picking side." A desk officer in the Department said that he preferred as many direct relations with the press as possible, with fewer and fewer intermediaries: "You get a better feel this way; you keep better control over what the State Department is saying publicly." And from the public affairs area of the State Department: "If we want a reporter to have our viewpoint, we've got to give it to him." It is not an exaggeration to say that there are those who "naturally" find it easy to deal with the press—to establish the "confidential relationships" with correspondents—while others find it so difficult that they consistently manage to avoid all contact with reporters; and the latter quite apparently outnumber the former. Considering the size of the State Department alone, for example, and the small number of regular foreign affairs reporters, and the fact that they trace overlapping paths through the Department (there are few exclusive contacts between reporters and officials; the reporters need multiple sources both for verification and to cover their traces, and most officials act on the understanding that "you can't play favorites with reporters"), it is obvious that relatively few people in the State Department have the confidence to discuss policy issues regularly with the press. In one Bureau it was reported that only four people besides the Public Affairs Adviser talked regularly to the press: The Assistant Secretary, a country-desk man, a regional organisation man, and the economics specialist. "Individually, over a week, they will have from six to eight contacts with the press. Only the Assistant Secretary sees the press as a group—and then only once every two or three months, for a background briefing. So our regular contacts with the press are small."

It is sometimes argued that there are institutional factors at work here, in the sense that the top-level officials can talk to reporters with the confidence that comes from their positions of authority, while lower-level personnel are more reluctant to put their careers at risk in these encounters. This line of distinction is reported by a few State Department officials, and by some reporters, too, but the latter, despite their claim that the working-level "Indians" provide the best information, have a predilection for the more authoritative "chiefs", and thus their observations about the openness of officials may be colored by their preferred lines of access. Two sets of considerations can be introduced here, however, which suggest that confidence vis-a-vis correspondents is not a function solely or even substantially of rank, although this proposition cannot be regarded as explicitly testable by means of the data obtained in this study. In the first place, even on a random basis it is easy to find the confident-competent syndrome at all levels in the State Department, as well as fearful personalities at all levels, including the highest.

There are other institutional differences in attitude toward the press that are frequently put forward and deserve some scrutiny. It is sometimes argued, for example, that the P-area people—the Public Affairs Advisers, the men in the News Office and in the other offices and divisions of the Bureau of Public Affairs—who are professionally concerned with the State Department's public relations, are more likely to be favorably disposed toward the press, while the desk officers—the substantive people, the Foreign Service professionals—have a fundamental antipathy toward the press and other "outside" institutions. There is quite a bit of secondary evidence that supports the main burden of this distinction; most Foreign Service Officers are not in direct contact with the press, whether or not their instinct is to avoid it, as one of them asserted.

In the first place, the distinction itself is not wholly valid, since many persons in the P-area are Foreign Service Officers on normal assignment. Furthermore, since the P-area is conventionally suspected by reporters as the source of an official line, and held in low repute as "the gateway to the obvious," desk officers are cultivated as alternative sources of information; and thus there is circumstantial evidence that more than just a few desk officers *are* in contact with the press. The line of distinction that seems most valid here, as elsewhere, is not between P-area people and desk people, or even between political appointees and career officials, or between civil service personnel and Foreign Service Officers, but between those people in *all* classification, who are confident in their dealings with the press, and those who are not. Regardless of whether it is chiefly a matter of personality, or whether training and experience are also involved, the press-oriented personnel are a relatively small proportion of the total. As a very rough approximation, the State Department's contact with the press is regularly maintained by perhaps no more than 10 per cent of its staff, and probably considerably less than that.

The imprecisions and uncertainties that mark this discussion of patterns of confidence toward the press suggest the need for more extensive investigation of the subject. The problem is large in dimension, since large numbers of people are involved, and difficult in scope, since one suspects that the details of many contacts with the press will not be quickly volunteered. No doubt the managers prefer these contacts to be reasonably few, yet there is no apparent reason why anyone should prefer that the talents that sustain these contacts should be randomly or accidentally distributed throughout the Department. On the contrary, if more were known about their location and character, the State Department could easily make an effort to see that people with the requisite skills and personality attributes were regularly put into areas where the Department's public information needs were the greatest, and thus where they could do the Department the most good.

In fact, virtually all dimensions of this hostility directed at the press in the foreign policy field call for closer scrutiny; the negative feelings themselves are often expressed so generally that it is difficult to isolate or assign an underlying reason to them. And since hostility toward the press seems to be generalised from one policy area to another, it is difficult in cases where officials have more than one interest or responsibility to know whether evaluations of the foreign affairs performance of the press are the cause or the result of generalised press attitudes. Even the extent of governmental hostility toward the foreign policy press needs to be established in a more reliable way; the evidence at hand tells us that it is very widespread, slightly more than 50 per cent of our governmental respondents having taken the occasion to make negative evaluations of the press. (Only 40 per cent had expressed favorable attitudes, and about 20 per cent of the total were on both lists.) But were the rest being honest or merely cautious, which is surely an appropriate response in these circumstances? A very able and observant public affairs person remarked, a free press is absolutely essential to the democratic process, in this country or in any country. Most people believe this, but 90 per cent don't really mean it. This is obviously impressionistic, and perhaps hyperbolic, but it might turn out, under a more representative and more impersonal mode of data-gathering, to be a better approximation to reality than the 50 per cent figure.

What are some of the reasons behind the antagonism toward the press? A few lines of objection seem to be particularly salient; they may also be familiar, since they tend to be the converse of those supporting favourable images of the press. Among foreign policy officials in the Executive branch, the major complaints about the press are that it is unreliable, irresponsible, and "unhelpful." And like the constituents of the favorable attitudes, these three seem to be closely related, perhaps even being different manifestations of one large animus.

The theme heard most often was that press coverage in the foreign affairs field is unreliable, in the sense that the reporting is uninformed and inaccurate, and the reporters themselves unequal to the task; the news product as a result is distorted and untrustworthy. "If stories were based on fact all the time, they might not come out so well." "Most young reporters don't know what they are talking about in this field." "The press has distorted stories, has confused issues, and often jumped to wrong conclusions." "I give the guy [a magazine writer] the true facts, and he gets depressed: "That's not the way I heard it.' His trouble is, he's been reading the papers." Officials often supported their charges of "meretricious journalism" with examples drawn from newspapers no more than a week old, and in several instances only several hours old. The most violent criticism was directed against the *New York Times*, which published an AP story about an alleged new proposal that the reporter had been told was not true, and which joined it to a photograph of officials conferring elsewhere on a different subject. The official explained the story as the consequence of a UPI report: "The guy can't let the United Press report go unmentioned by Associated, so he writes this story, which implies that the State Department is planning a new... program, that `reports' of the plan are being made by Departmental personnel rather than the United Press, and that these guys in the picture are sitting around discussing it."

An obvious reason for this line of criticism lies in the greater access of policy officials to relevant information about issues; they know the "insides" of stories, or at least a *version* of the inside story, and they repeat with conviction the often heard complaint, "I've hardly ever seen a correct statement of a situation about which I knew the facts." Not only do they have more knowledge of the subject than the reporter, but they have some background of prior cases, and also some knowledge of the hit-and-run aspect of the reporter's relationship to any particular subject in the first place. So when they see news paper accounts of stories they know something about, they are likely to be skeptical about the adequacy of the reporting. Some of the officials are prepared to "set the reporter straight," on a background basis or perhaps when the story is no longer in the news; while others let the errors stand, on the ground that to alert the reporter to them is to give away too much information, and to encourage reporters to go on "fishing expeditions" in order to be told the "inside story." The extent of distrust that an official feels toward foreign affairs coverage, and its significance for his communications behavior, are less clear than one might expect, however. While a policy maker may repeat that no one can believe what he sees in the paper, and underscore his argument with a current example, he nonetheless is an avid and careful reader of foreign affairs news in his morning newspapers, and he extracts from them some very substantial and positive things. Perhaps the controlling hypothesis is that the less a policy maker knows about a subject or an issue, and the more remote it is from his area of professional interest, the more likely he is to accept a news account as reasonably accurate, at least pending positive evidence to the contrary. For if a foreign policy official automatically disbelieved *everything* he saw in the paper, he would be disoriented, cognitively unequipped to make the appropriate associations between his own areas of foreign policy work and all the others.

Closely related to the theme of unreliability is that of irresponsibility; and, as we noted earlier, the degree of a reporter's responsibility is also closely identified with the degree to which he is thought to have been helpful from the policy maker's point of view. But there is an independent sense in which the concept is used. Reporters are held to be irresponsible when they write their stories not in terms of manifest foreign policy content—the essential content as interpreted by the foreign affairs specialists—but rather in terms of news values like controversy, conflict, and sensationalism that are likely to capture headlines and front-page space; when, in other words, there is a "distortion" of emphasis and significance resulting from the application of different standards of evaluation. "If a reporter is fully briefed, and he then jazzes the story up and distorts it to get it on page one, for example, that is irresponsibility." Many of the foreign correspondents are quite unscrupulous and actually distort the news for the sake of headlines. The ethics of the press, unfortunately, are not too high." But most of the time, irresponsibility cannot easily be separated from notions of damage to particular foreign policies or to our general foreign policy position—again, an instrumental attitude. Some officials regard this kind of irresponsibility as an inherent feature of the press—one that flows from the independent existence of the institution and from its ruling criteria, rather than from the ethics of particular reporters, editors, or publishers. For example, the requirements of news writing are essentially opposed to the objectives of foreign policy. The major criterion of news is conflict; new concerns all the bad things in our international relationships. Our basic objective in foreign policy, on the other hand, is to find accommodations between countries.... We minimize our differences with countries outside the Communist circle... but the press wants to maximize conflict. So they make legitimate differences much larger, to the point where they become "conflict.'"

More often, however, officials are less philosophical and more particularistic in their criticisms. They complain that the press has not been helpful (i.e., has failed to publish material that would further particular foreign policy interests) or that it has been actively unhelpful (i.e., has published material that officials would prefer to have remained unpublished), in specific contexts. By "making life difficult" for those who are, in their own eyes, trying to do a constructive job in foreign policy, the press is regarded as behaving less than responsibly. Some of the correspondents were helpful.... However, there is something quite wrong with newspaper people. Sometimes they don't have any morality whatsoever. If they can steal a secret, they will, and then use it for what they want. For example, when we were consulting with our NATO partners about the integration of Greece and Turkey into the system, the whole story broke in the newspapers before we had completed our consultations. This made things pretty awkward for us. And this type of thing happens constantly." In the public affairs area one official said, "The press is always lousing things up...." And another: "The press throws a lot of sand in a lot of gears—in negotiations of policy within the State Department, as well as with other countries."

Perhaps the clearest illustration of how attitudes toward the press are related to a measure of its helpfulness or unhelpfulness is contained in a pair of observations by a person who was closely involved in foreign policy formulation in the State Department during the Truman Administration. First this official expressed himself in strongly negative terms, and told the following incident: "On several occasions we got into deep trouble with the press.

The pattern of Congressional hostility to the foreign affairs press differs in one important respect from this picture of the Executive pattern. Congressmen share the Executive officials' negative attitude toward the unreliability of newspaper accounts of foreign affairs developments, and toward the irresponsibility of the press as a consequence of what one Senate staff member called its "vested interest in controversy." The criticism makers at the unhelpfulness of the press, however, is a minor theme in the Congressional outlook, reflecting a smaller institutional concern with the problems of secrecy and of public relations in the foreign policy field. In place of the Executive official's hostility toward the press for "lousing things up," Congressmen and their staff assistants are perturbed by what they feel is a lack of objectivity in the press; the apparent biases of reporters and columnists, and their attempts to influence the shape of foreign policy—i.e., the manifestations of the press's "participant roles"—seem to the legislators to be inappropriate, whereas the Executive policy makers have long since become accustomed to them.

Significantly, there were very few negative, expressions of an ideological nature, such as might reflect dissatisfaction with the press's performance of its "obligations" to the electorate.

One can only conclude that here, too, the evidence supports the proposition that the grounds for disliking the press, as for liking it, are overwhelmingly instrumental rather than philosophical—one more dimension of the pragmatic character of American politics.

It seems clear that the basic ingredient in the foreign policy makers' reluctance to meet the press—the reverse of the sense of confidence and mastery that we noted among those who are the reporters' regular lines of access to foreign policy—is a pervading sense of fear. This fear grows out of the official s inability to control what the press will do with the information it gets. The opposite of the sense of confidence, then, is the sense of insecurity, an unwillingness to take any risks in the press's handling of information even at the loss of whatever policy advantages or initiatives might accrue as the consequence of good coverage. Even the confident people experience the fear that things will come out badly, but they are willing to run a few risks; and so they take their chances even as they try to lower the probabilities of disaster by choosing the reporters and the subject matter with some care. And they have a powerful ally in the general understanding among reporters that officials can shut off some sources of information if reprisals should be necessary. There is an egg-shell fragility to their sense of having good relations with the press at any particular time. Speaking of Acheson's unhappy experience with the press, a friend and colleague said, "The best of men can have the press turn on them quickly; they turn like tigers." Another view about the press is looked on as a dangerous, unattractive beast, which you can lead along for a little bit of the way, but which is likely to turn and bite you at the slightest opportunity."

6

The Utilisation of News

Contradictory and ambivalent themes mark the approach of foreign policy officials to the press, and these contradictions and inconsistencies have been reflected in prior pages. The negative attitudes toward the press and the strong depreciation of its standards and accuracy, the view that one cannot trust the newspapers or believe them or take them at face value, are all aspects of a cynical, wary outlook suggesting that the official is relatively impervious to the contents of the press, that he regards it as something vulgar that he cannot rub out of his life but that he will not permit to upset the rhythm of his work and the order of his day. But as intense and as widespread as these feelings are, readership of the press and reliance upon its foreign affairs content are just as widespread and intense. Indeed, the evidence in this chapter suggests that the foreign policy maker typically takes more out of the press than any one of them readily admits to, or may even be aware of. The familiar saw," All I know about foreign affairs is what I read in the *New York Times,"* is meant as a confession of limited competence, and when it was uttered by a Presidential hopeful in early 1960 it earned the scorn of reporters; yet if the reference to the *New York Times,"* is meant generically, there is more truth in the statement than most practitioners feel comfortable with. The press is not wholly responsible for their education, to be sure, but it does serve them in some very important ways, supplying material that is not supplied elsewhere. What are some of the things that policy makers get out of the press that have a bearing on the foreign policy environment? and how well are the purposes that bad policy makers to communicate through the press actually served by these patterns of extraction from it?

Information

For the Executive. Although he is surrounded by official and unofficial private networks of communication designed to keep him informed, the policy maker in the State Department still turns to the press for basic factual information about the international political world he living in a information from abroad as well as from his own immediate environment. Why should this be so? What can he learn from this general public source that he does not get from his established internal sources of information? To a great extent the answer depends on how the internal network of communication serves different needs or requirements of foreign policy officials at different levels and with varying functions and responsibilities. These officials have certain common requirements for information, and other needs that are functionally specific.

Except for the top foreign policy making officials, there is a specialisation of geographic men and/or function among the people in the State Department. The official network of communication from representatives abroad is designed to keep these specialists informed with respect to their own specialisation. As a Department official pointed out. "The embassies do not attempt to cover the news; they assume that people in the State Department and newspapers." A former high-level official said the same thing: "Most of the information you get, you get from the newspapers.... In the State Department the internal flow of communication is specialised; the broad scope of developments is found in the newspaper." The same point was made by a foreign aid official: "Of course, government employees get their information from the newspapers...." And from a former foreign aid official, "The *New York Times* is the primary information source for most of our foreign policy people." The press also provides an independent report, outside the diplomatic channel, on what is happening around the world. The State Department long ago considered and gave up the notion that it might compete with the major news agencies by running its own network of news reporters around the world. Having taken that course, the Department became dependent on the wire services, and on the major newspapers with their own staffs of foreign correspondents, for its basic coverage of world events, and for an independent check on the more limited and private flow of intelligence within the Department. "The *New York Times* and other newspapers with their own correspondents abroad have angles that you may not be aware of as a consequence of reading only the official reports."

Furthermore, the officials usually get their information sooner through the press than through official routes; owing to the coding and decoding procedures, official reports generally run behind press reports. Ultimately, of course, officials have to work with the information and analysis supplied by their own "reporters" in the missions abroad; but their contact with the rapidly changing contours of the international political world at any moment in time comes more through the press than through their own facilities. And the more rapidly the changes take place, the greater dependence there is upon the press. A close observer said that "In fast-breaking situations, the tickers beat cables by four or five hours—and in some cases by up to twenty-four hours." Another State Department official, who has the news tickers clipped and sent up to him steadily all day, concluded that "the State Department sources run about twenty-four hours behind the press." Radio news also has a competitive time advantage, in a limited situation: the early morning news roundups often have later information than appears in the morning newspaper, and officials listen to them at home, some hours before they get a chance to see any of the same material on the tickers in the Department. It is not unusual, consequently, for an official to make a reference to a late radio news item in the Secretary of State's morning staff conference, or in other morning conferences within the State Department. Under these circumstances, the press cannot help but have some impact on the way the men at the top initially define international situations. "Your vision of the world," one of them said, "comes at you from the paper, it hits you at breakfast." The press's definition of the structure of international affairs, or parts of that structure, may even become the prevailing definition among these top officials—indirectly, because it is the one so many other people accept; and by default, because these officials are physically unable to read everything that comes into the State Department through official channels.

It may be misleading here, in any event, to discuss the press accounts and the diplomatic reports as if they were two wholly independent streams of intelligence. The men who write the reports in the embassies are like regular newspaper reporters in the sense that they too are responsive to developments "in the news," and what they send in to the Department some hours later may be their own reaction to things they have seen on the tickers, or it may be in reply to requests from Washington that were first stimulated by news reports. In this sense the press's definition of issues and the content of its news stories have a direct bearing upon the internal system of reporting. Furthermore, the local press in the foreign country has an impact on reporting from the field. In developing his own reports, the diplomatic official gathers his information from a variety of sources, a prominent among them being the press of the country concerned. The embassies find out what the government to which they are accredited is doing, via the press. In other words, the significance of the press is not merely that it gets to the foreign policy people sooner and perhaps over a wider range of issues, helping to define situations, but that in getting there first it also helps to shape the subsequent diplomatic reporting on the same issues. It does seem clear, in any case, that the reporting function of the diplomat—one of the classic triad of functions: reporting, representation, and negotiation—stands in need of re-examination in the larger context of the total flow of foreign policy information from abroad to foreign policy officials. There are some other points of similarity in the generally held conceptions of the diplomat and the foreign correspondent—for example, in the notions of desirable training, competence, language facility, and the like; but the smaller the difference, in practice, between regular journalism and diplomatic reporting, and the closer and more intimate the connection between them, the greater the significance that we must attach to the press in the stream of foreign policy intelligence, and the more relevant to the processes of policy-making become the standards by which press coverage is made and measured.

For the foreign policy specialists, the desk men and others who work on a narrow front, the press also provides an independent and more rapid view of what is happening in their areas of interest. But since the internal flow of specialised material is great, the informational contribution that the press makes directly to their work is proportionately less. A desk officer described it this way: 'There will be a story in the *New York Times* from time to time which is *news* to us, and about which there is nothing on the cables from.

But it is usually the structural problem, not a particular event, that gives rise to this story." The press provides these people with other information, however: it tells them what is happening around the world in areas other than the one with which they are primarily concerned. Since they neither have access to, nor time to read, the official reports from all over the world, these specialists—up to, and sometimes including, the Assistant Secretaries of State—rely substantially upon the press for their broader knowledge of international developments. It would seem to be the case, however, that the narrower a man's area of specialisation, and the greater the distance between him and the staff level in the State Department, the greater is his dependence on the press for his larger view of the world.

The press also provides the specialist with domestic political information. The specialist lives in a bureaucratic world, and he is familiar with the political struggles that accompany policy ideas and proposals along the route to decision. Of necessity, he acquires internal sources of information about relevant developments and possibilities in proximate bureaucratic units, but here, too, his intelligence becomes more tenuous with increasing distance. And so he turns to the press for information about things that are happening and proposals that are being considered elsewhere in the foreign policy-making structure of the government. Every announcement in the newspapers that Japanese peace treaty discussions might be in the offing evoked a wave of interested and critical participation from West Coast Congressmen who were concerned about a treaty solution to the fisheries problem. Even the President keeps in touch with the administration of foreign affairs this way; a recent account described President Kennedy's phone conversation with a "top official" in which he discussed "a *New York Times* story dealing with expenditures of one of Chester Bowles' foreign journeys. Item by item, the President demanded explanations; the official, his brow wet with perspiration, dealt with them as best he could." A Foreign Service Officer tactfully explained how the situation looked from high up in the State Department: "You cannot divorce foreign policy from domestic political situations and political events. By and large the traditional departmental methods of informing departmental officers do not suffice, so the press plays an important role in factually informing officers."

For the Congress. The Congressmen's "need" for foreign affairs information is of a different order from that of official in the State Department; his interests are rarely as specialised as the official's, and he rarely has to respond immediately to developments abroad. Despite this, the press is at least as important to members of Congress as a source of foreign policy information as it is to State Department officials, because the Congressmen's alternative sources of information are not so extensive, and because for most Congressmen this is apparently the most congenial way of keeping broadly and generally informed.

The legislative policy maker who is at all interested in foreign affairs is not much different from an attentive citizen in his dependence upon the press; he reads the newspapers to find out what is going on in the world. A Senator remarked, "I can't overemphasize the informational function of the newspaper. We have to get our information just as the citizen gets his." The absorption of legislators in the press is legendary; Congressmen are always to be seen in the lounges reading newspapers or the news tickers, and the Senators and Representatives who have a specialisation or a reputation in the foreign policy field commonly begin their day by reading from two to six newspapers, spending as much as two hours on them. Staff specialists for these legislators are somewhat more introspective and articulate about the relative place of the press in the scheme of things than are the legislators themselves; this may be due in part to their better capacities for observation and generalisation than the Congressmen possess, and in part it may be a projection of their own experiences. The newspapers are part of your life, your existence. Things just soak in from the newspapers. Then you may pick up bits in articles here and there. "The newspaper is *the* source of foreign policy information. "On a day-to-day basis, of course, it is still the press that supplies the information." "The press remains the only way in which one can get the whole impact of the world around oneself."

Congressmen even look to the press as a source of information on what is going on in and around the Congress. Matthews' observation to this effect holds up in the foreign policy area, where the newspaper seems to be a convenient and economical substitute for the heavy investment required to read Congressional studies, reports, and hearings. One Senate staff assistant ascribed this pattern to Congressmen's being "primarily `mouth and ear' men—i.e., they pay more attention to what they hear than what they read. Most of what they read is likely to be in the mass media." Congressmen even treat foreign affairs information in newspapers with the deference, and accord it the authority, that those on the "outside" (including reporters) commonly accord to the information that comes *out* of Congressional studies or deliberations. The newspapers often provide the material that enables legislators, according to their own testimony, to ask intelligent questions of witnesses during hearings. And according to a member of the House Foreign Affairs Committee, Committee members regularly bring newspaper clippings into their sessions to authenticate points and to clarify problems or raise them for questioning.

In all of these cases, the "press" modified scarcely at all by the addition of constituency newspapers. For most Congressmen, unless they are from eastern metropolitan areas, constituency newspapers are not a source of foreign affairs news, either because their coverage is relatively skimpy—"only the bigger papers have the facts"—or because they arrive in Washington too late. A midwestern Representative said, "No citizen or legislator could rely on any—[home state] newspapers as sources for policy or for broadly based knowledge as a citizen." When constituency newspapers do arrive, they are used for different purposes, which are amply summed up in this remark of a Democratic Senator's Legislative Counsel: "Local newspapers are read for their state political news, for their news about employment conditions, general or new business developments, and for what they say about the Senator."

It may seem obvious at this point, if it has not earlier, that the press serves foreign policy makers in both the Executive and Legislative branches as a basic, standard source of factual information about foreign affairs and also about political developments within the American government that are relevant to foreign policy. Yet it is of more than passing significance that even though the press gives the policy maker his "big picture" and a large number of his smaller ones, this particular service does not constitute one of the standards by which press roles or performances are defined or judged. The informational role of the press—its central function—is aimed at the citizen; even the reporters on the prestige papers, while they presume that the reading public is intelligent and well informed and may even include policy officials, generally have a relatively unspecialised public audience in mind as the group they are trying to serve. (The participant roles of the press, on the other hand, which *are* aimed at the policy makers, are defined in political rather than educational terms; foreign policy interpretations and preferences of newspapermen, rather than substantive information, are introduced into the policy-making process). Although many reporters see the foreign policy official as an important part of their audience, nowhere do newspapermen seriously argue that an important role of foreign affairs reporting is, or should be, the provision of information to officials. Thus the informational standards of the press, even the "prestige press," are set by the assumption that the chief market for every-day reporting is the citizen rather than the responsible specialist; the latter is, accordingly, fed a popular diet for breakfast, and with that initial intellectual nourishment he is supposed to go forth to his office and do battle with giants.

IDEAS, EVALUATION, ANALYSIS, INTERPRETATION

For the Executive. We can recall that most foreign affairs reporters and columnists are eager to be heard by policy makers; in their activist or reformist moments, they value participation as an important role for the press and as a useful outlet for their own interests and capacities. How much encouragement in this role do they get in practice from foreign policy officials (among whom we found very mixed attitudes toward newsmen and toward the press as an institution)? How well do these officials acknowledge the propriety of the correspondents' aspirations, as measured by the value they attach to their product? How open are the policy makers to the press as a source of intellectual stimulation and inspiration?

Policy makers quite obviously turn to the press not only for information but also for analysis and evaluation of developments and proposals, and sometimes even for new ideas on how to deal with the range of problems that confront them. Their attitudes toward the intellectual contribution of the columnists and reporters fall handily into three patterns, outlined below. The correlates of these attitudes are not readily apparent; in the data available neither political party nor rank in the policy-making hierarchy, the two most obvious variables, seems to make any difference in the receptivity of officials to ideas from the press. The implication seems to be that the differences are highly individual, much as we found competence in the handling of the press to be.

(1) While men who are professionally involved in foreign policy decision-making are quick to acknowledge their constant readership of foreign affairs analysts in the press, some of them are extremely reluctant to attach any great importance to the evaluations of these columnists or to admit that they contribute anything to the development of their own thinking. For instance, a former sub-Cabinet official described the effect of these writers as "mostly negative. They contributed very few constructive ideas." Another official of the same rank said that "none of them, Lippmann and the Alsops included," were important. "Their ideas had very little substance and merit. They were of trivial influence." There may be professional pride involved here—as in a Foreign Service Officer's view that "it is damned infrequent that the Foreign Service would miss something"—as well as jealousy, an unwillingness to accord to any outside source the distinction of equality with, or superiority to, the thinking that goes on inside the foreign policy institutions. There may also be, in this attitude, a trace of suspicion that the columnists are grinding the axes of other, unidentified, participants in the policy-making process.

(2) A step above this negative position is occupied by officials who grudgingly acknowledge that sometimes the newspapermen do have something to say that is worthwhile. For example, "Occasionally some columnist will drop a new idea that will get picked up in Washington, but this doesn't happen too often." A former Assistant Secretary of State described his encounters with reporters in these terms: "Some of them would come to see you—even pester you. There would be an

exchange of ideas. They often tried out a variety of ideas on you, most of which you wouldn't pay much attention to."

(3) And then there are the officials who willingly give correspondents and columnists due credit for an important, if limited, creative role in the making of foreign policy. A number of high-ranking policy makers have said, in effect, that reading the columnists is part of their job, and that their columns have often been discussed at staff conferences. An Assistant Secretary of State remarked, "Our policy is made by intelligent men who will read the views of... thoughtful and informed columnists." The judgment of men like Lippmann, Reston, and Baldwin is valued because they offer interesting ideas from time to time. A foreign aid official reported that State Department personnel will "often times" draft arguments that take their line of reasoning from a recent article by one of the columnists; and a public affairs official in the State Department displayed a fresh newspaper clipping with some ideas on an educational exchange program, which the official was using as the basis of a memorandum proposing action along the same lines. The relevant attitude seems to be that good foreign policy ideas are scarce enough so that one should seek them out and exploit them wherever they may be found; if the columnists have the edge over academic or other outside specialists in this process—and it is not absolutely clear that they do have, although it seems so—it may be because they are easier to exploit, being right at hand and writing as if they were a part of the foreign policy establishment.

On balance, then, it appears that the press is a steady and somewhat fertile source of policy analysis and ideas, affecting even people who claim to be unaffected by it. One might entertain the proposition that the impact of the columnists' views is in inverse proportion to the number and diversity of competent specialists who take part in the competition over policy alternatives. Where the specialist market is thin, as it has been on many occasions in both foreign and military policy, the remarks of the columnists seem to weigh more heavily in the balance than they do where the competition is active and intense.

The press also provides the foreign policy official with another kind of evaluation, which is no less important for being less obvious. It is commonly understood that, in the policy realm, what is *thought* to be true is often a more relevant source of political inspiration than what is true. A former State Department official who has always been a very close observer of foreign policy-making put it this way: "The freedom of action of the diplomat is greatly limited: he has to work with the realities of the way people interpret events. The newspaperman is of the utmost importance in that field." A Foreign Service Officer involved in high-level decision-making argued more explicitly that the policy appraisals made by persons outside the Department, representing a wider range of policy understandings, are themselves a vital part of the over-all problem that is being considered within the Department: "In assessing a given situation, you can't rely exclusively on Foreign Service reporting, or on staff papers prepared below in the Department. You have to rely to a great extent on analyses from outside—from newspapers, editorial reaction, Congressional statements, etc.—all of which reach us via the daily press. These are not primary considerations in our decisions, but you can't leave them out." Succeeding sections of this chapter will amplify this point by explaining how foreign policy makers extract from the press a sense of the way reality is perceived elsewhere in the political system—and, hence, a sense of political reality itself.

For the Congress. Members of Congress and their staff assistants are almost unanimous in acknowledging the usefulness of the press, and especially the major columnists, as sources of ideas, insights, and interpretations in the field of foreign affairs. The legislative personnel by and large lack a personal competence and *expertise,* lack their own resources for the analysis of foreign policy problems. They do have staff research facilities at their disposal, including the Legislative Reference Service of the Library of Congress, but these are not designed to provide the interpreta-tions, the speculations, the new thoughts about current develop-ments that are the daily food of politicians and the stock in trade of political columnists. The Congressman is interested in knowing what others are thinking about these unfolding events and their possibilities, as a convenient basis for locating and formulating his own thoughts. There are boundless examples absorbing the foreign policy ideas and reflecting the stimulation of columnists, ranging from the well-known relationship between Senator Vandentberg and James Reston to the daily and unremarked culling of ideas for policy speeches. Interestingly, the strongest and most explicit argument from anyone on the legislative side against the usefulness of the analytical content of the foreign affairs commentators came from a Senate staff person whose formative governmental experience in foreign affairs had been to the State Department.

Both Congressional and Executive people agree that Congressmen are more susceptible to the foreign policy suggestions of columnists than are Executive officials. In the eyes of officials, this susceptibility makes the press a desirable vehicle for exporting ideas to the Congress, in the hope of improving the chances for Congressional approval of Executive policy proposals. It also heightens the Executive officials interest in the content of the columns, as we shall note in a subsequent section, because they learn what the Congressmen are reading and thus are likely to be thinking in the immediate future.

Foreign policy interpretation in the press has different implications for the policy making system than are suggested by foreign affairs information in the press. We noted earlier that policy makers draw foreign policy information from a press that aims to supply it to non-specialised readers. In the case of analysis and interpretation, however, the audience assumptions of the journalists are more in line with the uses made of their product, for the work of columnists in comment, evaluation, and analysis is explicitly aimed at the policy makers as well as at the ordinary citizen. The reader may recall, from our earlier discussion of the roles of the press, that the interpretive function is generally regarded as an extension of the information role vis-a-vis the general reader, on the ground that "the facts" are meaningless without some interpretation. But the functions of criticism, of advocacy, of asking unanswered questions, and of participating in the policy deliberations and in the exchange of policy ideas are all aspects of the larger participant roles, which assume a dialogue between the correspondents and columnists on one side and the government officials and legislators on the other. This is not to argue, though, that what is done deliberately and knowingly by reporters is therefore done well; indeed, the attention that commentators turn to policy ideas is generally as wandering, haphazard, and capricious as the attention that their brother reporters turn to accounts of foreign affairs events or developments. The same uncertainty of standards as to what is newsworthy lies behind them both.

Importance

For the Executive. Policy makers also draw from the press some measure of the comparative importance of events in the eyes of others—that is, the significance that is being attached to particular developments or issues as a result of evaluations made elsewhere in the political system. In their official capacities, policy makers are constantly processing large amounts of information from internal sources and from other specialised sources; these items have generally been evaluated, explicitly or implicitly, at their points of origin, but the officials at the receiving end still attach their own criteria of significance to them. They then may wish to check their own judgments of significance with still other people, or they may have the judgments of others brought forcefully to their attention whether they want them or not. The same kind of evaluative problem exists, though to a lesser degree, with respect to the information they draw all day long from the wire service tickers. Despite the processes of selection and editing to which wire service news is subjected (which itself constitutes one external measure of its importance), the material still comes out of the machines as a steady flow of relatively raw copy, and much of it has to be put into further order—to have final importance attached to it according to criteria that will hold up in the marketplace of ideas.

The newspaper, and the wire service news budget, supply a large part of this independent ordering of the importance of events. The editorial choices of a given newspaper represent the ultimate evaluative process in the cycle of news. The editors, on the basis of their own best judgments of what constitutes news—helped, of course, by the judgments of the wire service editors—attach orders of priority to news items, which they make manifest by the place in the paper to which they assign the items, by the amount of space they allocate to them, and by the size and character of the headlines they write to call attention to them. In turning to the newspaper press, policy makers are seeking (or receiving) a comparative evaluation of the importance of events; and in turning to particular newspapers or directly to the wire service budgets, they are seeking the evaluation of editors whose bellwether powers they respect, and / or of editors in whose theories of what is news they have some tested faith.

One can distinguish several different aspects of this search for comparative evaluation. The first is the simple one of ascertaining whether or not a subject has been brought into the newspaper (or onto the ticker) in the first place. An issue may have received no coverage because officials have succeeded in keeping it under wraps, or despite the officials' best efforts to bring it to public attention, or only because reporters or editors have not thought it newsworthy. In any case, policy makers are entitled to draw reasonable inferences about the political environment of decision-making when the issues have not been put on public display. whether they have contrived to keep an issue "unimportant", or whether they have been unable to communicate to reporters their own sense of its importance, the absence of coverage tells them something about the salience of the issue in the world outside their halls.

Once a subject has "hit the papers", a more obvious aspect of the search for external judgments of its significance consists in discovering how the press rates it in comparison with all the other events and situations that are occurring at the same time. A State Department official who was once a newspaperman stressed the meaning that this use of the press held for him: "The press is more important here than the cables. There is a big difference in seeing a story on the front page, in comparison with all the other stories there, from St. Louis and everywhere else, and in the specialisation of the cables.... The impact of the cables is not felt until it is seen in juxtaposition with other stories, on the front page of the *New York Times.*" The *Times* is not the only benchmark, of course; all newspapers that foreign policy officials see serve the same end. Officials who read the *Times* and the *Washington Post* in the morning, and other papers in the course of the day, will read the *Washington Star* in the evening in order, as one official put it, "to see how the news of the day is played in the evening papers." And the two-page morning roundup or summary of foreign policy stories in the "prestige papers" that is prepared for the top officials in the State Department contains, for each story, its location in each newspaper that runs it.

Another manifestation of this particular use of the press is not properly the *search* for outside judgments of importance through the press, but their *imposition,* with the press attaching such importance to an item of news that government officials are obliged to take special cognizance of it. In other words, under certain circumstances the order of priority that the press attaches to policy items may be superimposed upon the significance originally or ordinarily attached to them in the State Department and elsewhere, and eventually even come to supersede those original estimations. This is readily apparent, of course, when the issue takes on scandalous attributes, or when the press coverage stirs up unsuspected opportunities for partisan political advantage. But less dramatically, and less obviously, it takes place all the time. This constant process whereby policy officials adapt their own concerns to the priorities of the press may be seen in two ordinary contexts.

First, whenever foreign policy officials meet the press in more or less formal and open conference, they customarily prepare themselves ahead of time by a thorough exposure to the current questions of interest to the reporters, as revealed by contemporary newspapers. "We pull together the questions we know will be asked of him, so that he doesn't go in there unprepared." This is a wholly reasonable and obvious mode of preparation, but its consequence is that the official is indoctrinated, so to speak, in the momentary foreign policy perspectives of the press and he has to organize, or if necessary reorganize, his thinking to match that perspective. "You know that a story that is scattered in newspapers across the country will stir up a certain reaction."

Second, and more important, the constant access that reporters have to foreign policy officials means that the newsmen are an integral part of the policy-making structure, and on an hour-by-hour basis their passing concerns, their conceptions of reader interest and news values, their notions of a story, are translated into questions that are fed steadily into the "policy machine" and cause it to shape its interests and activities in order to produce the answers. The daily and substantial process of preparation for the noon briefing of reporters should be understood as part of the continuous effort to understand and stay in step with the problems that seem to be bothering the press and presumably the public. This process reaches all the way up in the Department; the public affairs people, working with the two-page summary of the foreign policy news in the morning papers, raise some of the items for discussion in the Executive Staff meeting every morning. According to one of these officials, "Sometimes other people in the meetings will raise one of the items. These are items we may have to do something about.... There may be a story or an analysis that raises a question of policy. We may raise it at the meeting because we know we will be asked about it today, and we have to think about how to reply to it when we are asked." But this is more than just a morning preoccupation culminating in the noon briefing. At any time of the day a wire service item may bring the reporters into the News Office with questions, and when they come, "the people upstairs [i.e., the policy people] have to put their heads together to figure out how to field it." A public affairs man in one of the regional Bureaus offered a fresh example of how the policy officials have to adapt to the world of foreign policy in the press: "We are always calling news stories to the attention of the policy people. Today, for example, there is a United Press report of a US submarine observed off the—coast, which is reported to be armed with a nuclear capability. Well, we know what kinds of questions we are going to get asked tomorrow by the press. Have we cleared this with the—Government? This is part of... [our treaty arrangements] which has never really come up yet, and it will have to be interpreted." As we noticed at the end of the preceding chapter, their very success in foreseeing the questions that will come up is the best evidence that State Department officials, in thinking like correspondents, have assimilated many of their implicit criteria of importance.

Thus the press, in giving prominence to an issue, helps to nudge it somewhat higher on the list of items claiming the attention of foreign policy officials. This may then get translated into still further pressure on the State Department, into still another outside measure of importance, when members of Congress call up the Department to ask, "What about this problem I see in the paper?" There is great incentive, consequently, for the policy makers to turn to the newspaper to make sure that they know what is about to become important to them because people elsewhere think it is important—after their newspaper implicitly told them it was.

For the Congress. Congressmen understand the capacity of the press to lend significance to whatever issues are being discussed in its pages, just as they understand how they personally can use the press to create supportive publicity for themselves. In part, this understanding reflects the resignation of legislators in the face of a foreign policy environment over which they have no strong influence. Thus a Senator defined the principal role of the press as "picking up ideas that officials have dropped and then building up great publicity about those ideas." And a Represen-tative attributed the lack of sophistication about foreign affairs in the House, and its attendant lack of impact on foreign policy, to the "great thrusts of attitudes they [the Representatives] cannot control." But we have made it clear in earlier contexts that legislators realize full well that the press can be an ally in gaining prominence for policy ideas in the Congress as well as in the Executive branch.

Every body is conscious of the power of the press in raising up issues, but less aware than the Executive officials of the extent to which their daily notions of what they have to think about in the foreign policy field are influenced by the press. Where Executive foreign policy officials often turn to the press precisely to see how issues are being played, the congressmen seem to be more willing to accept the order of priorities in the press as the "natural" order. It would seem that their own dependence on the press is so complete that they absorb most of the ordering of importance that takes place in the newspaper as an original formulation of reality, rather than as an outside source of evaluation that might compel them to alter other and preferred priorities, as is often the case with the Executive. In other words, the order that is in the press becomes *their* order, and as such its capacity to impress itself upon foreign policy officials in the Executive branch is augmented. This is manifested in the daily response of Congressmen, on and off the Floor, to the contents of the day's paper, as well as in the calls they make and the memos they send to the State Department. It is also reflected in their conviction that reporters should stick to the objective facts about an objective set of events, and allow these news events to speak for themselves. In other words, they believe that a responsible newspaper depicts an incandescent reality that the responsible legislator has to soak up and to which he must respond.

STANDARDS

For the Executive

The eastern metropolitan newspapers, alone and in conjunction with other newspapers from more remote constituencies, provide foreign policy makers in various parts of the government with standards by which to measure or judge what others involved in the political process are reading about foreign affairs. This is an important source of their insight into the way foreign policy issues are being perceived and assimilated into political structures, foreign as well as domestic.

In the State Department, the New York and Washington newspapers especially provide a guide to what groups elsewhere in the foreign policy universe are reading; this is one way in which the State Department keeps track of changes in the foreign policy perceptions of some of its most relevant audiences. In the higher reaches of the Department, it is claimed that the *Washington Post* editorials are read "because we know they are read on Capitol Hill." And at all levels in the Department—including the desk level, where there is the most direct contact with specific country problems—the *New York Times* is studied carefully (not merely read) because Department officials know that foreign embassy personnel in Washington accord it very great attention as the leading American newspaper and the one that is reputed to have the closest connections with the State Department. A desk officer put it this way: "A *New York Times* editorial has more weight with us *because* it has more weight with our clients, the embassies. This is why we have to read the *Times*. The embassy people read it too, and it becomes a common point of departure for their reactions and for ours." The columnists, too, are read with more care than the manifest content of their work might warrant, just because the officials know that they are read widely in Washington and also by attentive people all across the nation. "Reston almost makes foreign policy, to many people..."

For the Congress

The press is even more useful to legislators than to State Department officials as a standard because of the very great differences that exist among the newspapers they see regularly. We have noted earlier that the eastern metropolitan newspapers serve the Congressmen as their foreign policy news source, and that, when the Congressmen do not come from these eastern metropolitan areas, their district newspapers serve as their source of state and local political and economic information and opinion. In time the differences that create these separate functions appear to be magnified, and the Congressmen begin to use the New York and Washington newspapers as a yardstick to measure what their constituents are—or are not—reading. This is not simply a way of comparing what they themselves are reading about the world around them with what their constituents are reading; in addition, they seem to accept the foreign affairs coverage in the leading eastern papers as the benchmark of top quality, and use it to measure the inadequacies of local press coverage. Thus a Senator commented, "I get an entirely different picture of priorities from my local newspapers than from the Washington papers. I want to know what the newspapers are telling *my* constituents about what is important in the world. I have to judge whether the emphases are accurate. ..." And a Representative complained that "There is no rhyme or reason to foreign policy coverage in the _______ [constituency] papers. A story may get a big headline there, and just one inch of coverage in the *New York Times*. Some idiot of a night editor plays a story up out of all proportions." Another Senator said that he attempts to discover what the home district press is thinking, and then compares this with the views of "the more reputable papers." This suggests, then, that whereas Executive officials are relativistic and instrumental in their extraction of standards from the press scrutinizing material with special care becauss othere are known or presumed to pay special heed to it,

Congressmen derive from the major newspapers a more absolute standard of quality or adequacy of foreign affairs coverage. In other words, the Executive's use of the press in this sphere does not necessarily require the officials to accept as valid the degree of importance that the papers in question assign to various subjects; all that matters is that other people are reading the same things at more or less the same time. But the Congressional uses do suggest, once again, that the Congressmen have accepted the measures of importance that the New York and Washington papers have assigned to various topics as being normal, correct, accurate representations of reality.

Congressmen also turn to the syndicated columnists as another way of discovering what their constituents are reading in the foreign policy field. It has been seen that the stories of syndicated columnists have an impact upon the mail that Congressmen receive from their districts, and hence they are "of marked effect in the political atmosphere of the capital." By reading the columnists the same day they appear in the constituency papers, the Congressmen gain some slight time advantage, some advance notice of what these particular political stimuli look like.

OPINIONS AND REACTIONS

For the Executive

Lastly, the press provides policy makers with the ingredient that has long been assumed to be its chief contribution: a measure of public opinion. Opinions in the press—editorial opinions; the viewpoints of columnists and commentators; the positions or reactions, spontaneous or elicited, of other policy officials and "newsworthy" individuals and groups that are reported in the news columns; even the views of the editors concerning the relative importance of items in the news—constitute one of the leading channels by which foreign policy officials can regularly and continuously tap an informed and articulate segment of public opinion. To be sure, this is not the only way in which policy makers gain an understanding of public responses to foreign policy, nor is it always the most relevant way. But lacking any other *daily* link to the outside, any other *daily* measure of how people are reacting to the ebb and flow of foreign policy developments, the policy makers reaches for the newspaper as an important source of public opinion, as the instrument of "feedback." In fact, in any officials treat the press and public opinion as synonymous, either explicitly equating them or using them interchangeably. The over-all political impact of the press in this respect was described by one official as follows: "The newspaper is a source of a daily `feel' as to what is going on, and the public reaction to it." Perhaps a better way to put this is to say that the press, which has elaborated the task of independently recording and criticizing the actions of government officials, is thereby the most important of the public audiences before whom the foreign policy makers act. This is the policy makers' major segment of public opinion, a daily referendum of articulate opinion, a surrogate for the body of plastic notions held by the general public that tell the foreign policy makers very little about public feeling and public preferences. In other words, the policy makers reciprocate and support the reporters' contention that they represent and speak for the public in the democratic dialogue between the government and the governed.

That the press is used as a major source of opinion about foreign policy is both widely acknowledged and well understood. *How* it is used, however, is less clearly understood; there are important variations both in the way press opinion is perceived and in its political impact and utilisation, and these merit our attention.

In the State Department, individual reactions to press opinion range from the extreme of apparently total rejection (after careful reading!) to the view that at times Department policy is fashioned in direct response to press opinion. The former is exemplified by the individual who, after identifying press opinion as public opinion.

The large middle ground points of view is occupied by two basic orientations to press opinion that are more in tune with the uncertainties of political decision-making, with the absence of any large and clear majorities of opinion, and with the recurring need to build effective majorities or at least to read persuasive public support in the signs and signals of opinion reaching policy makers. For convenience we might call these orientations, which are not at all exclusive, the evaluative and the manipulative.

The evaluative orientation looks to press opinion for clues to the structure of actual or potential political support for alternative policies. Where policy is relatively firm, "the daily trend of editorial opinion," according to a desk officer, "is less significant." But where there is flux, he went on, "we are interested in seeing editorials, to see what is behind them, who wrote them, what weight they represent." Another official, whose work entailed a wider area of political interest and participation, sought the same end by the opposite route: "The editorials are anonymous so that one can't tell who actually writes them. The articles of the syndicated columnists are in a way more important than the editorials." The policy officials at the higher levels are also on the look-out for signs of potential opposition or support in the Congress; these signs are more eagerly sought where the official has used the press explicitly for the purpose of testing reactions to new departures in policy. But in the ordinary way, too, the press is a source of comment on the things that come out of the Congress as well as out of the Executive; and by eavesdropping, so to speak, on the Congressional fragment of the dialogue between the public and the government, the foreign policy officials in the Executive branch get insight into the potential strength of Congressional sentiments.

In the State Department the manipulative or instrumental orientation seems to be at least as pervasive as the evaluative orientation; it is certainly not limited to those officials whose primary responsibility is the Department's public relations, although these people do have a special investment in it. The manipulative orientation looks to the press for clues to the way policy is being received by newspapermen, in order to determine whether such policy needs to be better justified or explained. In the public affairs area, the reading of editorial opinion has often led to make strenuous efforts, formal and informal, to give editors all across the country what one official called "the feel of what we try to do." That editorial and press opinions were "the true measure of the relative success or failure of our own public relations function. The higher-level policy people are equally concerned with these questions, as we have pointed out before. The following observation, from a vantage point close to the top of the State Department's policy-making structure, is an excellent statement of this instrumental use of press opinion and reactions: "The main use of the press in making foreign policy decisions is alerting you to public reactions and to public interest—to the necessity for considering how policy decisions need to be interpreted when they are made public. You can only set forth the reasons [behind a policy] in an intelligent fashion if you know what the public is worried about. The press that we read here is the major source of our knowledge of public opinion." One might question whether this is in fact the "main use" of the press, even at levels in the Department where internal information flows abundantly, but the relevance of this employment of the press to political purpose is plain in any case.

For the Congress. It can be expected of elected representatives that they will steep themselves in the public opinion that they find in the newspapers. Newspapers give us editorial reactions, personal reactions, of people who are informed, people whose reactions are an important gauge of the significance of developments abroad. Surprisingly, however, this use of the press for opinion information does not extend equally to foreign policy opinions, especially for those who are especially interested in foreign policy.

One apparent reason for the relative downgrading of local press opinion is that in many district newspapers there is no editorial coverage of foreign affairs or other expression of the foreign policy opinions that circulate within the constituency, while in many other papers there is only occasional and scant opinion information. If the representative is interested in keeping in touch with general editorial opinion on foreign affairs, he turns as a matter of convenience to those papers close at hand that print a lot of opinion information. Another reason for non-reliance upon the constituency press is that some Congressmen feel that press editorials on foreign policy matters have no resonance in the local communities. They are looking for the "informed opinion" of more than just one editorial writer. Where they suspect, rightly or wrongly, that the editor himself has no audience, that his views are not going to create a wider body of opinion and hence do not anticipate or reflect such a body of opinion, the Congressmen are likely to rely more heavily on the eastern newspapers that are presumed to have a wide and significant audience for their foreign policy editorial opinion. A midwestern Representative expressed this well when he said that "Reading the local paper doesn't give me any opinion information, because no matter how good the editorial columns—and they are *the* foreign policy columns in the paper—I know that nobody reads them." In the same vein, a number of staff assistants remarked on the sensitivity of members of Congress to opinions that they think *do* have a market, even if they are not themselves part of it; one Senator's assistant observed, for example, that "Columnists are read for their opinions because they are so widely distributed." Still another reason lies in the content of the editorials that do appear in the district papers; the smaller the paper, the less likely is it to have editorial writers who can comment on abstruse or specialised foreign policy subjects, or who can say new and different things on more familiar subjects. Thus a Representative found most editorials worthless because they were "on the *obvious,* not the subtle, aspects of policy, and along the general thrust of attitudes.... Several of the great newspapers will discuss editorially the more important but less notorious aspects of foreign policy, but generally it is not done."

The near-absence of opinion information on foreign affairs in the district papers compels the representative to look elsewhere if he wishes to ascertain constituency opinion on foreign policy. But the absence of foreign policy news and opinion information in the local press also tends to cut down on the stimuli that will be reflected in whatever other conduits of opinion within his district the representative might employ. And beyond this, of course, if the representative avoids editorial opinion on foreign policy in his constituency papers because he thinks of it as politically meaningless even when it is substantively competent, then he is cut off still further from articulate opinion back home.

Conclusion

It remains here to link this discussion of the classes of things that people in the government take from the press with our prior discussions of some of the characteristics of press coverage of foreign affairs. In taking information, ideas, standards, opinions, and a measure of importance from the daily parade of words in the newspaper, how are foreign policy officials and legislators affected by the things that reporters write about foreign affairs, by the way they write about them, and by the things that other officials and legislators try to get them to write?

We noted earlier that foreign affairs reporters tend to cluster around the story or stories that are getting the biggest "play" in the newspapers; that the biggest play is likely to be given to the dramatic, the controversial, the contentious, the personal element; and that this pattern of story choice has the effect of muffling other stories, on a day-to-day basis and also over extended periods of time. We pointed out, further, that in hopping from issue to issue, from crisis to crisis, the correspondent deals in political discontinuities. In drawing information from the press, then, the policy official confronts a grossly uneven, often misleading picture of the world and its political relationships and problems. And in extracting a sense of the public importance of foreign policy issues from the newspapers, policy makers are responding to criteria that, no matter what their merits, are not systematically relevant to the problems of American foreign policy that otherwise seem most urgent to them at any particular time. This is not to argue that these issues may not be important in the sense that public apprehensions, interests, and energies have been focused on them; it is rather to indiate that the priorities of the official, which do bear at least some relationship to a coherent pattern of foreign relations, are modified by the priorities of the reporter, which are responsive to no such coherent pattern, and which reflect rather the problems involved in assimilating foreign affairs to the standards of a mass market. We may still believe that foreign policy ought to be responsive somehow to some order of political values that arises in the public marketplace, even when those political values have no intellectual rigor or coherence. But this leaves open the question whether the reporter's priorities should be accepted as the most relevant ones within the marketplace, or whether a more consciously responsible and responsive political leadership might have a larger share in the task of defining these political values.

Another relevant feature of press coverage of foreign affairs is its anchorage in the immediate present, in the wake of those things that can be observed to have happened. The foreign affairs correspondents, in terms of their own *modus operandi*, have only a limited freedom to move in various directions, asking more anticipatory or developmental questions about political issues or possibilities, much as a boat at anchor can maneuver in a very circumscribed arc. (And, to be sure, the policy official is not often willing to talk in these "hypothetical" terms either.) Consequently, information and ideas relevant to policy generally enter the stream of intelligence after a situation has developed rather than in anticipation of it. There are exceptions to this, of course; an obvious exception is where policy officials sense a developing problem and for their own (generally unarticulated) purposes make a major effort to get correspondents to treat it as news. But under more common circumstances, where officials are cautious in the release of information, the opinions and reactions relevant to foreign policy that are stirred up by press discussion, and that officials then take from the press, concern policy developments that are comparatively mature and are therefore resistant to a large variety of external pressures. The opinions and reactions that officials learn about, consequently, are less capable of being integrated into the stream of policy thinking and policy choice than would be the case if newspaper stories were built upon foresight and facilitated foreknowledge of the possible patterns and procedures of political choice. (This may, of course, be the reason for the caution of officials in the first place.)

There is perhaps a closer fit between the things that some officials try to contribute to the press in the foreign policy field and the things that other officials take from it, than there is between the ordinary needs of the officials for substantive and political information and the routine contribution of the reporter. The efforts that individuals make by way of institutional, personal, and policy promotion reach home, so to speak, in the information, the ideas, the measures of importance that other policy officials take from the press. We noted earlier, for example, in a different context, how an official might use the press to claim the attention of higher policy levels in the State Department for an idea or a problem that he could not bring to the top through regular internal channels. This process is constrained only slightly by the anonymity of sources of stories or ideas or viewpoints. In some cases the source, or at least the political location, of stories may be known to other policy makers, or surmised by them, and in other cases it may not even matter whether these things are known at first, so far as their import for others is concerned. The use of the press by officials to test reactions to specific possibilities is, of course, a more-or-less complete process in itself; for every input there is an output, even if it tells the official that no one is paying attention to him.

But in a larger sense the policy makers' continuous combing of newspapers to discover reactions to policy developments tends to generalize and extend the significance of the "trial balloon" far beyond whatever narrow purposes might originally have been entertained.

Contributions to the press that are meant to divert reporters from more troublesome problems that policy makers wish to keep under wraps may have serious consequences to the extent that they succeed in diverting other officials as well as reporters. These kinds of diversions, which reach officials in the form of daily estimates of what others in high positions are thinking about or preoccupied with, must be added to the distractions that the reporters themselves provide in their eternal pursuit of the "big story" and of popular "news values." Together they suggest a daily surge of stimuli that impinge on the foreign policy official but have no necessary connection with the longer-range problems of political relations that define the floor, the walls, and the roof of the house he lives in.

There are finally, some observations to be made here on the subject of policy coordination growing out of common exposures to political stimuli, no matter how discontinuous, or distractive, or irrelevant those stimuli may seem to be. When one ponders the utilisation of the press in foreign policy-making, one cannot help but be struck by how much real coordination of policy in an otherwise decentralised political system is provided by the institution of the press. Common exposure, on a continuous basis, to large amounts of information on foreign affairs, and common understandings of the apparent importance of various issues, help to provide a common context for the specialised efforts of large numbers of participants in the enterprise of foreign policy-making.

Without depreciating in the least the impact of the press upon even the specialists in the Executive branch, one might say that there is greater significance in the fact that Congressmen draw their understanding of the world of foreign affairs from a common pool than in the fact that Executive officials do the same. For one thing, the Executive official does not have the Congressman's constituency problem. The Congressman, as a political specialist, is constituency-oriented; and in the course of his ordinary local routine his exposure to foreign affairs information and salience would come to him in large part through constituency or regional media. Living in Washington, however, usually deprives a Congressman of ready access to the local media, and particularly to his local newspaper on the day of issue; but it does provide him, as a part of the new community he lives in, with a new set of newspapers that reflect the dominant public and political interests of that community. The result is clear: despite the wide range of individual backgrounds, despite the low coverage of foreign affairs and the diversity of emphasis that would be found among constituency papers, Congressmen in Washington are exposed in common to a larger amount of information about the world of foreign affairs, and they are also exposed to uniform measures of salience or importance. To be sure, these men bring diverse attitudes and policy orientations with them that help to condition the way they seek and utilize information about foreign affairs; yet one might speculate that Congressional consideration of foreign policy might be considerably more acrimonious and unfocused and less consistent and relevant than it now is if its participants were differentially, rather than commonly, informed.

By giving policy makers in both branches an insight into the political perceptions of men with important roles in the political process, the press helps to create common understandings or interpretations of political reality. There is thus some significance for the governmental—and hence public-debate on foreign policy in the fact that both Executive officials and Congressmen draw on approximately the same sources for their wider knowledge of "what is going on in the world," and how important it seems to be. Certain kinds of behavior can thus be reasonably predicted, and mutual expectation can become the basis for policy planning. Despite the specialised and confidential character of the State Department's diplomatic channels of information, continuous and meaningful discourse among foreign policy-making officials in all parts of the government, at all times and at all levels, is possible within the bounds set by this independent source of information and intellectual structuring of policy.

No matter what latitude a Congressman may have in general to vote according to his conscience or to go along with his party on various policy issues, he may still find it necessary to try to "touch base" now and again with opinion in his constituency. But the parochialism that lurks in this necessity, and that is enforced on American politics by the electoral system, seems to be somewhat counterbalanced in the case of foreign policy, perhaps by the continuous tapping of a different stratum of opinion in the leading metropolitan newspapers that circulate in Washington. In this respect, the press may be helping to create for all Congressmen a common constituency that is a little closer to the national constituency of the Executive branch and that is commensurate with the national responsibility inherent in the shaping of American foreign policy.

7

The Outward Flow of News

In this chapter, we shall look at the policy makers themselves as sources of news by virtue of the things they choose to say about American foreign relations. The attitudes that foreign policy officials entertain toward the press—the animosity and the fear, the confidence and ambivalence—are ultimately reflected in the flow of information from these officials to the press. An official is also a source of news by dint of his action. In the light of very widespread instrumental attitudes toward the press, and the prevalence of negative feelings about it, what can we say about the flow of news out, about the foreign policy officials' contribution to press coverage of foreign affairs?

In discussing the policy makers' contribution to the fund of information and ideas out of which the daily newspaper is formed, we have to keep in mind a simple distinction between what we might call voluntary and involuntary contributions—between those freely offered and those yielded up in response to varying amounts of extractive pressure and skill. The former represent a range of initiatives on the part of policy makers, the latter a range of initiatives on the part of the correspondents. But in either case the officials who make the contributions are among that small number who have regular contacts with the press—those whom hostility or fear has not driven into a protective isolation. On any given day, the policy makers' contribution to press coverage of foreign affairs is a mixture of voluntary and involuntary elements, in varying compounds.

We can distinguish three different kinds of voluntary contributions to foreign affairs coverage, representing three different levels of *exploitation of the press* in the service of foreign policy.

The first of these is the "handout," or the formal statement or release, offered to correspondents, who generally regard it either as a form of official propaganda or as unimportant and irrelevant information—and sometimes as both. The handout puts the greatest strain on the wire service reporter, who interprets his obligation to report "hard news" so that it includes much of what the officials give out as news. One of these reporters, as he went over his notes after a State Department briefing, muttered angrily adding that the official who handled the briefing was "the only person who went around saying that the Western Allies were in no real disagreement [in late 1958] about how to approach the Soviets in negotiations over Berlin." But despite his feelings on the subject, he still phoned the story in to his office. The men who are responsible for the handouts are aware of the negative sentiments that surround their work. A few of them are so sensitive to the propaganda overtones of the handout that they lean over backwards to strip the releases of any major policy significance; for example, "The news we give them [the reporters] on our own initiative is news of visits of foreign dignitaries, economic aid programs, and agreements with other nations." But in general the handout is designed to give the correspondents "Stuff that might not come to their attention." These help to "set the story straight" as far as the Department is concerned, although they do little to alter the reporters' image of the handout as propaganda.

The second level of voluntary contribution to foreign affairs coverage includes the more serious efforts to keep correspondents informed on major or continuing aspects of foreign relations. These are invariably *ad hoc* efforts through informal channels, and their general purposes may be summarized as letting the leading correspondents and analysts—particularly those who are read by other correspondents—

know what is going on in crucial areas, and what the state of Departmental thinking is in these problem areas, so that newspaper comment will not get divorced from reality as the officials see it. One "Danger" in such a divorce, is that the policy makers may subsequently be forced to adapt themselves to the correspondents' view of reality. Stated this way, the instrumental component in these informational efforts is obvious; it is equally apparent in many of the voluntary contacts between correspondents and informed working level officials, where the very act of informing the reporter in a particular context inescapably involves communicating a particular ordering and interpretation of a set of facts. But these instrumental elements should not obscure our understanding that this is the context in which the press is unobtrusively kept informed—not for attribution and sometimes not even for publication—of the developments that are currently sensitive and therefore not likely to be the subject of official releases or statements.

The third type of voluntary contribution consists of the deliberate instrumental use of the press in order to achieve specific foreign policy objectives. The identification of these occasions, in which information on particular issues is fed to particular reporters or newspapers, is generally difficult, because so many of them are either not acknowledged, or never described in the detail that permits the observer to discriminate among their varied purposes. They usually represent unorthodox political maneuvers, designed to influence the decision-making of particular individuals by shaping their communications environment; hence they are treated with the degree of secrecy commonly associated with security classifications, lest the maneuver backfire or the channels through which information has been flowing be compromised. Because of the secrecy that surrounds them, it is impossible to know just how frequently they occur, and therefore what their comparative importance is among the various types of contributions to the press. For the same reason it is also difficult, from a distance, to distinguish in particular cases between this type and the second type of voluntary contribution.

The staple in the diet of the foreign affairs correspondents, however, consists not of the dishes they are offered but rather of the bones they manage to dig up for themselves. This is the result of the fortuitous intersection of their own preferences and those of foreign policy officials. Unless the reporter's co-operation has been enlisted in the service of a foreign policy cause that he is informed about and sympathetic to, he is inclined to be suspicious when "significant" information is freely offered to him; he wonders what the motive is, and where "truth" lies, and he is not satisfied until he has gone digging around on his own, checking with other sources, and extracted the information that he thinks approximates the true story. A highly respected correspondent phrased it as follows: "I think one's attitude to the State Department.... depends on whether they can come to you with a piece of information, or whether you go to them with a request for some information. If they come to you, there are grounds for skepticism or caution." The foreign policy officials, on the other hand, are not disposed to give away information on current policies unless some instrumental purpose can be served by doing so. The policy officials would rather let the reporters come to them with specific questions; in that way they protect themselves against the possibility of giving out information for which there is no present "demand," as well as having the protection afforded by the recourse to "no comment." Both the correspondents and the officials, then, prefer to work on the principle that foreign affairs reporting is extractive. Even in the public affairs area of the State Department, it is acknowledged that "our contacts with correspondents are usually a result of their initiative."

An important consequence of this preference for "involuntary" contributions to foreign affairs coverage is that, as the initiative is passed to the correspondents, so is a large part of the responsibility for the definition of news; here is created the need to keep a few leading correspondents informed on a personal and informal basis, to keep them "on the track." Furthermore, with the initiative in the hands of the reporter, an important task of the State Department official is to "keep up with the news"—i.e., with what is already in the newspapers—so they will know what to expect by way of further requests for information. It would not be a great exaggeration to define the government's basic public information programs in the foreign policy area in these same terms. The important phases of those programs, especially the press conferences and news releases, are substantially guided by a process that might be called "playing reporter"—that is, the officials prepare for the reporters' initiatives by going through the same steps as the reporter does in *his* search for news. By thoroughly, exposing themselves to the current market in news, they can predict with reasonable accuracy the questions that the correspondents will be asking on any particular day. On the basis of these predictions they are able to make sensible advance preparations of their answers. The major influence on the daily pattern of public information out of Washington on foreign policy comes, circuitously, from the press rather than from the officials responsible for foreign affairs. There is a larger political significance in this, involving questions of public participation and political control in a democratic society. Those who are concerned about "managed news," about the control that the government exercises over the citizen's view of the world, may find comfort in the fact that in ordinary circumstances the press still bears the largest responsibility for the shape of foreign policy information. But those who are concerned about the substance of those images of the world will note that the way the press goes about shaping that pattern of public information is not characterized by any orderly or systematic approach to the substance of foreign affairs, nor by any explicit understanding of what public information might usefully consist in.

The press coverage of foreign affairs is a similar mixture of voluntary and involuntary contributions, but here the extractive principle is the more usual. The number of Congressmen involved is small, and the total contribution is much less—three observations that follow from our prior discussion of the pattern of Congressional attitudes toward the foreign policy press. Even the foreign policy leaders in the Congress, those who can summon reporters, feel inhibited in the foreign policy area, and prefer to "answer questions" rather than to "call in reporters," although they will of course give them advance copies of occasional foreign policy speeches in order to maximize publicity. On their part, the reporters themselves are more interested in the foreign policy votes than the foreign policy views of the large majority of Congressmen; they reserve their efforts for those few people, on the foreign affairs committees or in leadership positions, who are likely to have reliable information about foreign policy itself or about legislative possibilities concerning foreign policy issues.

THE CHANNELS OF NEWS

An elaborate network of formal and informal channels is at hand for use by officials in their efforts to feed information to the press, and by correspondents in their attempts to elicit information and comment from officials. Most of the institutions that sustain or comprise these channels have been abundantly described elsewhere; the only point in discussing them further is to delineate their usefulness to the men involved in them.

The most important of the formal organizations within the Department of State is the Office of News, formerly the News Division, the Director of which is the person most frequently identified in reporters' accounts as "a State Department spokesman." The Office of News has a staff of about twenty men, who have geographically and functionally organized responsibilities for news distribution, who monitor the teletypes, and who run the latest news through the Department. The Office is the reporters' formal point of access to the Department; the Director holds a "briefing," a small-scale news conference, every day at noon, which provides the Department with a regular outlet for routine statements, announcements, charges, replies, and so forth, and which offers the reporters an opportunity to ask some of the more obvious questions that the morning newspapers will have generated. The noon briefing, an outgrowth of Secretary of State Hull's daily meetings with the press is attended by approximately 30 reporters, mostly from the leading domestic and foreign wire services, syndicates, and newspapers, and most of them will depreciate its importance, given the slightest opportunity. One of them remarked, "Some days...we sit out there all day and get propaganda. Other days we get nothing from them." After the morning flurry of preparation for the noon meeting with the correspondents, the staff has the time to "field" the less obvious questions that individual reporters may put to them in more private audience. And when the News Office cannot handle a question satisfactorily, either alone or after consultation with the policy people, it will put the reporter in touch with officials in the Department who are closer to the substantive problem.

Another formal channel of news is the Public Affairs Adviser attached to each geographical and functional bureau in State Department. The Public Affairs Adviser's (PAA's) primary responsibility is, in the words of one of them, "to flag the substantive people, and force them to focus on the public relations problems of our foreign policy." In practice, however, the PAA himself handles many of the public relations problems, and "we have to field a lot of hot ones the press hands us." The PAA's are also an important point of access for the reporter, if they cannot effectively work out an answer to an inquiry in consultation with the country desk, they will put a correspondent in direct touch with the appropriate political officers. This self-appraisal is shared by most of the reporters, who also see the PAA's as lesser parts of the "handout" system, as cogs in the Department's propaganda machine. We can recall here a reporter's characterization, quoted earlier, of the PAA's as "a gateway to the obvious."

The formal press conference is another important institutional channel of news, but a comparatively infrequent one. Few Secretaries of State in recent years have met the press as regularly and often as John Foster Dulles. His press conferences were generally scheduled the day before the President's, and were approximately as frequent; they were also well covered by reporters. Part of the interest in those conferences developed from the fact that Dulles was likely to answer questions by enunciating new lines of policy, often taking his staff by surprise. For most Secretaries, however, the press conference has been an occasional device, and their obvious lack of enthusiasm for it has been reciprocated by the correspondents, whose reportorial habits and notions of journalistic skill do not easily accommodate to the increasingly public nature and public functions of the press conference. Some of the leading correspondents, in fact, make a point of not attending press conferences. Within the confines of the questions raised by the reporters, the press conference offers the Department a chance to state its positions; and the Secretary is free to make whatever additional statements he wishes. Most observers in the Department are prone to call the conference a "vital and important" institution; but the view from the top is a little different. The man on the spot is likely to be more impressed by the potential difficulties and dangers than by the opportunities and advantages, which is why Secretaries of State have had such little recourse to it, on the whole. A former Secretary of State-criticized the institution on the grounds that news was made "by the reporters asking questions, not by the President or the Secretary of State who wants or has something to say." A high official in the State Department called the press conference a "dubious sport": "The problem arises because of the disparity of your audiences. It is like having just one vaudeville act for both a men's smoker and a church social." There are, of course, other functions and purposes that are served by formal press conferences—the often-drawn parallel with the British Question Hour is suggestive of these—and there are other lines of criticism that would need to be brought into an over-all assessment of press conferences, but we are not attempting such an assessment here. Our present purpose is rather to point out those gross features of the press conference that bear upon its usefulness as a channel for the dissemination of foreign policy information.

Speeches constitute another formal device through which officials can contribute to press coverage of foreign affairs. Talks by policy officials may constitute official declarations of policy, or merely explanations and restatements of it; the chief difficulty with these as a way of getting wide distribution of the views enunciated is the official's lack of control over the uses made of them at the receiving end. The task of getting good newspaper coverage of speeches may be facilitated by preparing good press releases that tell the reporters what the speaker's important points are meant to be, and by some judicious phone calls reminding reporters of the talk and conveying some sense of its significance. But even then most officials habitually describe press coverage of their speeches as capricious. One official reported the following experience: "I gave a major speech in Kentucky once...which got no publicity. Six weeks later, I gave much of the substance of it in an off-the-cuff address here in Washington, and it got big press coverage with no effort on my part. In the first instance, there was even a good press release, and yet it was not picked up nationally—only locally in Kentucky. and then you appear here casually, and you get wide coverage. I wouldn't say there is no rhyme or reason to it—just that it is hard to know what the rhyme or reason is." The reporters, however, take refuge in the concept of "news", and if their passing judgment is that they are being treated not to important declarations of policy but rather to restatements of position, their disposition either to accept it as "news" or to ignore it as "propaganda" is strongly influenced by the number and nature of the other things that are "in the news" that day.

It should be clear from these remarks that the formal lines of news distribution in the State Department and in other agencies having foreign policy responsibilities are adequate and satisfactory only for the more formal or routine types of messages about foreign affairs, and for the declaratory aspects of foreign policy—that is, when the announcement of an official position is itself an important or even an essential part of the policy. Since there are many of these items in contemporary foreign policy, these lines are busy most of the time. They are much less efficacious for the not-for attribution material relating to on-going foreign relations or the non-declaratory phases of policy; and so they are not the channels that are used by officials in offering, or by correspondents in eliciting, these kinds of information. And while the correspondents have to cover the former class of material in the performance of their neutral role as objective recorders of daily history, they are usually more interested in the latter class and so they work hard at the cultivation of the necessary informal channels.

These informal connections range from the structured background briefings that Department officials will manage on particular occasions, to the casual private conversations on a personal level between a correspondent and an official. The former are sometimes hard to distinguish from press conferences, the latter from ordinary discourse between individuals. The distinctive feature of a "backgrounder" is that the material given the reporter cannot be quoted or attributed to particular officials, or identified as the official viewpoint of the Department, nor is it considered binding. The purpose, most generally, is to enlighten and instruct the reporters, to let them share the thinking and perspectives of the policy officials, "so that they know what they should know about important policy matters"; "so they will act responsibly"; "so they will not go off half-cocked." Another important purpose is to get politically useful information into circulation without revealing the source. Some officials insist that only the Office of News gives out news, and that in their own background discussions with reporters they provide only a context or perspective; but apart from the non-attributability of the latter the distinction may be meaningless to a reporter. Context or perspective lends meaning to events, and may be "newsworthy" in itself. In fact, the distribution of the foreign affairs correspondent's time as between the News Office and his own contacts throughout the Department shows that the distinction between news and perspective is a distinction without a difference.

Informal sessions with reporters can be varied to meet almost any kind of circumstance. Assistant Secretaries of State have regularly held background briefings of a relatively well-structured sort. Secretary Dulles would often have a dinner discussion with a small group of correspondents, senior in status, who stood by, as it were, ever ready for a hint from on high that the Secretary would welcome a dinner invitation. Some of Dulles' critics suggest that the hints came whenever the Secretary was getting especially rough treatment in the press. The practice itself, however, is a common one, and many friends of Secretary Acheson attribute his difficulties with the press to his refusal to "play favorites" among the foreign affairs correspondents in this fashion. The luncheon conversation with a reporter is another very common practice among policy officials, but it is only one variety of what an official called "backgrounding *a deux*"; other forms are curricular, in the sense that they are a sanctioned use of the working time to those officials who have the inclination and competence to deal directly with the reporters. And, of course, there are extensive personal friendships between correspondents and officials, of a kind that facilitates the interchange of information not otherwise shared between the two institutions. There are thus multiple opportunities for officials to "plant a story" in private, and as a result there is a steady flow of information pertaining to current developments in foreign relations—called "leaks" by people who have not given it out themselves—from all sides of the Department.

CRITERIA GOVERNING THE DISTRIBUTION OF NEWS

The foreign policy official who has some reason for talking to reporters has no trouble finding a way. There are, to be sure, some fine points that he may want to consider in making his choice of the most appropriate channels—whether to make a public speech, for example, or to make a statement at the start of a press conference; whether to pass the word along to a small number of leading columnists, or to talk to a particular one; or whether to prepare a handout, etc.—but these are not separable from the specific issues of substance that he wants to discuss and the reasons that lie behind them, since his choice will be shaped in some measure by his estimate of the effects of handling particular policy ideas in particular ways. Questions of purpose, therefore, are relevant in any consideration of approaches to the press. What kinds of regularities can we discover in the reasons for the distribution of foreign policy information? What are some of the criteria governing the channeling of foreign affairs news to the press?

Ideological Considerations

The point was made in the preceding chapter that ideological or philosophical reasons for being favorably disposed toward the press are weak, and subordinate to instrumental reasons. The same rank ordering exists among the two sets of considerations with respect to the actual distribution of particular items of information, although a new factor is involved. Decisions to release or reveal specific bits of "news" are more likely to be made—or at least justified—on general ideological grounds, the more their content is routine and declaratory or peripheral to policy matters. The public affairs personnel, partly because they are responsible for the bulk of the routine material, and partly because their jobs are defined in this fashion, are much more likely than the policy people to advance the general criterion of "informing the public" as the basis for decisions on what information is to be given to reporters. But even in the public affairs area the rationale is perfunctory and suspect; since anything that is given to the press serves to "inform the public", the criterion itself is non-discriminating. It may even be worse than that: because the criterion embodies democratic virtues that are politically equivalent to "home" and "mother," it permits the user to embrace any kind of public information policy or practice he wants, releasing or withholding information on other bases but justifying the output as a desire "to make more and more information available to the public." This is not to argue that manipulators of public understanding are deliberately hiding behind the mask of a democratic philosophy, but rather that the philosophy itself induces an unknowing self-deception among people who have extremely difficult decisions to make, and have no other way of explaining or justifying their choices; they sincerely believe that their selections are motivated by an effort to inform the public—"we try to keep the public honestly informed"—but that would be the case no matter what selections they made.

There are other versions of ideological criteria that are less comprehensive in a philosophical sense but more effective and honest discriminators of information that should or should not be given out. These are articulated more frequently by officials with policy responsibility and they reflect a greater concern with practical questions and with purposeful or instrumental reasons for "informing the public." One of these is a concern that the American public be alerted to developing problems, "to clouds on the foreign horizon which may, indeed, threaten our very existence," in the hope that responses to crises can be carefully fashioned in advance rather than convulsively adopted in the midst of the event. The choice of news to this end, to "directing the attention of the public to certain items," seems to be made after estimating the extent of Congressional and public participation in particular acts of policy-making, and the likely direction that these involvements will take if left along. It is also motivated by longer-run concerns about the stability and continuity of American foreign policy, by desires to put American participation in international politics on a predictable and sustaining basis. Another yardstick of this kind—i.e., a practical concern with the state of public information—is provided by rough estimates of the level of public anxiety. If the public, whether sampled through the press or by other means, seems to be worried about particular aspects or manifestations of American foreign policy, then these suggest obvious guides to the choice of subjects and of materials to be discussed with correspondents.

Promotional Considerations

The capacity of the foreign policy maker actually to get material into the newspaper is a product of several factors that we have already discussed, and it seems a worthwhile digression at this point to recapitulate a few of the more salient ones. Working *for* the official who approaches the correspondent with some information are all those features of the reporter's orientation that we summarized in Chapter II as the neutral roles of the Press. We pointed out that one consequence of the reporter's felt obligation to transmit information "objectively" was to make him peculiarly susceptible to being "used" by policy makers who come bearing information shaped to suit their own purposes. coming *against* the official, however serve their own purposes. As a Senator observed, "The best politics is to inform the people about policies and problems." Where we can account for these situations, we shall; but where latent criteria are not apparent, as is most often the case, there is little we can do but keep the possible interconnections in mind, focus on the manifest content of the considerations that are put forth, and treat the varieties of promotion as if they were distinct types.

Policy Promotion

The advancement of policy interests is by far the most frequently articulated motivation behind the distribution of foreign policy news; it is expressed about as often as institutional and personal advancement combined. Even so, it is hard to know exactly how much oil one has struck here; the main pool of policy promotion is probably hidden from view under layers and layers of private inhibitions against disclosure, inhibitions that are reinforced by Congress's well-known dislike for anything that might resemble domestic "propaganda." So the closer one gets to the possible use of the press on behalf of policies not yet stamped with the official, the more one feels that the well of reliable information has begun to run dry. There are no inhibitions, however, against supplying information to the press in order to organize general public support—usually defined no closer than that—for policies that are agreed and adopted, and may thus be regarded as official. On the contrary, this is thought to be part of the continuing problem of citizen education in the foreign policy field, and an obligation rather than a competitive challenge for the State Department.

Despite all the reasons for reticence, there is still ample evidence that the press is used extensively to gain broad public and political support for policies and programs that are not yet official or authoritative, in the sense that they have not yet been approved by Congress, as well as to strengthen ever-fragile declaratory policies by clarifying and restating the positions and intentions of authoritative (if unidentified) officials. On still another level, the press is used to build up support, or at least some political resonance, for proposals that are still contesting for acceptance as policies within the Administration.

Institutional Promotion

The promotion of foreign policy institutions within the general political system is like most institutional advertising with which the reader is familiar; it involves the use of the press not to pursue a particular policy directly, but rather to "sell" the organization that produces it, thus creating a favorable environment for existing policies and for future ones. The building provides for institutional advertising in foreign affairs include the quality of the personnel as well as the achievements of the past, which are projected into the future in the form of over-all trends of policy. And like other organizations trying to build up their corporate image, the foreign policy institutions are concerned about the presentation and handling of the materials on these subjects—the packaging of its various policies.

The press is also used to try to build up the position of foreign policy institutions within the governmental circle. The careful programming and staging of Congressional hearings to maximize favorable coverage are an obvious example, but substantially greater opportunities to create an institutional image exist in the Executive branch. The need is also greater there, because of the competition from other Executive agencies and because of the dependence on the Congress for agency funds. A Washington correspondent has described the period from January to June each year as "the period when Congress is considering appropriations and each agency is passing out carefully selected information to make itself look good." How much is actually accomplished this way, however, is a matter for further study; in an environment where all institutions are understood to have a deep interest in the outcome of all competitions in which they are involved, the information they release may be received with skepticism, if not suspicion. As a Congressman put it, "One knows that Hagerty, Lincoln White, and Murray Snyder are doing a selling job, so one discounts it." It is a common feature of Congressional criticism that the State Department "uses the press as the organ for its propaganda program." But even if the intended audience is not entirely convinced, it may still be the case that a residue remains, and also that the less perceptive citizen who reads from a political as well as a geographical distance is getting a picture of reality that is drawn by an interplay of divergent institutional interests that are not all apparent to him.

Personal Promotion

It is sometimes difficult to distinguish incidents and possibilities of personal advancement from the other varieties of promotion, especially since personal interests are almost always associated with institutional or policy interests and are not likely to be made explicit by the person involved. Personal promotion may be regarded as one manifestation of politics, both electoral and administrative, in which a variety of interests may be served at one time. Despite the hazards of attributing any particular resort to the media in the foreign policy field primarily to considerations of personal advancement, such interpretations of political motivation on the part of others are being made all the time by participants in the foreign policy process.

Congressional use of the press for these purposes is relatively easy to observe, even though there is not a great deal of it in the foreign policy field. Efforts of Congressmen to get favorable publicity for their speeches are well known, as is their introduction of foreign policy resolutions that are meant only as a sop to their constituencies. The members of the Foreign Relations Committee are often described as feeling more responsible for American foreign policy than most of their colleagues, yet even there, "Members who want to cultivate the press leave hints around, and the reporters can develop a story." And one frequently runs across suggestions that the few Senators who have achieved national prominence as foreign affairs specialists in the post World War II period, like Vandenberg and George, have done so partly through their mutually accommodating relations with reporters.

On the upper levels in the Executive branch, where the stakes in political ambitions and political reputations are high, there have been some spectacular illustrations of personal promotion as an apparent criterion governing the distribution of foreign policy news. The long-drawn-out dispute in 1957 between Secretary Dulles and Harold Stassen, Special Assistant to the President, on US approaches to disarmament and arms control was often joined in the news columns, as first one and then the other would give his version of the issues and his thoughts on his opponent's position to reporters in background conferences contemporary observers.

It would be a distortion to conclude that foreign policy news is heavily shaped by these personal considerations. Yet if foreign policy keeps increasing in importance among the live issues in American politics, we may expect to see more people trying to establish their political reputations by dealing in foreign policy information. And the problem of determining the relevant "reality" through the public prints will be that much greater.

External Policy Considerations

Paralleling the uses of the press to promote foreign policies at home are its uses to promote policies abroad; here we shall bring together the external, or foreign policy, purposes behind the distribution of foreign affairs information.

There are two sides to the coin of external policy considerations, two manifestations that seem to be of equal importance. There is the giving of specific material to reporters as an instrument of policy to influence the behavior of others in foreign countries, and there is the withholding of specific material from reporters in order to prevent undesired influences on behavior abroad. Since the international impact of foreign affairs information is cited as the chief reason for restraint in the release of information at home, it is appropriate to consider these negative criteria along with the positive ones.

Foreign policy officials are reluctant to discuss in detail the active uses of the press to promote particular foreign policy interests, and so one ordinarily hears more about the restrictions that external policy requirements impose upon a domestic public information policy than about the opportunities they offer.

The reasons for the general reluctance to talk this way are twofold at least. For government officials to acknowledge that some news items—those that are not so obvious that they need no acknowledgment—have foreign policy objectives is to involve the American government explicitly in enterprises that look like "interference" in the internal affairs of other countries, running the risk that the efforts will backfire and also that future attempts to communicate with foreign governments through the press might be excessively discounted. And for officials to acknowledge these things is also to complicate and compromise their relations with the correspondents upon whom they depend to give prominence to the items. These correspondents may or may not understand the latent significance of a particular story, and that they themselves are being used for policy purposes; but even if they do understand and accept these things, the moral requirements of objectivity and independence for the press mean that they cannot passively accept their being made explicit. Indeed, James Reston has claimed that the "whole controversy" between the press and the government during the Cuban blockade arose only when Assistant Secretary Sylvester made the government's intention explicit: "As long as the officials merely didn't tell the whole truth, very few of us complained; but as soon as Sylvester told the truth, the editors fell on him like a fumble."

As negative criteria—as reasons governing the non-distribution of information to correspondents—external policy considerations affect a sizable range of topics. The most obvious, perhaps, involve diplomatic actions and negotiations, where political advantages or bargaining positions might be undermined or lost if they were given out too early, or where the opportunities for slow and delicate compromise in sensitive areas might disappear if they became the subject of daily newspaper discussion. "We don't expect General Motors to issue descriptions or pictures of its new automobiles to its competitors months in advance of their release; why should the United States government be put in that kind of a position with respect of *its* competitors?" "You cannot carry on negotiations for a missile tracking station on a small island... if there are going to be constant newspaper announcements about it." The constraints on the distribution of information to reporters during the blockade of Cuba in the fall of 1962 are an especially vivid illustration of this criterion.

Secondly, there are subjects that fall under the ban for reasons best summarized as the sensitivity of other peoples or governments, which is to say that large aspects of our foreign relations are dependent on "good will," and hence that the propriety of revelation may be a more significant criterion than the truth as far as foreign governments, policies, and officials are concerned. Governments, like private persons, do not publicly call attention to the frailties or infidelities of people they have to live and work with; nor do they publicly reveal their true thoughts about someone else's manners, intentions, and aspirations when to do so would be disruptive of ordinary good relations; nor can they claim full public credit for good works if the persons thus benefited are embarrassed by the revelations.

As a third class of subjects calling for restraint we might include the range of foreign policies still to be bargained for and negotiated at home; just as there are points where publicity may help one out in the process of policy-making, there are times when to tip one's hand is to guarantee victory to one's competitors. These are not always external policy considerations, to be sure, but one suspects that foreign policy officials sometimes handle them as such because secrecy in the name of the national interest has social sanction, while secrecy for the sake of narrow political advantage is always under attack from the press.

As positive criteria—as reasons governing the distribution of information to reporters—external policy considerations are no doubt more potent than an outside observer can judge (or than a participant can record). We can easily discover the important use of the press, however, in declaratory policy or declaratory aspects of policy, where the statement or announcement of intentions, of programs, of past performances—indeed, of any aspect of foreign relations—is itself a vital element in the policy. The wide dissemination of information about Christmas food packages abroad, about the Congo troop airlift, about aid programs where the economic effects will not be felt for months or years; the more focused communication through the press to foreign governments, dropping hints about a willingness to talk or restating firm obligations of support or deliberately obscuring our likely responses by ambiguous forecasts (e.g., a "keep-them-guessing" policy such as we have relied on for the defense of Quemoy and Matsu)—these are a few examples of the communicative or declaratory aspects of foreign policy. They illustrate how the press as a system of communication has become an integral part of the battery of instruments by means of which American foreign policy makers try to influence the expectations and the behaviors of other peoples and governments—friends and allies as well as potential enemies and countries with wandering affections.

It is not always possible to distinguish between the substantive political component of policies and their declaratory overtones, because some courses of action must be verbally communicated before they can begin to be effective and thus the declaratory aspects are essential parts of the policy. On the other hand, there is little possibility for confusion about the use of the press for the direct exchange of remarks and viewpoints with foreign governments, where the discourse itself constitutes the entire political relationship; this scoring of minor points in an endless exchange of charges, denials, and countercharges has been a characteristic policy weapon always with all nations. The press may also be employed in countless other ways to support particular policies or lines of policy, ways that are neither declaratory nor propagandistic. Cater points out how it has been used to focus public attention (and thus political attention) quickly on potentially dangerous situations, and to put pressure on an ally in order to induce concessions in subsequent negotiations. The practical effect of these uses of the press is to alter the political pressures on our competitors or opponents, or at least their perceptions of future degrees of opposition or support; Secretary Dulles' news conference warning to the French of an "agonizing reappraisal" of American policy if the French defeated EDC is a good example.

The Testing of Reactions

The "trial balloon," the calculated indiscretion that is designed to test reactions to new policy ideas, constitutes one of the best—or at least the most widely—understood reasons for the distribution of foreign policy information, even though it is far from the most common use made of the press by foreign policy makers. By definition the technique is reserved for new, potentially unpopular decisions; these may be ones for which there are reasonable alternatives, so that if the reaction turns out to be adverse, then a different decision can be made. But policies can be tested that will be put into effect in any case, the results of the testing providing data on which to base public information programs to make the policy choice more palatable. Implicitly, also, the flotation of trial balloons is the province chiefly of the higher levels in the foreign policy establishment, where authoritative decisions can be made on the basis of the data that the testing has provided.

Foreign policy officials defend as a practical necessity the use of the press to measure reactions both abroad and at home, but they give it far less attention than they pay to other reasons for releasing information to reporters. Among its very considerable advantages for foreign policy officials are the speed of the data collection and the possibility of tailoring it to a very precise set of potential policy specifications. Alternative systems exist for estimating public reactions, particularly of wide and distant publics; for example, polls, the mail, local party officials, organizational representations and literature, and day-by-day scrutiny of ordinary press coverage. They are, however, much slower, and unless they are specifically undertaken by officials with particular questions in mind, they have the further weakness that they can be applied to new policy possibilities only as a result of inference and extrapolation from other and perhaps crucially different issues. But even among the near-by political community, the trial balloon can elicit within hours a sample of political responses to specific proposals that would require a greater degree of commitment as well as much more time and effort to evoke by such means as private exploratory discussions, for example. To be sure, there are problems in the interpretation of reactions that are stirred up by trial balloons in the press, too, but after some experience with the technique, the very pattern of reactions—the sources, the intensity, and so forth—itself furnishes clues to the way that the proposals will be received.

While the interview data at hand do not refer to it, one can imagine a situation where Executive testing of foreign reactions through the press might conveniently take place through the agency of a friendly Congressman. Testing out foreign reactions to new policy developments may be less disruptive of existing relations if the overtures seem to come from the Congress; if the response from abroad is too severe, the suggestion can be more easily disavowed and the official foreign policy agencies of the government are less likely to feel the chill wind from abroad.

Conclusion

These varied considerations that shape the foreign policy official's approach to the distribution of news are presented here largely in a classificatory way, with little attempt at ordering or locating them in an on-going political structure. Hence they do not pretend to explain the press behavior of particular officials at particular times, but only to point out the range and character of the influences that come to bear on the release of foreign policy information. These criteria are interwoven in a fabric of discourse between officials and correspondents, in which the initiative most often rests with the reporter and the official has to make the best of his opportunities to achieve the "mix" of interests that seems reasonable to him. A more elaborate study is clearly indicated, to ascertain the magnitude, location, and relative significance of the different motivations behind this active use of the press.

Perhaps the most compelling argument for more systematic knowledge of these motivations is that they are helping to shape our daily image of what is relevant and important in foreign policy; and in the absence of satisfactory knowledge about the reasons why these particular segments of reality are the ones that "make history" today, we cannot properly evaluate the information contained in the news stories. Are we reading about a potential crisis, for example, because there is a high probability that it will actually materialize, or because there is a high probability that it will facilitate a Congressional appropriation, or strengthen someone's hand in a forthcoming negotiation? A better understanding of how the press serves a multitude of political and policy-making purposes might well diminish its efficacy with respect to some of those purposes; but we are not even in a position to begin to judge the net balance of advantage and disadvantage on the basis of our present inadequate knowledge of the motivations and of the degree to which they serve their purposes in practice. We may get a better comprehension of the latter problem, however, if we turn now to what is taken *out* of the press by foreign policy officials.

8

Libel

A. LIBELS COMMITTED BY THE PRESS

The greater its audience, the heavier weighs a defamation. The large circulation of the press has led, therefore, in many countries to special regulations regarding libels committed by newspapers. Often they are the main part of the press laws. In fact, the defamation perpetrated by the press has been at all times the real press offence overshadowing all other infringements of which a periodical may render itself guilty. The notion of this offence was and is most far-reaching in the Anglo-Saxon countries; it involves there not only the defamation of private persons, but also of church, government, sovereign, members of the cabinet, and includes any comment on public or private events which may chance to give offence to anyone.

1. TREMENDOUS POWER OF THE PRINTED WORD

The rigorous punishment, to which newspapers are liable according to these laws, reflects the importance attributed to the printed word. He whom the newspaper praises is thereby elevated, while he whom it exposes to contempt might as well be annihilated. This idea, which is not necessarily correct, has been alive in millions of people since there have been newspapers. In fact, it is perhaps the greatest power wielded by the press. Just as it is the nightmare of many people to find their name printed in a newspaper one day in an unpleasant connection, it is, on the other hand, their most ardent desire to receive an honourable mention in these columns. Every day the readers see evidence of this power. In innumerable cases the disaster does not follow from the sentence of the court, but from the report of it, which may cause an imprisonment of one week to become a life-long condemnation. Unpleasant family matters, if published, may grow into big affairs, which bring misfortune to the people concerned. A commercial incident may lead to bankruptcy if it is mentioned by the newspaper. No wonder that particular legal protection against the abuse of this power has been demanded.

The press has never denied its influence. On the contrary, it is at pains to show its readers continually what a powerful organ speaks to them. Indeed, is it not the general impression that the newspaper is above all public institutions? Newspapers both teach and criticise parties, governments and even parliament itself. A minister who has not met with the approval of a journal resigns and the readers are convinced and confirmed therein by the newspaper that it was its editorial comment which led to his dismissal. The paper mentions a candidate, whom it credits with the abilities for the position to which he aspires and whose good chances it knows. The next day he is appointed. Thus the newspaper appears to be an institution, from which favour and reprimand go out and which may bring honour to some and to others the pillory.

In view of this great authority which the press exercises, a defamation committed by a newspaper has always been considered a serious offence, which must be judged more strictly than an attack upon honour and reputation carried out by other means. But even in countries where the proceedings take place according to the ordinary rules of law, the publicity caused by the publication is regarded as an aggravating circumstance. Private life must be protected. He who avoids public attention should not be exposed to contempt or ridicule.

Prosecution in Respect of Libels

Outside the countries governed by the common law it is

left, as a rule, to the libelled person to institute the prosecution of the offence. The press law of Estonia makes an exception by prohibiting 'publications which may impair the reputation of a citizen' (art. 16(6)). Therefore, in the case of a defamation the accusation against the responsible newspaper-man is brought by the public prosecutor. In other countries a defamation is indeed a punishable offence, but proceedings only take place if the offended person brings an action. In Chile, if he is absent, his relatives may sue for him (1872, art. 7).

In the Anglo-Saxon world, however, defamation is chiefly the subject of a civil action, by which the offended person claims damages for the damage done to his reputation. Only in a few cases of a particularly serious defamation may the public prosecutor move the prosecution of the offender, but, as a rule, damages are also claimed in a civil action. In this way, two law suits are instituted at the same time. In the United States the courts are more frequently called upon to try criminal libels than in Great Britain.

Regulations on criminal libel are in force in several states of the American Union, e.g. in Indiana (s. 10-3201) or in Michigan (s. 16.812) where a person, who publishes or knowingly aids in publishing a libel or a false charge accusing another person of a crime or of a degrading or infamous act, shall be deemed guilty of criminal libel. In South Dakota (pars. 4082/3) 'any malicious injury to good name, other than by words orally spoken, is a criminal libel, and every person, who wilfully and with a malicious intent to injure another, publishes any criminal libel, is guilty of a misdemeanour.'

Defamation and Insult

A defamation may appear in one of various forms which cannot always be distinguished. The French law draws a distinction between an insult (*injure*) and the proper defamation (*diffamation*). The former renders a person liable to contempt without accusing him of a special offence; the latter, however, contains a concrete charge, for instance, of having committed a dishonourable act. It is an insult to call someone a 'fool,' while the expression 'liar' is a defamation. In both cases the intention to cause damage must be presumed.

In the Anglo-Saxon countries statements, by which a person is exposed to ridicule, hatred, or contempt, or his reputation is damaged, are regarded as defamatory. The expressions used need not be *per se* defamatory, but may be misrepresentations of facts, malicious comments, even harmless words which, however, in a certain circle are conceived to be injurious. In general, a defamation by the press may be defined in the Anglo-Saxon world as a statement which, considering the circumstances of the publication, arouses in reasonable people the impression of a defamation.

2. DAMAGES FOR LIBEL IN GREAT BRITAIN

In the countries of the British Empire, particularly in Great Britain, juries are inclined to award high damages in libel actions, incomparably higher than in the United States of America, although, on the whole, the legal basis for such awards is the same. The question why juries in Great Britain tend to award such high damages cannot be answered easily; various circumstances are responsible.

Reputation as a Commercial Asset

Defamation impairs the reputation enjoyed by a person in the circle in which he is living. Reputation does not stand for personal qualities of character, but only for the esteem in which a person is held. This reputation is gained, often in the course of a long time, by corresponding conduct and represents, therefore, a possession of which people are proud and which they try to preserve not less carefully than their health. Reputation is an important means of existence. Certainly it may involve moral considerations, but, as a rule, society sees in it chiefly the result of professional conduct. Both are taken into account in the phrase 'the merchant of repute,' 'the physician,' or 'farmer,' and so on, 'of repute.' Often much money is spent in order to establish a reputation: working capital for a business or a professional practice, educational expenses, and so on. Some may therefore connect the reputation of a 'citizen of repute' with the commercial values involved and may feel in a position to assess the damages resulting from defamation.

Commercial Considerations in Assessing Damage to Reputation

It is obvious that in a country like England, where the greater part of the population is either engaged in business or has grown up in commercial traditions, considerations of this kind play an important part in assessing the amount of damages in actions for defamation. But even if among the twelve members of a jury men of business should be in the minority, their opinion will claim the strongest attention. They are experienced, skilful, and capable of convincing others. Their votes will therefore decide the issue within the jury in cases where the commercial reputation of a person is injured and his credit shaken. But being men who are accustomed to think in figures, they will also be heard if the defamation concerns personal character. The measure laid down in cases of this kind of defamation is not very different. In the first case commercial, in the second social connections are endangered; in the first case financial credit is shaken, in the second social expulsion may take place.

Thus commercial considerations are applied even where they do not appear to be justified, and damages are awarded in cases of defamation which cause great surprise outside the jury—not least among the judges.

The Leading Libel Cases

The most discussed judgment in a case of press libel which has always been felt by the British newspaper world as extremely disquieting, arose from the famous suit of Artemus Jones against the publishers, E. Hulton & Co. The case is quoted as *Hulton* v. *Jones,* because Jones was the respondent when the case came before the higher courts. It was finally decided in the House of Lords in 1909.

Its importance justifies some remarks. The *Sunday chronicle* published an amusing article one Sunday about the behaviour of Englishmen who crossed the Channel to attend the motor festival in Dieppe. The passages which led to the action run as follows :

'Whist! there is Artemus Jones with a woman who is not his wife, who must be, you know, the other thing!' Whispers a fair neighbour of mine excitedly in her bosom friend's ear. Really, is it not surprising how certain of our fellow countrymen behave when they come abroad? who would suppose, by his going on, that he was a churchwarden at Peckham? No one, indeed, would assume that Jones in the atmosphere of London would take on so austere a job as the duties of a churchwarden. Here, in the atmosphere of Dieppe, on the French side of the Channel, he is the life and soul of a gay little band that haunts the casino and turns night into day, besides betraying a most unholy delight in the society of female butterflies.'

Artemus Jones was a fictitious name. The author, who was the French correspondent of the paper, chose the unusual Christian name because a well-known humorist (Artemus Ward) bore it. But it happened that an Artemus Jones felt offended by the article and brought an action. It was true, he was not a churchwarden, he did not live in Peckham, was not married, and had taken no part in the Dieppe festival; but witnesses stated they had referred the story to him. The jury awarded him £1,750 and the higher courts upheld the judgment.

The decision involves a great risk to publishers, as Artemus Jones' success may encourage other persons to look in fictions for doubtful characters whose names happen to be identical with their own and to take their chance on bringing a libel action.

This risk was even extended by a judgment given in a similar libel case (*Newstead* v. *London Express Newspaper Ltd.* (1940)). A court report in the *Daily Express* (London) under the heading 'Why do people commit bigamy?' started: 'Harold Newstead, 30 years' old Camberwell man, who was jailed for nine months, liked having two wives at once.' the story was true. It chanced, however, that another man of the same name and age lived in Camberwell and sued the paper. Counsel of the newspaper pointed out that the principles laid down in *Hulton* v. *Jones* were not applicable because in that case a fictitious, while in this a real person was involved, and because this time the story was true. But the court, below and the Court of Appeal did not accept this view. Thus the principle of *Hulton* v. *Jones* applies if the publication truly relates to a certain real person and is thought to refer to another real person.

The second ruling newspaper libel case (*Cassidy* v. *Daily Mirror*) (1929)) was caused by the publication of a photograph in the London *Daily Mirror* of Mr. C. and Miss X with the caption beneath it. 'Mr. C., the race-horse owner, and Miss X., whose engagement has been announced.' But Mr. C. was married and his wife claimed damages for libel because in the circle where she lived and was reputed as C.'s lawful wife, she would be regarded after that publication as his mistress.

The jury awarded to her £500 and the Court of Appeal upheld the judgment.

In a similar case of late (*Hough* v. *London Express Newspaper Ltd.* (1940)) an even more hostile attitude towards newspapers can be seen. In *Cassidy* v. *Daily Mirror* three witnesses were called to prove that they had understood the photograph and its caption as an imputation to Mrs. C. In the recent case mentioned above damages were awarded although no evidence at all was tendered.

The defamation concerned again a married woman who did not live with her husband. In the *Daily Express* a paragraph appeared telling the story of a boxer's 'curly-headed wife' who saw every fight of her 'husband.' However, she was not his wife, but lived with him. The lawful wife, whose hair was not curled, claimed damages for her reputation as the notice could create the impression that she had children by the boxer without having been married to him. She was awarded 50 guineas. In *Cassidy* v. *Daily Mirror* the jury returned a verdict for the plaintiff because reasonable persons understood the words published in the newspaper as defamatory. Equally in *Hough* v. *London Express,* the jury decided against the newspaper as they assumed that the publication might be understood in this sense.

Judges on Newspaper Work

How is journalistic work affected by these two pairs of judgments? The newspapers concerned had no intention of defaming the plaintiffs. But in the opinion of the courts it does not matter what the authors mean. The meaning is to be discovered from the expressions which are put into permanent form on paper.

Regarding *Hulton* v. *Jones,* an apology was published at once. It was stated that the Artemus Jones of the article was a fictitious person and that there was no intention of insulting the plaintiff. Moreover, the defamatory character of the incriminating words was strongly contested. One judge of the Court of Appeal declared that 'some people may regard an allegation of immorality of the kind as comparatively immaterial.' Besides, Jones was described in the article in a manner that those who knew the real Jones well could not have been mistaken. Nevertheless, the judgment of the jury was upheld. How can a newspaper-man avoid such a mishap? 'His remedy is to abstain from defamatory words,' stated one of the judges in the House of Lords. This suggestion may perhaps be interpreted as advice to newspapers, to abstain altogether from criticism.

In *Cassidy* v. *Daily Mirror,* too, every reasonable care which may be expected from a newspaper was taken. The information that Mr. Cassidy has been engaged came from the fiance himself, and there was no reason to believe that he was not speaking the truth. No newspaper would make further inquiries in such a case. But jury and judges did not let this view pass. In their opinion it is immaterial whether the defendant newspaper-man did not know that his statement contained a defamation. He must take the risk of that and is liable unless he took all reasonable care to verify what he wrote. One judge of the Court of Appeal even made the following contemptuous remark on newspaper work: 'From a business point of view, no doubt, it may pay them not to spend time or money in making inquries, or verifying statements before publication; but if they had not made a false statement, they would not now be suffering in damages. They are paying a price for their methods of business.'

The Power of the Jury

The assessment of damages lies within the exclusive competence of the jury. Reputation is said to be property the evaluation of which is made by the public; therefore the public, represented by the jury, should assess the damage caused by the offending person. This leading principle was formulated by Lord Herschell, L.C., in *Davis* v. *Shepstone* (1886) as follows: 'The assessment of damages is peculiarly the province of the jury in an action of libel.'

It even happened that a judge in a case of commercial defamation went so far as to declare himself incompetent. He said: 'Everyone of you gentlemen knows more about damages than I do; certainly, twelve heads are better than one.' In order to be quite clear, he added: 'That is a matter entirely for you.' The jury used this liberty and awarded £3,000 to the plaintiff (*Barber* v. *Deutsche Bank* (1919)).

What Should be the Amount of Damages?

The general rule is that damages should be neither unreasonably large nor unreasonably small. Translated into practice, this means that damages should be as high or as low as can be expected from the judgment of twelve reasonable men. such a definition opens wide possibilities of interpretation. Sometimes high damages awarded by juries have moved judges of the higher courts to express their criticism and even their censure.

In the above-mentioned case, *Hulton* v. *Jones*, a judge of the Court of Appeal called the verdict of the jury 'absolutely perverse.' Similar denouncements occurred in other cases. Sometimes the comment made by judges of higher courts is restricted to the statement that they would have awarded smaller damages than the jury.

The Court of Appeal interferes very rarely with the assessment of damages, and does not reverse an award in the courts below for the reason only that in its opinion the damages are too high or too low. 'In reviewing the assessment of damages,' says the leading English law book, 'the discretion of the Court of Appeal is governed by the general rule that some substantial wrong or miscarriage of justice must have been occasioned by the verdict complained of. Where the damages awarded by a jury are excessive, a new trial will be granted if the Court of Appeal... comes to the conclusion... that the damages awarded are so large'—or so small — 'that a sensible jury could not reasonably have awarded them.'

But when are damages too large or too small? The judges themselves often disagree: damages considered by one member of the court as satisfactory may be found by another judge as out of proportion.

Punitive Damages

If damages are awarded which exceed the material loss suffered by the plaintiff, then such damages assume the character of a fine. In such cases one speaks of punitive or vindictive or exemplary damages. These damages have provoked sharp criticism in the newspaper world of the Empire and the United States. First of all, it is objected that it is an anomaly to impose fines in a civil case. This, it is said, is the task of criminal courts. If an offence is so serious that punitive damages alone would represent a just reparation, the civil court should declare itself incompetent. But jurists object that punitive damages are not a fine but compensatory damages which, according to the character of the defamation, may be increased so as to appear as a more or less rigorous admonition.

The courts have repeatedly and in incontestable form upheld the right of the jury to award punitive damages to the offended person, just as they are entitled to assess 'contemptuous' damages amounting to one farthing which means the plaintiff's defeat. It is, as a rule, the intention of the juries to show by the amount of damages the untruth of the imputation and the seriousness of the charge. But in the assessment of punitive damages factors are apparently considered which do not favour an objective judgment. A few years ago a high judge showed little respect for the motives which prompt juries to award punitive damages; they 'are so likely in present days to be the result of the special skill of an advocate in cross-examination or his remarkable powers of invective rather than any other real cause, that I think a Court of Appeal ought not to be too reluctant to exercise his powers' (Maugham, L.J., in *Ley* v. *Hamilton* (1933)).

Often juries express even their dislike toward the defendant by awarding punitive damages.

Some Reasons for High Assessment

English juries are influenced by various circumstances in their inclination to award high damages. England is the country of the biggest circulation of newspapers in the world. Counsels of the offended parties do not omit to point out that owing to this factor defamations become known to a vast public.

References to the great financial resources of newspapers often made by counsels for the plaintiffs may also exercise a certain influence upon some members of the jury. Add to this the frequent experience that it affords a great satisfaction to the man in the street to be in the position of sitting as a judge in a case involving a powerful institution, the influence and importance of which always appeared overwhelming to him and to make it clear to the newspaper that this time it is on the defensive. In addition, the following circumstance may be stressed. If the criticism which the newspaper is called upon to justify is unpopular and not shared by the jury or by even some of its eloquent members, then the willingness to give high damages will be strengthened by feelings of antipathy, whatever the intrinsic merits of the criticism may be. On the whole, an unfriendly attitude toward a certain paper or the press in general may play an important part in the assessment of damages.

The generosity of juries has caused the plaintiffs to see the proper reparation in the highest possible damages. In *Rook* v. *Fairrie* (1941) the plaintiff 'wanted the full damages to which he would be entitled, not because he wanted the money, but because he wanted that award of damages as something which would show that his character was established....' This means that even if the plaintiff is not materially interested in the sum he claims, he invites the jury to find high damages in order to prove to the public, accustomed to extraordinarily high damages, that his reputation has been completely re-established.

In several libel cases which came before the higher courts the judges expressed their astonishment that juries awarded damages although there was no reason for any damages at all. One of the best known cases of this kind, although not being a newspaper libel, is the award of £25,000 to Princess Irina Alexandrowna of Russia, on the ground that in the film *Rasputin* she was wrongly represented as having been seduced by the above-mentioned monk. 'No doubt,' said a Lord Justice in the Court of Appeal, 'the damages are very large for a lady, who lives in Paris, and who has not lost, so far as we know, a single friend, and has not been able to show that her reputation has in any way suffered.' (*Youssoupoff* v. *Metro-Goldwyn-Mayer* (1933-34)).

Many a counsel of defendant newspaper-men has always stressed the point that the papers, after having received the complaint, inserted in the next issue a disclaimer in terms which either left no possible doubt that the plaintiff was not referred to in the article, or gave some other explanation which fully restored the plaintiff's reputation. An apology was given, too. It is remarkable that in contrast to the practice in the United States and other countries British juries seem unaffected by excuses and withdrawals. A Lord Justice who had to judge in *Hulton* v. *Jones* tried to give some reasons:

'It is difficult,' he said, 'to estimate the consequences of libel in a newspaper. Those who read it may never read the subsequent explanation or the report of the trial; and some of those who read both may forget the result, and be left with a general recollection that the plaintiff was the man of whom a discreditable story was reported in the paper.'

Difficulties in Assessing Damages

Compensation for an injured reputation cannot easily be assessed. By the time the case comes before the court, the damage has perhaps not yet been apparent and may show its consequences later. But it is likewise possible that the libel will not have any consequences detrimental to the plaintiff. 'It is impossible to track the scandal,' said a judge in the House of Lords, 'to know what quarters the poison may reach; it is impossible to weigh at all closely the compensation, which will recompense a man or woman for the insult offered or the pain of a false accusation.'

Neither law nor practice give any direction for the assessment of the money-value of defamations; they put one limit only: the damages awarded must be reasonable in amount. But in awarding damages juries and judges endeavour to put a money-figure upon several different things which are not easily capable of being assessed. Sir Wilfrid Greene, as he then was, recently analysed the considerations preceding the assessment. 'One is considering,' he said, 'the injury which the plaintiff has suffered, which may or may not be capable of pecuniary valuation. One is considering the deterrent effect, and so forth...

one is dealing with a type of damages, upon which there may be a very wide divergence of opinion without either of two extremes falling into what may be described as "an entirely erroneous estimate."

No doubt invisible factors play a part in the assessment of damages in actions for defamation. Dislike of or sympathy with the plaintiff or defendant or a counsel is sometimes expressed in the award. Two American lawyers relate how circumstances which have nothing to do with the subject concerned might be considered in assessing damages. A member of the jury in a libel action had previously decided to oppose the award of damages to the plaintiff, who was of the same nationality but of whose conduct he disapproved, and to persuade his colleagues to do the same. But at the outset of the deliberation he became annoyed by an insulting remark of another member of the jury regarding the plaintiff's race and, forgoing his intention, he did not rest until the plaintiff was awarded a considerable sum.

Thus the assessment of damages is often but a game of chance. Juries cannot be blamed too much, for they are sometimes faced with a problem which the learned judges cannot solve.

One thing is incontestable: juries generally award far higher damages than learned judges would do. A recent example is significant.

The Assessment by a Judge Sitting Alone

Libel actions in wartime are tried in England by a judge sitting alone. In the case of *Rook* v. *Fairrie* the defamation was so grave that it would certainly have induced a jury to increase the amount of damages beyond the actual loss suffered by the plaintiff, expressing in this way the condemnation of the defendant. Meanwhile Atkinson, J., assessed the damages at £550, which the plaintiff thought to be an incomparably low amount. However, the judge, in delivering judgment, expressed his opinion of the defendant's conduct by a censure.

The plaintiff appealed. This was the first case in which the Court of Appeal had to consider the position with regard to an award of damages in a libel action given by a judge sitting alone - but the appeal was dismissed. It was said that whereas a jury can express condemnation of a defendant only by awarding heavy damages, a judge is not so limited and, in the circumstances of the present case, the sum awarded should not be interfered with.

Equally in another case (*Citrine and Others* v. *Pountney* 1940) where the judge was sitting alone, the amount of damages awarded to the plaintiff was relatively low, although the defamation was very grave. The reason given was similar to that in the preceding case: 'A jury could only express their view of a case in pounds, shillings and pence, and they awarded exemplary damages for that purpose. But the judge could express his views in terms much clearer than was possible in money.'

This trend to moderate damages seemed to be discontinued, when a judge who was also sitting without a jury awarded £3,500 to the plaintiff in the libel action *Knupffer* v. *The London Express Newspaper Ltd.* (1942), although the defamation was rather doubtful. In the article complained of a certain group was criticised, but the plaintiff was not mentioned and the defendant contended that the article did not refer to him. The Court of Appeal reversed this judgment and called the amount of damages awarded by the trial judge 'extravagant.' 'It is notorious,' stated MacKinnon, L.J., in the Court of Appeal, 'that juries have often awarded utterly extravagant sums in such cases. Under our present arrangements such cases are heard by a judge alone, sitting without a jury I cannot think it is right for a judge when he has to assess the damages to attempt to attune his mind to what he imagines would be the extravagant impulse of a jury....' The House of Lords upheld the judgment of the Court of Appeal.

These cases do not indicate a change of practice, for if juries had assessed the damages, the result might have large sums. Therefore the prospect of a return to the usual practice of having damages assessed by juries after the war causes much anxiety in British newspaper circles.

In fact, the high damages awarded by juries have resulted in civil libel actions being more dreaded than prosecutions for criminal libel. Certainly this cannot be the intention of the law.

But the menace of such heavy penalties arising out of civil proceedings which may even provoke the peculiar wish to be summoned rather before a criminal court — if this were possible—and there to find mercy, is not the only disadvantage. In criminal law the old principle that the accused must be given the benefit of the doubt holds good. Many doubtful actions for civil libel resulted in high damages; sometimes the defamatory character of the statement in question was not at all clear. There are certain criminal laws according to which a reparation of a misdemeanour before the beginning of the prosecution stops the proceedings. But a retraction of a defamation by newspapers and an apology does not always save defendants from considerable damages. He who can prove before the criminal court — where it is competent — that he had no intention to defame, is not to be prosecuted. This differs from the practice of the civil courts. Even if the defamation has been due to mistake or to incorrect information or to inadvertence, civil courts have come to the conclusion that intention is irrelevant, but that the fact of defamation is conclusive, and have awarded high damages.

Finally, another factor which contributes to the awarding of high damages should not be overlooked. It is well known that laymen are inclined to go to the extremes in both directions as regards the measure of penalties. Therefore, in many countries juries are called upon to decide the question of guilt only, while the learned judge fixes the extent of the penalty. If in Anglo-Saxon countries the learned judges had been entrusted with the duty of assessing damages, they would have awarded lower, very much lower damages, even in cases where, in their opinion, punitive damages should have been awarded.

Demands for a Revision of the Law of Libel

The newspaper world's criticism of the law of libel, as it stands at present, is chiefly directed against the measure of damages in cases where the plaintiff has not suffered any damage by the defamation. In fact, this is one of the weakest points in the administration of justice, as contradicts the principle of private law that damage should be compensated only if damage has been caused.

Therefore British newspapers and other circles suggest an amendment of the libel laws which have remained unchanged for more than fifty years. In 1938 Mr. A.P. Herbert (as he then was), M.P., introduced a Bill aiming at the abolition of some of the hardships caused by the administration of the law. According to this Bill, no libel action should succeed unless the defendant newspaper-man had the intention of referring to the plaintiff or, at the time of the publication, had or could have, by taking reasonable care, knowledge of his existence. Equally, a libel action should be dismissed unless the defendant newspaperman, at the time of the publication, foresaw or could foresee that the defamation could be referred to the plaintiff. It is obvious that these proposals are related to the case of *Hulton* v. *Jones*. If there are several defendants, the Bill proposed that the damages awarded should be apportioned among them according to their responsibility.

Some months later (1939) another Member of Parliament, Sir Stanley Reed, introduced a Law of Libel Amendment Bill, the cardinal point of which was that no plaintiff in a libel case should be awarded damages unless he could prove that his reputation had or might suffer damage owing to the defamation. In order to put an end to libel actions of doubtful persons, it was proposed that the defendant should be entitled to communicate to the plaintiff his intention of asking him in court about previous convictions.

According to both Bills, the time of prescription was to be reduced from six years to one year.

In the course of the deliberations in the House, the Lord Chancellor appointed a committee for the revision of the Law of Defamation, with Lord Porter as chairman.

3. THE LIBEL LAWS IN THE UNITED STATES OF AMERICA

The law of defamation in the United States seeks to prevent high damages. Juries are unfettered in their discretion to assess damages only in cases of grave insults and provided either that the malicious character of the defamation cannot be doubted, or that the newspaper refuses to retract.

The following examples of excessive damages are mentioned: The award of $25,000 to a married woman who was charged in a highly sensational manner with entertaining adulterous relations, although the story was completely untrue; or of $20,000 for the groundless charge of arson with the alleged purpose of obtaining insurance money. But even in such cases the higher courts usually reduce the amounts awarded if, in their opinion, the juries have gone too far. A New York magistrate was awarded $40,000 by a jury as a result of a statement by a New York Newspaper, which had charged him in a series of articles with flagrant misconduct in the discharge of his official duties. But the higher court found the damages excessive and reduced them to $25,000. In another case, where a person who had been charged with conspiracy to defraud an insurance company, asked for $36,000, the court awarded $20,0000.

Award of Actual Damages Only

There are various regulations in the United States which aim at stopping speculative libel actions. Some of them meet the principal demands of the British newspaper world. Of special importance are the regulations, according to which in many kinds of libel cases mentioned by the law, only actual damages suffered by the offended person may be awarded. Usually these regulations run as follows:

'If it shall appear on the trial... that an article was published in good faith, that its falsity was due to mistake and misapprehension, and that a full correction or retraction was published, the plaintiff shall recover actual damages only.'

Sometimes the wording makes particular concessions to the necessities of editorial work by using terms such as 'if such libellous matter was published through misinformation or mistake' (Iowa), or 'by inadvertence' (Maine), or 'under a mistake as to facts' (Minnesota), or 'due to an honest mistake of the facts and that there were reasonable grounds for believing that the statements were true' (Ohio, North Carolina).

The principle that in certain libel cases only actual damage should be awarded, is also expressed in the following way: 'The defendant may give proof of intention' (to retract the defamation); 'and unless the plaintiff shall prove either malice in fact or that the defendant, after having been requested by him in writing to retract the libellous charge... failed to do so within a reasonable time, he shall recover nothing but such actual damages as he may have specially alleged and proved.'

Another way to stem the flood of libel actions is provided by regulations which order offended persons to inform the publishers of newspapers in which the defamation is published of their intention to bring an action, unless the insulting statements are retracted and corrected. The psychological value of such a step is obvious; personal contact usually brings adversaries nearer to each other and facilitates the settlement of disputes. The law assumes that both parties are inclined to do so, even those offended persons who otherwise would be anxious to obtain the highest possible damages, but who must now attempt a reconciliation, if they wish to qualify for any reparations.

The regulations in question are practically identical. The offended party shall, three or five days before filing the complaint in the intended suit, serve notice in writing on the publisher, specifying the statements which he alleges to be false and defamatory. If reasonable grounds for the article in question can be given, and a 'full and a fair retraction of any statement therein alleged to be erroneous is published... within three (five) days'- or within ten days if it be a weekly publication — then the plaintiff shall recover only actual damages.'

As a rule, the retraction should be published 'in a conspicuous place and type, in the same place where said original item appeared.' In this way libel actions aiming at excessive damages are frustrated. The fact that such statutes have been introduced recently, e.g. in Georgia in 1939, in an increasing number of states of the American Union, testifies to the satisfactory experience with such regulations.

Legal Consideration for Editorial Work

Consideration of the special difficulties of editorial work lies at the root of some other provisions in American statutes. In order to mitigate damages, the defendant in Iowa (s. 11172) may set forth in a distinct division of his answer any facts, of which evidence is legally admissible; in New Hampshire he may prove (ch. 335, s.6) 'that the writings complained of were the repetition of common report,' and in Virginia (s.6240a) he may adduce in evidence 'all the circumstances of the publication, including the source of the information in character as affording reasonable ground of reliance, any prior publication elsewhere of similar purport, the lack of negligence or malice.' The defence that the statement complained of originated from a source which could be regarded as reliable is allowed. This relieves the paper of the charge that it has not made inquiries regarding the truth of the statement concerned.

Even in cases where the statute does not compel the offended person to request the paper for a correction, the fact that he had taken the first step towards suggesting a retraction will be taken into account in the judgment. A plaintiff who, by his conduct, creates the impression that he is hunting for damages does not meet with the sympathy of the court. In addition, the fact that the defendant newspaper corrects or retracts the defamatory statement without being requested, or at least offers a publication of retraction to the plaintiff, will also be interpreted in his favour.

Regulations Concerning Mitigation of Damages

A regulation which may be found frequently says: 'The defendant... may prove... in mitigation of damages that he has retracted the charge and offered amends before suit by publishing an apology.....'

Among other statutes which deal with the advantages accruing to defendants in libel actions, the following regulations may be noted. 'If the defendant, before the answer is required to be filed therein, gives written notice to the plaintiff or to his attorney of his intention to publish a retraction of the libel, accompanied by a copy of the retraction, which he intends to publish, he may prove such publication in mitigation of damages. If, upon such notice, the plaintiff does not accept the offer to publish such retraction...; and unless the plaintiff proves actual malice or want of good faith.... He shall recover damages only for the actual injury sustained.'

The relevant provisions contained in the statutes of Wisconsin are very mindful of the interests of newspapers. It is said there: 'Any true statement, explanation, correction, or retraction, published without comment... within a reasonable time, may be introduced upon the trial of any such action as a sufficient defence against any imputation of malice and against the recovery of any damages except actual damages.'

The undesirability of actions brought by persons of doubtful reputation who only aim at damages, as their reputation cannot be repaired at all, is also dealt with in some statutes. In

Massachusetts (ch. 231, s.94) the defendant is allowed to set forth 'acts of the plaintiff which create a reasonable suspicion that the matters charged against him by the defendant are true.' Also in New Hampshire (ch. 335, s.6) 'the conduct of the plaintiff' must be considered, if there is reason for believing that the charges against him are founded. An English newspaper would run heavy risks if it followed such principles.

Many statutes in the United States refrain from providing detailed regulations and content themselves with the following provision: The defendant may allege 'any mitigating circumstances to reduce the amount of damages,' and it is for the learned judge to direct the jury accordingly.

A friendly attitude towards newspapers is also maintained by the statute of Delaware (s.4693). In libel actions where the truth is pleaded and given in evidence, if it 'be found that the libel was written or published properly for public information and with no malicious or mischievous motives, the jury may find for the defendant.' This wording gives the defendant many opportunities of claiming that the publications was made in the public interest and that the population is entitled to be properly informed. This regard for the needs of editorial work reaches its climax in Massachusetts, where 'in no action of libel shall exemplary or punitive damages be allowed' (ch. 231, s. 93).

According to these regulations, damages similar to those awarded in *Hulton* v. *Jones* and *Cassidy* v. *Daily Mirror & c.*, would never have been given in many states of the American Union. The plaintiffs would not have succeeded, as the defendants were either mistaken or had acted 'by inadvertence,' or because 'there were reasonable grounds for believing that the statements were true.' Besides, a defendant in these states could claim that he had acted 'in good faith' and a 'full retraction or apology was published.' In these circumstances no actual damages would be considered to have occurred and the action would have been dismissed with costs.

What are the actual damages? They include, according to the statutes of Indiana (s.2-1044), 'all damages that the plaintiff may have suffered in respect to his character, property, business, trade, profession, or occupation, and no other damages whatsoever.' In Michigan (s.14472), besides actual damages, also 'damages to feelings' are admissible, and the jury shall in all cases specify the amount for this purpose separately from the amount awarded for other damages.

Vexatious Provisions

But there are some exceptions to the benevolent attitude towards newspapers, generally shown by American statutes. According to some of them, retraction of the defamation in the aforementioned manner will not suffice in several states to avert excessive damages. There are particular provisions, the character and purpose of which may be called vexatious. In Kentucky (s. 2438b-1) 'a sufficient correction, retraction, explanation, or rectification 'has to be published 'in at least two successive issues... accompanied by editorials in which the alleged slander is specifically repudiated.' Still farther go the statutes of Utah (s.62-2-1), demanding that a retraction of the libel should be published 'at the head of the second column on the editorial page... for three days,' and a reference to such retraction should be 'made also on the local page.' If the libel was published in the Sunday edition — the daily papers in the United States have also a Sunday issue which has, as a rule, a bigger circulation — one of the three retractions must appear on Sunday.

Measures Against Unfounded Actions

Various regulations which aim at rendering more difficult unfounded actions and the protraction of proceedings do not allow the award of costs of the plaintiff in such actions. According to the statutes of Mississippi (s.671), the plaintiff shall not be awarded costs in libel actions if he recovers damages of less than $10:'In... actions sounding in damages where the plaintiff sues for more than $10 and recovers less than that sum, no more costs than the amount of damages recovered shall be awarded to him, unless the court be of the opinion that the plaintiff had reasonable cause to expect to recover more and that the action was brought for no other purpose than to be compensated for the wrong done.'

A similar regulation exists in New Jersey (s.239): If the plaintiff recovers damages of less than $50, he shall not be awarded a higher amount of costs. A drastic measure against unfounded actions is provided by the statute of Oklahoma (s.12-1446): '... if there be a verdict in favour of the defendant, and the jury find that the action was malicious or without reasonable provocation... judgment shall be rendered against the plaintiff and in favour of the defendant for his costs, including an attorney's fee of $100.' The same tendency is expressed by regulations which aim at preventing the plaintiff from putting the claim for damages too much into the foreground in his negotiations with the accused person. If in Alabama (s.7363) the defendant 'after or before suit brought, make the recantation and amends... and also tender to the plaintiff a compensation in money, and bring the same into court, the plaintiff can recover no costs, if the jury believe and find the tender was sufficient.'

In Massachusetts (ch. 231, par. 94) the defendant may allege and prove in mitigation of damages that the plaintiff 'has already recovered damages or has received or agreed to receive compensation' if he, despite of it, brought an action for the same libel.

If the plaintiff is a candidate for office at the time of the libellous publication, higher damages are usually awarded, and also the regulations about retraction and apology are more rigorous than in libels regarding private persons. In Iowa (s.12415) the retraction must be published 'in a conspicuous place on the editorial page... within two weeks next before the election.' Other statutes contain similar regulations. In the State of Minnesota the apology to the offended candidate must be headed 'Retraction' in a '18 point type or larger, (s.9397).

The comparatively mild practice in the United States is due to the efforts of the legislative bodies to secure the right of criticism, and not to prevent newspapers from expressing their opinion about public affairs. This principle is laid down in the Constitutions of most states of the American Union, which contain the regulation that 'the accused party shall be acquitted, if it shall appear that the alleged libellous matter was published for justifiable ends.' If only the 'end' has to be justified, some outspoken, even sharp, words may be tolerated.

4. LIBEL, A CRIMINAL OFFENCE ON THE EUROPEAN CONTINENT

The tradition of chivalry to the effect that a personal insult must be avenged with blood, survived on the Continent longer than in Anglo-Saxon countries. In the second half of the last century that tradition penetrated deeply even into the middle classes. The duel was popularised by compulsory military service in Central, Western and Southern Europe. It was a matter of course that officers of the army should settle their private disputes by means of arms; whoever withdrew from that duty was regarded as a coward and reduced to the ranks. Only if the offender was, according to the severe rules of the code for officers, incapable — owing to his social position — of giving satisfaction with arms, a duel was not admissible. However, even then officers did not always bring an action, but often procured the necessary satisfaction by attacking the offender corporally. It occurred not infrequently that officers who felt offended drew their swords and dealt with the offender on the spot, as they were entitled to do.

This form of settling private affairs was not restricted to officers on the active list. Every year thousands of officer cadets joined the army who were entitled to a shortened period of service and could become officers. After their return to civil life they remained officers on the reserve and were called up from time to time for military exercises which lasted some weeks. Many of them were proud of that status and felt enhanced in their social position; even in plain clothes they held themselves to be bound by the officer's code of honour, which ordered a duel in case of insult. Although civilians were prohibited from doing so, the courts appreciated the equivocal position of an officer of the reserve who had adopted the military attitude regarding honour, and passed mild judgment; most judges were former officers. Sometimes the ruler of the country concerned used his right and issued a decree of *nolle prosequi.*

The custom of challenging the offender to a duel became, thus, a prerogative, favoured by high circles, and was regarded as a proof of personal courage. Add to this that in the countries of Central Europe the associations of students cultivated the duel and required their members to settle their affairs with the sword.

Reluctance to Accept Damages for Libel

These circumstances may explain why the idea of compensating an insult by money could not take root in countries where the conception prevails that, if the circumstances so require, life must be staked in the fight for honour. The offender was regarded as a criminal, and his act as a criminal offence. Accordingly, there could be but one reparation for an insult: the punishment of the perpetrator. If the offence was committed by the press, the punishment had to be measured according to the extent to which the defamation had been disseminated.

In such a world of an artificially exaggerated sense of honour private law did not seem to be a sufficient means for combating defamations. Even the highest amount of money could not wipe out an insult which, according to social views, required a fight with lethal weapons. Moreover, offended persons would not have welcomed the idea that an offence against their honour should be assessed by a court. In the opinion of these circles, a new insult would thus be added to the defamation already suffered, if their moral values were to be assessed in money. Moreover, however high the assessment might be, it would be too low in the eyes of the offended persons and could only cause ironical remarks by the outside world. In fact, one meets in those countries of the Continent, where, besides criminal proceedings, damages for defamation can be applied for, a deep aversion against such damages, and it occurs frequently that offended persons content themselves with the punishment of the accused, but do not ask for any damages. 'My honour is priceless,' this is the meaning of such a gesture.

The same reluctance to accept money from the offending person can be found in settlements made before or out of court. As a rule, the plaintiff is satisfied with an apology; sometimes he demands damages, not exceeding a moderate limit, for a charitable purpose. As regards costs, the plaintiff not infrequently waives his claims to them if he is in good circumstances. In his opinion, however, honour should not be the object of gain or of any pecuniary transaction.

Advantages of Proceedings Before Criminal Courts

There are still other reasons which, on the Continent, render the hunt for damages inexpedient. The offended person, who applies to a civil court creates the impression that he does not consider his grievance important enough to submit the case to the criminal court. Proceedings before the civil court usually meet with little public interest; the newspapers do not publish reports about them and, consequently, an award of damages would not come to public knowledge. Besides, civil courts work slowly. Injured people who are anxious to obtain the quickest possible satisfaction reach their aim more speedily if they bring their suit in the criminal court. This procedure is also advantageous for the reason that it is cheap and gives the opportunity in some countries of connecting damages with the punishment of the offending person.

But there are, indeed, defamations which cannot form the object of a prosecution in a criminal court, but which, nevertheless, cause injury to the plaintiff. In such cases compensation must be recovered in the civil court. In most countries this claim is based upon the old-established rule, already laid down in ancient Roman law, that every act, causing damage to anyone, obliges the person by whose fault it has been done to reparation. But this right is rarely exercised for the reasons mentioned above.

The advantages of prosecuting libels before criminal courts disappear if juries have to judge in matters of defamation by the press, a procedure which was still prevalent in many European countries until some years ago. Apart from the fact that high costs arise in proceedings where juries are summoned, such proceedings and their result depend upon so many factors which cannot be foreseen that it is almost hazardous for the offended person to start such an action. There were, in Central Europe, newspapers which looked for such occasions, even provoked them, because they gave them welcome material to get popularity at the expense of the plaintiff. As a trial before a jury affords the opportunity of thoroughly elucidating the case and of scrutinising the life of the offended person, of unpleasant questions and evidence - that type of newspaper did everything which could cast suspicion on the plaintiff so that offended persons did not begin such suits, but used their right of reply instead.

Finally, the peculiar manner of selecting impecunious persons as responsible editors in European countries prevents the award of excessive damages in libel actions. Not the leading men of the newspaper are responsible for its contents, but an employee who is not accused of having committed a defamation, but of not having prevented its publication. His subordinate position is taken into account in the comparatively mild sentences. Thus the risk incurred by the newspaper is not heavy, even if owner and editor are liable for the payment of fines and damages to which the responsible person is sentenced.

The effect of these conditions on the Continent and in the Anglo-Saxon countries respectively becomes quite clear. On the Continent, people criticised by newspapers mostly use their right of reply in order to correct mistakes, and are glad to settle the matter in this way. Elsewhere the prospect of gaining high damages induces many people to look for mistakes in papers, or even for hints, which might possibly be interpreted as referring to them, for the sole purpose of suing and of being awarded a considerable sum of money.

Damages as Punishment

Special regulations regarding damages in libel actions are in force in several countries of Europe and other continents. The continuous interest in this problem is shown by the fact that some of these laws were passed in recent years. To begin with France, the classic country of press laws, from which the most valuable suggestions have come and have influenced the legislation of other countries: the Code Civil, in its Articles 1142 and 1149, provides that money compensation, corresponding to the damage sustained, should be paid to the offended person as a reparation. But in the course of time, chiefly under the influence of political conditions, other regulations were introduced which pushed the claim to damages into the background. Among them are to be mentioned the confiscation and destruction of the publication at the request of the offended party; further, the right of any person mentioned in a newspaper or in a periodical, either by name or indirectly, to reply to that statement, and finally the right of persons, offended by newspapers or periodicals, to publish the judgment against the offender in the publication concerned or in other papers, at the cost of the offending party.

Damages in France, granted according to the above-mentioned regulations of the Civil Code, are very moderate compared with the sums which are usual in the Anglo-Saxon countries. The highest damages which were ever assessed in France amounted to 50,000 francs, i.e. £260, according to the pre-war rate of exchange. All the same, that sum created a sensation and was considered an exception, *un monument de generosite.*

In Austria damages for libel committed by newspapers were introduced in 1929, but they are awarded only if the author is unknown and if the responsible editor, who is called to account for 'negligent omission of the necessary precaution,' pleads justification but fails. The regulation was intended to put an end to wilful protractions of libel actions by responsible editors who, without being able to do so, declared their readiness to prove the truth of their allegations and, by publishing this statement, created the impression that the defamation were well founded. They did not take any risk, since if they did not succeed only a fine for the above mentioned 'negligence' could be imposed. Meanwhile, they had been able to cause the plaintiffs considerable annoyance. The damages may amount to 10,000 Austrian shillings (£400); the editor and the owner of the paper are liable for their payment. At the same time the maximum fine for 'negligent omission of the necessary precaution' was raised to 2,500 Austrian shillings.

German law also knows damages, which are payable to the offended person up to an amount of 10,000 marks (£800 according to the pre-war rate of exchange). They can be imposed at the demand of the plaintiff, besides punishment, only in case of malicious defamation, and provided that the consequences of the defamation affect the economic position of the offended person.

Another solution is provided in the Czechoslovak press law of 1924 (art.17, *a,b,c*). In assessing damages, 'the court must consider how much the good name of the offended person has suffered; a higher amount will be fixed, if the accused has made obviously futile attempts to prove that his statements were true... aggravating the offence. A smaller amount must be assessed, or the payment of damages refused altogether, if the accused person has offered to give the plaintiff sufficient satisfaction which has been refused; or if it appears that the plaintiff is endeavouring to make a profit out of the action, which is not in proportion to the damage he has suffered.'

These regulations display a tendency of friendliness towards the press which is also proved by the fact that the highest amount of damages which the accused may have to pay to the person whose honour has been impugned is fixed at 10,000 Cz. crowns, corresponding to a sum of about £70 only. The courts usually award lower damages.

In Greece, too, proceedings involve partly the imposition of a fine and partly the award of damages. According to the law (1919, art. 1), 'any person injured by a punishable act beyond the loss which he has suffered from the offence, is entitled to demand also financial satisfaction for his injured honour or the moral distress.... The satisfaction being obligatorily imposed by the court in case of condemnation. The demand for financial satisfaction is definitely adjudged by the court trying the case, and in the same decision, the court not being allowed to transfer it to the civil courts. If the decision is an acquittal, all right to such financial satisfaction is excluded.' Thus damages are inseparable from the sentence.

In addition to the penalty, imposed according to the terms of the criminal law, a joint liability of the publisher of a newspaper and of the author of an injurious publication, relating to private life, is provided by the Greek Constitution of 1911 (art. 14). Both publisher and author are jointly liable 'fully to redress any loss occasioned and to indemnify the injured party by payment of a sum of money, determined at the discretion of the judge, but never less than 200 drachmas.'

A joint liability for payment of compensation to a third person, comprising author, editor and owner of the newspaper, and of the printer, but only in a subsidiary capacity, is also provided in the 'Books, Documents and Newspapers Law' of Siam (1922-23, art. 20).

The award of damages and a fine is provided for in the Polish press laws of 1928 and 1938. The fine, having the character of damages on compassionate grounds, is limited to Zloty 10,000 (about £400), according to Article 37 of the law of 1938, after having been fixed at Zloty 3,000 ten years before. While its award lies in the competence of the criminal courts, the offended party may claim 'supplementary' damages before the civil courts.

Some Provisions Regarding Damages as Compensation

In contrast, damages as compensation payable to offended persons in Hungary, Portugal, Turkey and Yugoslavia are entirely for loss of reputation.

According to the Hungarian press law (art. 39), the injured party 'has the right to claim, over and above compensation for the damage caused to his property by the press communication, corresponding reparation in cash for injury not affecting his property, but occasioned to him by the aforesaid communication. But such reparation may only be claimed when, after the circumstances have been taken into consideration, such reparation should be deemed equitable. The Court of Justice fixes the amount due for damages not affecting property, after having taken into consideration all circumstances, and especially the financial position of the respective interested parties. The injured party has also the right to claim compensation, even should the press communication not constitute an offence against the law. In this case, however, compensation can be claimed only by an appeal to civil law.'

The last-mentioned provision was adopted again in a Bill introduced by the government in 1929, which so far has not come into force. These regulations, which are in effect similar to the British practice, allow the plaintiff to claim damages for material or moral losses sustained by the defamation. A penalty may not be imposed, unless the plaintiff demands it. In the Hungarian law the amount of damages is not limited; in practice damages are, as a rule, not high.

In Yugoslavia the punishment for libels, directed against private persons, is imprisonment from one month to one year and payment of damages of at least 500 dinars, if the plaintiff so desires and if the court agrees thereto. It is remarkable that, as in Great Britain, the plaintiff need not prove that he has actually suffered damage (art. 30).

In Portugal heavy penalties (imprisonment of three months to two years) are inflicted for defamations by means of untrue statements. Moreover, damages are given, if the defendant is unable or unwilling to plead justification (1910, art. 18). In cases of newspaper libels Turkish courts combine damages, according to the moral or material loss to the plaintiff, with imprisonment or a fine (1909, art. 12).

5. GENERAL REGULATIONS CONCERNING NEWSPAPER LIBELS

Libels in Doubtful Form

In order to make it quite clear that also libels veiled in doubtful form are defamations, a recent French Ordinance (6th May, 1944) provides that the publication of defamatory statements is punishable, even if the persons or corporations aimed at are not expressly named, but if their identity may be guessed. Also a doubtful form given to defamations does not exempt the responsible persons from liability (art. 4).

The same Ordinance aims at stopping another frequent evil in the press: the reproduction of statements which have already been judged as defamatory by a court. Such a publication will be considered maliciously made, unless the author can prove the contrary (art. 7).

Defamation by Quoting Rumours

A newspaper will not be relieved of its responsibility if it gives the defamation an impersonal form and thereby the character of a rumour. In the Anglo-Saxon countries the courts have adhered to this principle at all times. Also in the press law of Panama (art. 2044), 'when an injurious or calumnious statement of an impersonal nature is published in the form of "it is said," "it is assured," "it is rumoured," or the like, it will be considered for the purposes of the cases that the statement has been made in a personal and peremptory manner by the person responsible for its publication.

Accessories to Libel

According to the libel laws in some countries, not only the persons who are responsible for the publication, but also accessories are made liable. These are; first of all, the persons who have given the newspaper the defamatory information. The laws of some states of the American Union declare persons, who wilfully transmit to a newspaper or periodical 'for publication therein any false or libellous statement concerning any person or corporation, and thereby secure the actual publication of the same, guilty of a misdemeanour.' Regulations of this kind are in force in the States of Montana (s. 10.999), Nevada (s.10.114), New York (pars. 1352/3), North Carolina (s. 4229), Virginia (par. 4427a). A prosecution can be instituted even if the information had not been published. In the State of Nevada the misdemeanour is assumed, if the communication to the newspaper in case of a publication 'would be a libel,' and in the States of New York and Virginia, if the mere intention is evident that the statements transmitted to the newspaper shall be published. In contrast to it, in the State of Montana and other American states the proceedings are instituted only, if the publication of the defamatory statement has taken place. Regarding the measure of punishment, the court is given a wide discretion, and in Montana the punishment may amount to 500 dollars or to six months' imprisonment, or both.

Besides the informants, also persons who have made 'a manuscript copy of a libel,' or have 'performed the manual labour of printing it,' may be made responsible if it is shown that they were 'actuated by a malicious design against the person defamed' (New Mexico (s.35-3511), and Texas (art. 1280). However, the law of New Mexico adds that 'the person for whose account or by whose order it was printed or copied, shall be presumed to have known the intent of the publication and shall be liable for the offence.'

Conspiracy in Libel Cases

A defamation committed by two or more persons who 'conspire together to maliciously publish... anything which exposes any living person or the memory of any deceased person to hatred, contempt, ridicule, or obloquy, or which causes or tends to cause any person to be shunned or avoided or which has a tendency to injure any person or association of persons in his or their business,' is considered in the State of North Dakota a felony (s. 9553).

Change of the Judge

American legislation has coped with the problem of libel very thoroughly and has contributed some interesting provisions which remain unique. In the State of Michigan, for instance, 'no justice shall have jurisdiction to try any person for a second or subsequent violation of this act' (libel law). The punishment amounts for the first offence to a fine not exceeding 100 dollars or imprisonment not exceeding 90 days, or both; for the second or subsequent violation of these regulations a fine of up to 500 dollars and imprisonment of up to three years, or both, are imposed (s. 16.813).

When is a Libel Considered to be Published?

The question when a libel by the press may be regarded from the technical point of view as having taken place is touched in some laws. Must the publication have been distributed so that it can be rightly assumed that its contents have been read? Or does it suffice that it was printed? The law of the State of Georgia (s.4430) states that 'a libel is published as soon as it is communicated to any person other than the party libelled.' According to the law of the State of Idaho (s.17-1505), which is much stricter, 'it is not needful that the words or things complained of should have been read or seen by another. It is enough that the accused knowingly parted with the immediate custody of the libel under circumstances which exposed it to be read or seen by any other person than himself.' A similar definition is given by the law of Minnesota (s.10.114). As a rule, the courts assume that a libel which has been printed has also been distributed, unless the contrary is proved during the trial. A provision of this kind is contained in the law of the State of New Mexico (s.35-3510).

In Guatemala 'printed matter is understood to be published, when more than six copies of the same have been carried out of the establishment, after the printing has been done' (art. 8).

Form of the Complaint

In the American State of Wyoming (s. 89-1039) the law orders that in an action for libel 'it shall not be necessary to set out any obscene word, but it shall be sufficient to state its substance.' As the statement of this complaint is read in court and consequently the report will be privileged, expressions which the law wants to withhold from the public might come to its knowledge.

6. MEASURE OF PUNISHMENT FOR LIBELS

As mentioned above, defamation is, as a rule, considered a punishable offence outside the Anglo-Saxon world and, apart from a few countries where the ordinary criminal law is competent, is tried according to special press regulations. Defamations show many degrees and shades. Consequently, the discretion of the courts in imposing penalties is very wide. According to some press laws, the courts are guided by certain directions in determining the measure of punishment.

The Swedish press law going back to 1812 gives a wise rule to those on whom 'the examination of a publication or of liability therefor' may devolve (par. 3). They 'should in doubtful cases rather acquit than condemn, should always pay more consideration to the illegality of the subject and thought rather than of the expression, and to the purpose of the publication rather than to the mode of presentation, and shall in no case have the right to draw uncertain conclusions from the expressions.'

In Greece, if any person is wilfully accused of a crime by a publication, the offender is punished with imprisonment of from six months to three years and with a fine. If the imputed act is a misdemeanour, the imprisonment will amount to from three months up to one year, and if the charge involves a violation of discipline or an offence, the imprisonment will not exceed three months. Besides, a fine will be imposed in the latter case (1919, art. 3).

In Egypt, too, punishment for defamation is measured according to the character of the charge made against the offended person (1910, art. 262).

In Chile and Peru defamations like other press offences are divided according to their severity into three degrees and punished accordingly. In the old press law of Peru (1823, art. 20) the first degree involving a penalty of three months and 200 pesos is the most severe; in the second degree the punishment drops to two months and 150 pesos, and in the third to one month and 75 pesos. In default of payment of the fine, the period of imprisonment in each case is to be doubled. In Chile (1872, art. 4) the first grade, with a fine of 50 dollars, is the lightest; in the second and third grade the fines amount to 100 and 300 dollars. The punishment for defamation in Guatemala is rather considerable. The authors of calumnious writings have to suffer the penalty of one year's major arrest when charged with a serious libel, and of six months if the transgression is less serious. In the first case two-thirds and in the second the whole term are commutable at the rate of two reals to five pesos per day, according to the pecuniary circumstances of the culprit (art. 35).

Equally, in Yugoslavia the penalties for press libels on private persons are rigorous, the minimum punishment being one month, the maximum one year. In some laws press libels are expressly contrasted with defamation committed by other means and punished severely. In the American State of Nebraska persons who commit a libel shall upon conviction be punished with not more than 500 dollars or six months or both. If, however, 'said libel is published in a newspaper, having a general circulation, the person so offending shall be punished with imprisonment... for not less than one year, nor more than three years' (s. 28-452). The law of the State of Georgia calls a libel committed by the press a 'newspaper libel' and thus emphasises its special character (s. 4431).

According to the penal law of Finland, the penalties for defamation which are very serious in general—imprisonment from one month up to one year or a fine of not less than 100 marks—are increased to double the amount if the offence is committed 'through print, writing or pictorial representation.' If, however, the libel is not perpetrated against better knowledge even if intentionally, and if ostensible grounds for the imputation or rumour cannot be produced, the upper limit of the penalty is reduced to one year. If only a fine is imposed, it should not fall under 100 marks (1889, art. 1 and 2).

7. DEFAMATION OF PUBLIC OFFICIALS

The defamation of civil servants, of members of the cabinet, of deputies and other public officials, also of authorities, courts, and public corporations is usually regarded more seriously than that of private persons. But some laws encourage the public to criticise such persons and institutions. They are considered servants or bodies of the people to whom they are responsible. According to this view, critical comment on their activities lies in the general interest, and, although these laws provide more severe penalties for unjustified defamations than in cases concerning private persons, no additional procedural obstacles are put in the way of the prosecution. Nobody should be deterred from venturing a frank and sometimes even ironic remark regarding errors and faults of persons engaged in matters of public interest.

According to the French press law, defamations against the following public institutions are to be tried in accordance with special regulations: courts, the Army and Navy, legislative bodies, above all the Senate and the Chamber, and also authorities of the public administration (art. 30). The defamations, however, must be directed against a certain authority or body, not against these institutions in general. Only a wholesale defamation of the Army suffices for the institutions of proceedings.

Amongst the public officials in respect of whom a prosecution may be instituted are deputies or senators, members of the cabinet, civil servants, officials of the administration, but also citizens exercising certain public functions, if they are attacked owing to these activities, and finally members of the jury and witnesses, if the latter are defamed for their depositions (art. 31). The law expressly assures the defamed for their depositions (art. 31). The law expressly assures the offender of his acquittal and of his exemption from claims on damages and court fees, if his statements prove true (art. 35).

The Egyptian law follows this example. If criticism, passed upon a civil servant in good faith, refers solely to the performance of his official duties, and if every fact alleged turns out to be true, the responsible person will be acquitted (1910, art. 261). Equally, the press law of Guatemala states that calumny and defamation directed against public officials on account of purely public acts do not constitute an offence (art. 33).

An unusual procedure is in force in Colombia in respect of a defamation of public officials. On the one hand wilful attacks against such persons are not encouraged, on the other hand people are not discouraged from making charges which can be justified. If, for instance, a public official is blamed for not properly 'handling public moneys,' and when, in accordance with the present law, he shall have justified his behaviour, the journalist must state whether the charges made have or have not been satisfactorily answered. This statement must appear in the next issue of the periodical, under penalty of a fine of from 50 to 100 pesos. If the statement is in the sense that, in the opinion of the journalist, the charges are not answered, or if the official is not satisfied, the journalist must bring an accusation against the official within ten days of the presentation of the official's justification, under penalty of a fine equal to that above mentioned. If after making the accusations the journalist is unable to prove the charge or charges made, he shall be liable to a fine from 100 to 500 pesos (1898, art. 19).

The measure of punishment in cases of libel of public officials differs, as a rule, from those of private persons. In France, for example, until 1944 the maximum penalty for insults to officials or authorities was imprisonment of three months or a fine of 500 francs or both, while insults to private persons were punishable with, at most, two months or 300 francs or both (art. 33). If the offence was qualified as defamation, the maximum penalties amounted in the former case to one year's imprisonment or to 3,000 francs or both, while for defamations of private persons at most imprisonment of six months or a fine of 2,000 francs or both were imposed (art. 32). By the Ordinance of 1944 mentioned above, the maximum fines for insults to and defamations of private persons and officials being indeed inconsiderable were increased to 200,000 francs and in certain cases to 500,000 francs (art. 1).

The same Ordinance also provides that a defamation of a public official concerning his private life is now to be treated like a defamation of a private person (art. 5).

In Colombia, too, the measure of punishment is graded in a similar way. The punishment for calumny committed against public officials, ministers of religion, or public bodies is more severe (imprisonment of from 20 days to four months and a fine of from 20 to 200 pesos) than for calumny of private individuals (15 days to three months and 10 to 100 pesos) (articles 21 and 22). Also insults to officials or corporations are punished with imprisonment of from ten days to two months and with a fine of from 5 to 100 pesos, while for insults to private persons five days to one month and 3 to 50 pesos are to be imposed (art. 25). We find the same idea in Norway, where the maximum penalty for defamations of private persons amounts to six months' imprisonment and for defamations of officials to one year.

Who May Sue for Libels on Officials?

The regulations regarding the right to bring an action, when public officials and institutions are defamed, differ from each other in various countries. In France and elsewhere the defamed civil servant is not permitted to sue in person, but his principal or the Ministry must do it. If the injury is inflicted on a corporate body, the prosecution can only be instituted by a resolution of its general meeting. In most Central European and other countries the defamation of officials is a criminal offence the prosecution of which lies in the hands of the public prosecutor. In Chile, too, the prosecution in such cases lies with the public ministry concerned (art. 7). In Finland, however, the law orders that libel cases may not be brought by the public prosecutor, if the plaintiff or the authority injured has not instituted proceedings (1889, art. 8).

The new Czechoslovak law for the Protection of the Honour (1933, par. 5) has very much extended the right of authorities and corporations to sue for libel. According to it, the legislative bodies, their presidencies and committees, all authorities and bodies of public administrations, also the armed forces, the police and the corporations exercising public activities, the periodical publications and others, are entitled to bring actions for libel.

8. DEFAMATION OF NEWSPAPERS

It is usual in libel cases to see newspaper-men accused. But sometimes the journal appears as a plaintiff, suing, as a rule, another newspaper for defamation. This happens often in countries where vehement polemics are fought among newspapers for political reasons or for reasons of competition.

Actions of this kind are usually dismissed on formal grounds, because the newspaper has no *locus standi* and, consequently, no cause for complaint. However, it is left to the editor or to the responsible person to bring the action against the offender of the newspaper. Legal circles in France hold the view that defamations of a newspaper are to be tried in the same way as attacks against a commercial undertaking: at the request of the owner of the defamed newspaper or of the company to which the journal belongs, the prosecution may be instituted. If the attacks aim at the owner, or editor, or at the members of the editorial staff, they must bring actions and may claim damages.

According to a judgment of the French Court of Cassation (of 10th July, 1937), even if the libel is directed against the newspaper and no individual, juridical or private, nor the company which owns the journal, nor its manager, editor, or journalists in its employ are mentioned, the courts, nevertheless, may decide that the defamations against the paper are, in fact, directed against the company which owns it and injure its reputation and honour.

In contrast to this opinion, the Czechoslovak press law (1924 art. 27) expressly provides the right of a newspaper to sue for libel committed by the press. A newspaper which has been injured, so states the regulation, may also institute a prosecution on the ground that its reputation has been impugned or that those responsible for the conduct of another newspaper have been guilty of culpable negligence. The application for prosecution lies with the publisher; but if the latter fails to make an application within four weeks of the publication of the offending paragraph, then the responsible editor may do so. In this way, the editorial staff is guaranteed the opportunity to fight out the issue even if the publisher should have no interest in it. The leading newspapers have called for such a law as a protection against attacks in the press, which for national, political, and social reasons were not infrequent in Czechoslovakia.

In some respect this law was amended by the Act for the Protection of the Honour (par. 5). The right of newspapers to protect their reputation was extended by the regulation to the effect that not only defamations by the press, but also those committed in well-attended meetings, may become the subject of an action; on the other hand this protection is limited as proceedings can be instituted only for evil report and calumny; a newspaper cannot sue any longer for a simple defamation. While the previous regulations allowed only the editor and responsible editor to appear in court for a periodical publication, now the owner is also permitted to do so (par. 16(2)). In Estonia newspapers are relieved of the pains to defend their reputation against press attacks, since the law (art. 16(7)) prohibits 'polemical articles' which expose other periodicals to ridicule or defame them. Equally, caricatures serving this purpose are not permitted.

Judgments of the courts in the Anglo-Saxon countries do not convey a clear picture. It may be premised that in Great Britain the press rather excels in politeness, and vehement polemics are not frequent. But even if strong words are used, the courts do not easily conceive them as defamations. It is, for instance, not considered an injury to reputation if one newspaper calls another one 'the most vulgar, ignorant and scurrilous journal ever published in Great Britain.' It is, however, a defamation to say of a newspaper that 'it is the lowest now in circulation; and we submit the fact to the consideration of advertisers,' for that affects the sale of the newspaper and the profits that might be made from advertisements.

In another judgment the view is expressed that not every charge against a newspaper constitutes a personal attack on a person who is associated with the journal. But a South African court held recently that the defamation of a newspaper disparaging its editorial conduct is regarded as a defamation of of the editor.

In the United States the Codes of associations of publishers and journalists warn newspaper-men 'not to speak disparagingly through editorials or news columns of competing papers or editors.'

9. LIBELS ON CLASSES OF CITIZENS

Attacks on certain parts of the population owing to their race, religion, colour, or to their occupation, e.g. on aristocrats, 'bourgeois,' clergymen, judges, military officers, landowners, merchants, and so on, have been an almost permanent feature of the newspapers of the Old and New World. The press law, apart from a few exceptions, do not provide regulations against defamations of this kind; they were prosecuted according to the ordinary criminal law, if they were liable to disturb public order or arouse contempt and hatred against a certain class of citizens.

'Classes Cannot be Defamed'

When in France the suggestion was discussed to include in the press law of 1822 regulations regarding attacks on groups of the population, the philosopher and politician, Royer-Collard said that no classes exist and, therefore, no protection is needed for them. Classes are notions and not actual beings. Since groups of the population cannot be punished, it is, according to Royer-Collard, quite impossible to grant to them a particular legal protection. Moreover, general accusations are not defamations of individuals. If general faults are attributed to a certain calling, these are not the personal defects of those who practise the occupation.

In Great Britain, according to a judgment passed in 1858 (*Eastwood* v. *Holmes*), the courts follow similar deliberations and declare the defamation of a group of persons also as neither actionable nor punishable. 'If a man wrote,' it was stated in that judgment, 'that all lawyers were thieves, no particular lawyer could sue him, unless there is something to point to that particular individual.' In contrast to this opinion, however, the courts in Germany and in some other countries hold that the defamation of a class affects also each of its members. But such actions have been in Germany successful merely if the class concerned enjoyed undue favours, e.g. officers of the Armed Forces.

Only in the French press law of 1881 and afterwards in other press regulations, too, provisions were included which made punishable attacks on the army, judges, and on public officials. In default of such press laws the group concerned has usually the benefit of the protection of the ordinary criminal law.

Recent tegulations

In some press laws the instigation to hatred against nations and religions is declared to be inadmissible. In Germany, for instance, regulations from pre-Nazi times made punishable the public incitement of various classes of the population against each other with imprisonment of up to two years and with a fine, if thereby the public peace was endangered. The Egyptian press law (1910) makes anyone committing this offence liable to imprisonment up to one year or to a fine (art. 153). In Estonia, too, contributions are not permitted which, by their malicious demagogic or inciting tone, might sow discord between the various classes, political or other groups (art. 16(5)). Finally, the Yugoslav press law (1926) declares the instigation to hatred against nations or religions as an offence.

As a consequence of the violent attacks of some newspapers and periodicals on various groups of the Dutch population, particularly on the Jews, the Second Chamber of the Netherlands passed alterations of the Penal Law in 1934. Accordingly, a person who injures a group of the population by words, writings or pictures, is punishable with imprisonment of up to one year or with a fine of up to 300 florins. He who distributes, affixes, or exhibits publications of this kind and knew or could know their contents, may be punished with imprisonment of up to six months and with a fine of up to 300 florins. If a person commits one of the offences mentioned above while practising certain callings and five years have not yet elapsed since a previous conviction had taken place, it will be regarded as an aggravating circumstance (art. 137).

A provision of the Tunisian press law (1936, art. 22(4)) aims at preventing anti-Semitic propaganda. Any person, the regulation states, who instigates to race hatred, is punishable with imprisonment of from two months up to three years and with a fine. In Switzerland the cantons and the federation are empowered by the Constitution (1874, art. 50 (2)) to take the necessary steps in order to protect the various religious communities from attacks. When the council of the Canton Geneva banned anti-Semitic publications, the Swiss Federal Court upheld this decision (1936) according to the Constitution, whereupon in other cantons, too, similar resolutions were passed. After two years the matter was uniformly settled, since a federal law (5th December, 1938) prohibited publications of the above mentioned kind and made them liable to imprisonment of up to three months or to a fine of up to 2,000 fr., or both.

10. LIBELS DURING ELECTIONS

Prior to political elections the candidates suddenly come into the limelight. Their records and abilities are appreciated by followers and criticised by adversaries. Often the criticism becomes a reprimand and even a defamation.

While the press law of 1881 was deliberated in the French parliament, it was proposed there that a defamation of a political candidate should be treated in the same way as if a public official were defamed. But the motion was rejected and so were subsequent suggestions, which attempted to bring into accordance the right to criticise, so necessary in times of election, with the respect for the public and private life of candidates. But the French Court of Cassation held the view of the ordinary law. Newspapers and electors should have their right uncurtailed to deal with the candidates, their opinions and actions, but they should not abuse it to the extent of defamations. French courts, which had often the opportunity of judging libel actions of this kind, have held the opinion that even provocation does not justify defamation in electoral contests.

In Great Britain candidates are protected against falsehoods, which could damage their prospects, by two Acts, the Corrupt and Illegal Practices Prevention Act (1895), which applies to parliamentary elections, and the Municipal Elections (Corrupt and Illegal Practices) Act (1911), relating to municipal elections. According to them, 'no person shall, for the purpose of affecting the return of any candidate at an election, make or publish false statements of fact in relation to the personal character or conduct of such candidate.' Expressions of opinion are not affected by this regulation. Contraventions are punishable with a fine not exceeding £100 and the persons liable shall be incapable of voting for five years.

Also in most states of the American Union strict regulations are in force, which aim at preventing wilful defamations of political candidates. In the States of Montana (s. 10.800) and Oregon (s. 36-2434), if a publication relating to elections 'shall contain a false statement or charges reflecting on any candidate's character, morality, or integrity, the author thereof and every person printing or knowingly assisting in the circulation shall be guilty of political criminal libel' and punished by imprisonment in the penitentiary for one to three years. It will be sufficient defence to such charge if the person accused 'shall prove on his trial that he had reasonable grounds to believe such charge was true, and did believe it was true, and that he was not actuated by malice in making such publication.' But in that event, and as a part of such defence, the author and the printer or publisher must also prove that, at least fifteen days before the publication was printed, 'he or they caused to be served personally and in person upon the candidate to whom it relates a copy thereof in writing, and calling his attention particularly to the charges contained therein, and that before printing, publishing, or circulating such charges, they received and read any denial, defence or explanation' from the candidate within ten days after the service of such charge upon the accused person.

In Great Britain a regulation, which also aims at checking defamations of candidates, provides that election printed matter, e.g. bills, placards or posters, 'must bear on the face thereof the name of the printer and publisher.' (Corrupt and Illegal Practices Prevention Act, 1883). The same restriction is contained among others in the statutes of Montana (s. 10.800), Oregon (s. 36-2434), Pennsylvania (s. 18-535).

According to the last-mentioned statute, 'in all criminal prosecutions or indictments for libel no conviction shall be allowed if the subject matter of the publication... relates to candidates for public office or to the official conduct of public officers, and is found to the satisfaction of the jury to be proper for public information or investigation and not to have been maliciously or negligently made' (s. 18-533).

The criticism should not be restricted too much. 'It is no offence', states the law of the State of New Mexico (s. 35-3514/5), 'to make true statements of facts or express opinions as to the qualifications of a candidate for any office or public place or appointment,' and it is also no offence 'to publish true statements of fact as to the qualities of any person for any occupation, profession or trade.'

The Supreme Court of Michigan decided that 'the public are interested in knowing the character of candidates for Congress, and while no one can lawfully destroy the reputation of a candidate by falsehood, yet if an honest error is made in an honest attempt to enlighten the public, it must reduce the damages to a minimum if the fault itself is not serious.' Similar views were held by courts in Pennsylvania and Texas.

11. DEFAMATION OF WOMEN

In several states of the American Union a defamation of innocent women by words, writings or printing, if they are charged with incontinence, is tried according to special regulations. They aim, as it is stated in the law of North Carolina, at stopping the practice of people 'who may attempt in a wanton and malicious manner to destroy the reputation of innocent and unprotected women, whose very existence in society depends upon the unsullied purity of their character' (s. 2432).

The qualification of such defamations varies. In Alabama (s. 4923), Georgia (s.343), Indiana (s. 10-3201), Michigan (s.16.812), Utah (s. 103-38-9), Virginia (par. 4536a), and other states it is regarded as an offence and liable to penalties, which amount in Michigan at most to 100 dollars or 90 days' imprisonment, or both, in Alabama to 500 dollars or six months' imprisonment, or both, and in Utah to 1,000 dollars or one year's imprisonment, or both.

In other states, however, such a defamation can be only made the subject of a civil action, e.g. in South Carolina (s.8659) and Tennessee (s.9310), but it also happens that criminal and civil proceedings may be carried on simultaneously, as in Alabama (s.4923 and s.7359), Indiana (s.10-3201 and s. 38815) and North Carolina (s.2432 and s. 4230). The claim to damages need not be supported by the evidence of special damage caused by the defamation.

In the State of Georgia it is prohibited 'to publish... or cause to be published... the name or identity of any female who may have been raped or upon whom an assault with intent to commit a rape may have been made' (s. 28-2105).

The right of a married woman to claim damages for a defamation inflicted upon her is laid down in the State of Indiana as her own right (s. 38-115). She may bring and maintain an action in her own name, the law states, against any person or body corporate for damages 'as if she were sole'; and 'the money received shall be her separate property, and her husband, in such case, shall not be liable for costs.'

12. INSERTION OF THE JUDGMENT IN A LIBEL CASE

The plaintiff who has carried his cause in a libel case is, as a rule, greatly interested in having published the judgment in the newspaper, where the defamation appeared, and perhaps in other journals, too. However, there are judgments which, even if they are in the interest of the offended person, contain passages which are not favourable to him, e.g. the statement that the defendant succeeded in proving the truth of the defamatory publication in one or another unpleasant point.

For this reason, in many laws the decision as to whether the judgment should be published is left to the plaintiff. For example, according to the Hungarian law, 'the Court of Justice, at the request of the party injured by a newspaper libel, will order the libeller to publish the sentence pronounced together with the grounds thereof in a Hungarian paper chosen by the Court of Justice' (art. 43). Also the Turkish press law (art. 12) provides a reproduction of the judgment in libel cases at the order of the court, but the request of the offended person is not necessary. The judgment must be published in the first or second edition after it has been passed; the reproduction may also be ordered in other newspapers at the cost of the guilty person.

According to the Polish press law, the fact that the truth of the defamatory passages has not been proven, may be published at the request of the plaintiff along with the judgment. The cost must be borne by the publisher or editor of the publication.

In Colombia the publication of judgments in cases of calumny depends on the offended person. 'Should the aggrieved party so desire, the editors or directors of periodicals in which calumnies have been published shall insert in them, within the period of time laid down by the law... or by the tribunal which pronounces judgment shall be published in an official newspaper if the calumniated person so desires (Penal Code, arts. 748 and 752). In such cases the person responsible must pay the cost of the insertion of the judgment in at least three periodicals, at the discretion of the judge (1898, art. 24).

An unusual regulation of the press laws in Czarist Russia and Denmark may be added: If in the former country a person felt offended by a newspaper, he was entitled to publish therein his suit against the journal, which had to insert it without cost (art. 23). Since Russian proceedings took a time, the publication of the action was at least a swift vindication. According to the Danish press law, a person who considers himself attacked in a periodical publication 'may demand the insertion therein, without payment, of a notice of the institution of proceedings in consequence of the attack, as well as of the result of the proceedings' (art. 11).

French courts have declared that it is left to the plaintiff in a libel case to publish the judgment, the insertion of which in some newspapers was ordered by the court, also in other journals at his cost, without exposing himself to penalties or damages for libel.

13. DEFAMATION OF FOREIGN HEADS OF STATE

Reasons for their Protection

Regulations regarding the protection of foreign heads of state and diplomats from defamatory attacks in newspapers had been included in the press laws a long time ago. The reasons given were merely of a general nature; the obligation of politeness and the care for the maintenance of good relations with foreign states make it necessary, it was said, not to permit such publications. The real motives go deeper. A defamation of the, let us say, Roumanian King by the Greek press might easily lead to replies in Roumania, which would injure the Greek monarch. The result is that the reputation of both, and what seems to be still worse, the monarchic idea had suffered. Moreover, if in both states newspapers are prohibited from publishing such contributions, a frequent case of disturbed diplomatic relations would disappear.

The laws concerned are usually applied only, if also in the other country the same regulations are in force. The request for the prosecution of the journal must be made through the foreign office of the state the head of which has been attacked. In France as early as in the press law of 1819, when a king, Louis XVIII, ruled, such a regulation was introduced. The wording of the law had, therefore, regard to the protection of sovereigns. The constitution now in force was issued in 1818, i.e. in the times of the Third Republic, and the expression 'Sovereign' was replaced by 'Chief of the Foreign State.' The sense of the law, however, has not changed thereby. The Turkish (art. 27) and the Persian press law (art. 40) restrict the protection to rulers of 'friendly' powers. In Belgium, following the example of France, the heads of foreign governments ('Presidents of the cabinet') are mentioned besides the sovereigns, but the protection is not only granted in the case of a defamation, but also if the 'authority' of the persons mentioned is attacked (decree of 1852, 20th December). In Roumania also royal families are included in the protection.

Libels on Diplomats

The protection granted to diplomatic representatives of foreign countries relates to attacks on their private life as well as on their official activities. The plea of justification is not allowed. Consuls, however, are not affected by these regulations. In the last two decades the question was sometimes discussed whether sovereigns in exile, who were a frequent target for newspaper attacks, may claim the protection of such laws. But it was held generally that the regulations mentioned referred to active rulers only.

The penalties for defamations of heads of state and diplomats are relatively heavy. In Belgium they amount to imprisonment of from three months to two years and to a fine; in a subsequent case the loss of civic rights is added. In Turkey it is imprisonment of from one month to one year, in Yugoslavia of from one to six months, and in Portugal 33 days, while in Switzerland the public insult to a sovereign or to a foreign government as well as the defamations of a foreign nation are punishable with a fine and imprisonment. In France imprisonment of from three months to one year or a fine or both may be imposed. Similar penalties are provided for in Persia, Roumania, Colombia and in other countries. The defamation of foreign diplomats is punished more mildly.

In Great Britain words, which may expose a foreign government to contempt or hatred, or may cause disquiet in some way, are not punishable, unless they contain an incitement to commit violent acts.

Lese-Majesty

The defamation of the sovereign in his own country is tried, as a rule, according to the criminal law. If press laws contain special regulations about it, they are usually stricter than the ordinary law. Frequently the families of the rulers are included in this protection.

In the Netherlands and in Greece, besides the King, the Queen is mentioned whose defamation is punished as severely as that of the King, namely, in the Netherlands with imprisonment up to five years or with a fine of 300 florins if the insult is intentionally inflicted (art. 111), and in Greece with imprisonment from one to seven years (1837, articles 1 and 2).

The Japanese law does not assume the possibility of a defamation of or of an insult to the Emperor, but speaks of 'items disrespectful towards the Imperial House' (art. 42).

In France lese-majesty was differently judged, according to the constitution now being in force. In 1819 the defamation of the King committed by a publication was punishable with imprisonment of from six months to five years and with a fine of from 500 to 10,000 francs (art. 9). This law was abolished after the fall of the monarchy in 1848, but already in the next year a new law was promulgated, which contained regulations against defamations of the President of the Republic, and in 1858 another law followed providing the protection of the Emperor from abusive language.

When the law of 1881 was deliberated in parliament, the view was held that every insult committed by the press to the President of the Republic and also to the Republic, to the Senate or Chamber should be punished with imprisonment of from six months to two years or with a fine or both. But strong objections were raised, since such a regulation might recall the times of the political reaction during the monarchy. A counter-proposal was to the effect that insults to the Republic but not to its President should be punished. Finally a motion was made to punish insults to the Republic, Senate, Chamber, and to the President. The four offences were voted separately, but only the insult to the President was declared as punishable, while 'Republic,' 'Senate' and 'Chamber' were regarded as abstract notions, which cannot become the subject of a defamation. Moreover, the Senate superseded the expression 'insult' by 'offence.' Thus the regulation concerned (art. 26) states that a defamation of the President of the Republic by word or writing, by distribution or posting of publications, placards, pictures and so on is to be punished with imprisonment of from three months to one year and with a fine. Plea of justification is not admitted.

Many press laws include in the protection of the sovereign from defamations still other persons of public position or public institutions, such as courts and administrative authorities in Sweden and Egypt. Constitution, legislation, and religion, also the legislative bodies, are protected in Roumania (1862, art. 45 to 47), while officials of the state administration, judges, professors (!) and military officers enjoy protection in Portugal (1910, art. 10). The French press law, too, contains regulations regarding defamations of these and similar kinds, but not in connection with lese-majesty.

14. LIBELS ON DECEASED PERSONS

Malicious comments do not even cease with the life of the victim. Personal or political hatred often pursues him in the newspapers after his death. Still worse is it if, after years, scandalous affairs are dug up from the life of a person who is dead, and filth is thrown at him, when he can no longer defend himself.

Two different opinions regarding the judicial prosecution of such cases prevail in the press laws. The French law (1881, art. 34 amended in 1919, 29th September) states that defamation of and insults to deceased persons may only be prosecuted if they were made with the intention of injuring the reputation of a living descendant, spouse, or heir, who, at any rate, will have the right of reply according to the press law.

Thorough deliberations and careful considerations preceded, this wording. The old French law contained a regulation traced back to the Roman law, according to which the heir may claim damages from a person who disparages by calumnies the memory of one who is dead. But this provision was neither adopted by the French Code Penal nor by the press law of 1819. When in 1881 the French legislation again intended to introduce a protection of the memory of deceased persons, in the senate M. Pelletan gave some ingenious reasons for a new way of solving this problem. Roughly speaking, he said :

'In a case of defamation the defamed, and no other person, is, as long as he lives, entitled to bring an action against the offender. Therefore, the law providing actions for defamations of deceased persons assumes that the defamed ceded his right before his death to someone who, at that time, may not yet have been born; in this heir the dead one revives and wishes, perhaps after a century, to obtain retaliation for a calumny which he had known and despised whilst alive. And how would it be if by chance one heir sued and another one, related in the same degree, would not, because it might be more damaging than useful to the memory of the deceased? To whom should the court do justice?

'A man has gone from the scene of action', M. Pelletan continued, 'he has played his part well or otherwise and has found, after troubled activities, his rest in the grave, but also that other not less precious repose: oblivion. Should it really depend upon some remote cousin, whether he will be dragged out from his grave and brought to court to give a plaintiff and a defendant the opportunity of searching in the depth of a tomb and of raising dust?'

Pelletan's arguments did not fail to impress Chamber and Senate. In both the law was passed in the moved version. Accordingly, calumnies or defamations of deceased persons are not punishable. Only when they are directed against the living heirs, these may bring actions just as if they themselves had been defamed. However, they are entitled as if they themselves had been defamed. However, they are entitled to claim damages in civil actions or to continue proceedings which were instituted by the deceased plaintiff.

The press law of Syria has taken over these regulations (art. 36), and also the press laws of Colombia and Yugoslavia follow the French view. The Colombian law (art. 26) stresses still more the principal idea. 'The penalties for calumny or insult against the memory of deceased persons shall not be imposed on the persons responsible, except when there is proof of an intent to wound thereby the honour of the living heirs, family and relatives.' Thus the circle of persons who are entitled to bring an action is wider in the Colombian law than in the French one, and is not restricted to 'living heirs.' The Yugoslav law is less distinct, but expresses the same opinion (1904, art. 33).

Trials Exposing the Memory of Deceased

In contrast to the opinions expressed in the press laws mentioned above, the German Penal Code (par. 189) makes liable to imprisonment up to six months or, in the case of extenuating circumstances, to a fine, a person who insults the memory of one who is dead by contending or distributing against better knowledge untrue statements which, if he lived, would expose him to contempt or disregard. The prosecution is only instituted at the request of the parents, children or spouse of the deceased.

Accordingly, the insult to the deceased is considered an offence, even if thereby the reputation of the next relatives—the expression 'heirs' is not used—is not affected. However, it must be an insult, not only a defamation; the statement must also be untrue and made against better knowledge. But the truth is to be proved in court. In some embittered lawsuits the proof of the truth has been fought out, and in this way the private life of the deceased, and also the memory of other persons exposed. The French law wanted to avoid just this effect.

The regulations of the Netherlandish Penal Code (articles 270/1) resemble very much those of the German law. The penalty is a little more lenient (up to 300 florins or up to three months' imprisonment); only one of the relations by consanguinity or affinity of the deceased person in the direct or collateral line to the second decree, or the husband or wife may bring actions.

One of the most recent regulations of this kind might be the Czechoslovak law for the Protection of The Honour (1933), which also provides actions for the defamation of deceased persons (art. 5). Equally, the Finnish law follows this course, but it is more precise (Penal Law, 1889, art. 4). According to this regulation, the offence is not only committed 'by falsely accusing the dead man, against better knowledge, of a definite offence or certain kind of offence or other such act which, were he alive, would be calculated to bring contempt upon him,' but also by spreading 'fictitious or false reports concerning him.'

The plea of justification is admissible in Finland, for in this way only will it be stated, whether the defamatory statements are false and invented. In contrast to the laws dealt with so far, it is ordered by the Finnish law that, if the defamed person has been dead for 20 years or more.

Another deviation from the general direction is provided by the regulation of the Finnish law to the effect that the memory of a 'dead man,' and not, as usual, of a 'dead person' is to be protected. The legislator could not foresee in 1889, when the law was promulgated, that a time would come when women would step out from domestic life and thus, like men, might become an object of defamations.

Punishable Offence in Great Britain and in the United States

English courts consider the defamation of a deceased person punishable only if its tendency clearly aims at stirring up his relatives so deeply that, in order to avenge the reputation of the family, they would be prepared to commit an act which might disturb the public peace. Such a defamation must be, or course, very serious indeed. Just in England, where reserve and self-control are regarded as natural virtues, one will not easily be brought into a state which might make one capable of committing a breach of peace. A rather considerable amount of contempt must be thrown on the family, if the action is to be considered justifiable. At any rate, according to the judgments of English courts, expressions which injure the character of the deceased, but do not affect the family, are not considered a sufficient basis for an action. In Great Britain a judge said once: '... to discuss the characters of deceased statesmen and noblemen as a matter of history is no crime.'

Serious defamations of deceased persons are tried in Great Britain as criminal libels are punished by fines and imprisonment. The proceedings are instituted by an indictment of the relatives. Nobody must claim damages. As it is not always easy to prove the malice of the offender or his tendency to a breach of peace, such prosecutions occur rarely in England. In a case which aroused interest owing to the personality of the defamed, the decision of the court was reached in another way. A biography of Gladstone, published in 1927, contained a remark about his relations with the female sex, which was felt by his sons as a defamation of their father. But they had no illusions about the prospects of a prosecution of the author, since they would hardly be able to prove that they, being over 70, might forget themselves so far as to commit a breach of peace against the far younger author. As they, however, wanted to clear the memory of their father in court proceedings, they wrote to the club, of which the offender and also they themselves were members, a letter calling him liar and coward. The author had no other way than to bring an action against them, but he lost his suit and, moreover, the jury added to the verdict of acquittal the remark that they could satisfy themselves of Gladstone's high character.

The case led to various discussions in juridical and literary circles, as a result of which the demand for a revision of the penal regulations concerned was asked. For the prosecution of the offender it should not be necessary to prove malice or the tendency to a breach of peace, if the defamation is intended to injure or provoke living persons. Moreover, the defamation should be examined as to whether the charges against the deceased had already been known in his lifetime or were produced only after his death, when he could not defend himself. In such a case the proof of malice would be admitted. Finally, the suggestion was made that the law should distinguish between attacks on persons of public life whose activities aroused comments, and on private persons who should enjoy greater protection.

A somewhat similar case was tried by a court in Paris a year later. The grand-daughter of the French novel-writer, George Sand, claimed damages from her biographer Jacques Boulenger, who made some personal remarks concerning the author's relations with the male sex. (The return of the sexual motive is noticeable). The court, however, declared that such a claim was unfounded and dismissed the action.

In the United States the practice of law takes, on the whole, the same line as in England. The defamation of dead persons is regarded, according to the ordinary law, and, moreover, in more than twenty states of the American Union according to special statute laws, as an offence liable to punishment by fine and imprisonment, but it must be proved that the article was written with malice and intended for exposing the family to contempt. According to the wording of some laws in the United

States, such a defamation is assumed, if the statements made are maliciously untrue and may 'blacken the memory of one who is dead,' as, for instance, in Arizona (s. 4617), Arkansas (s.3015), California (par. 248), Colorado (ch.48, par. 199). Other American laws provide that the defamation must be still more serious to cause a prosecution, namely, 'designed to blacken and vilify the memory of one who is dead, and tending to scandalise or provoke his surviving relatives and friends,' e.g. Kansas (ch. 21, s.2401), Maine (ch. 141, s.1), and others. In some states the relatives are entitled to institute the prosecution, if the memory of the dead is exposed 'to hatred, contempt, ridicule, or obloquy,' for instance, in Minnesota (s. 10.112).

In contrast to English law, prosecution in the United States is facilitated, since the defamation must not be so serious that it might provoke a breach of peace. As in England claims for damages are not granted. An American judgment gives the following reason for it: Since a person cannot claim damages for the defamation of a relative, he can still less do so if the defamed relative is dead. Only the offended person himself, if alive, is entitled to such a claim.

PLEA OF JUSTIFICATION

If follows of necessity from the right of the press to comment on events in public life that a newspaper-man is entitled to prove the truth of his statements, if he is called to account for his criticism. A prohibition of this defence would impair the critical activity of newspapers, and thus endanger the freedom of the press. Therefore most American statutes when pronouncing the liberty of the press declare that newspaper-men, who are charged with criminal or civil libel or calumny, may plead justification.

No Justification in the Case of a an Insult

Since this plea must be based upon facts, it cannot be admitted in the case of an 'insult,' which is defined in most criminal laws as a kind of outrageous defamation, e.g. 'idiot,' 'mangy dog,' 'jail-bird,' and others. Whether a person deserves one of these attributes can hardly be proved in court. Should the accused person be permitted to give evidence, he would be enabled to make statements which would add to the previous insults. Such a justification must also be rejected for moral reasons, since an insult, however true it may be in a certain case, is a censurable act. The decision of a court to enter into a discussion about the truth of an insult would involve a new, heavy insult to the plaintiff.

The rules concerning the ban on the plea of justification in cases of insult are chiefly contained in the ordinary criminal law. But some press laws deal also with the matter, e.g. that of Colombia, which states that 'the proof of the truth of an insult is not to be brought before the court, and in no case exempts from punishment' (art. 28). In some states of the American Union it is laid down that, in prosecutions for a libel-tending to expose the natural defects of persons, the truth thereof may not be given in evidence (Colorado, ch. 48, par. 199, and others).

Protection of Private Persons from Disclosures in Court

In most countries, apart from the English-speaking world, justification in libel actions which concern private life is also inadmissible. The most recent rule of this kind, introduced in France in 1944 (6th May), prohibits justification in the following libel cases :

1. When the defamation concerns the private life of the plaintiff;
2. When it refers to facts, which occurred more than ten years before;
3. When it relates to a fact constituting a minor offence which is covered by an amnesty or by prescription, or which was the object of a sentence that has been purged or quashed.

In France the principle laid down in the Ordinance mentioned above is of long standing. Already the press law of 1819, which was followed in other countries, adopted the rule of Royer-Collard: 'The private life should be walled off.' 'It is the task of justice,' said M. de Serres, one of the authors of the law of 1819 in his report, 'to restore the reputation of the defamed, and not to deal a new blow at him as happens if such evidence is given. Is it just to sacrifice an irreproachable man in favour of one who is not? Should we not by allowing this evidence.' Serres pointed out further, 'promote the idea of bringing to light our private life, of disclosing our most intimate relations, our most painful and most secret wounds at the first offending word? Should we not perceive in the evidence a decoy for defamations, an open arena for piracy and malice? These considerations have caused us to suggest a prohibition of justification.'

However, French lawyers agreed that this ban also involves some disadvantages. The decent man, against whom a defamation based upon incorrect facts is directed, cannot show that he is wronged, since just as the offender is not permitted to prove the truth, he, the defamed, cannot prove the contrary, namely his honesty. But in the opinion of Barbier, one of the most important French lawyers, these inconveniences, however considerable they may be, weigh less than a legal system. which would admit the proof of the truth in all libel cases.

French courts have not always held this view. The Court of Toulouse declared in a judgment of 1881 (16th June) that the plaintiff should be given the right to prove the falsehood of the defamation for the following reasons: The prohibition of the plea of justification is designed to protect the defamed person from inquiries which might disturb the domestic peace, and not to prevent him from proving his honesty and decency. While the plea of justification may constitute a danger to family life, the proof of the falsehood of the defamation amounts to the exercise of the natural right to parry an unjustified attack. But as other courts did not accord to the plaintiff the right to adduce evidence to counter the plea, in the end both parties remained deprived of the right to plead justification.

French lawyers advance a striking argument in order to

show that the admission of justification in libel cases would be unjust and immoral: Let us suppose that many years ago a person has committed, a violation of the law and was punished accordingly. Out of malice or for similar reasons the matter is revived later on and broadcast to the world. If the plea of justification is admitted, the offender must be acquitted and the defamed person is again stigmatised. Thus persons who once did wrong would be unable to retrieve their reputation by good conduct.

Of course, there may be cases where certain circumstances plead for the offender. When he was making the defamatory statements, he was perhaps moved by good intentions, or may have based his attack upon official documents, or he may have believed that he was acting in the public interest. Should an examination of the facts be excluded by the court even in such cases, and the accused person be treated in the same manner as the calumniator who has maliciously made false statements? French courts, objecting to this argument, point out that the accused will always be given the opportunity of stating those facts, which will prove his good faith without going into the truth or falsehood of the offending statements. Thus the judge can obtain an idea of the motives and intentions of the accused, and can express his impression in the sentence, the measure of which is determined by him according to the circumstances of the case.

The main points raised in these discussions have now been embodied in the French Ordinance of 1944 mentioned above.

The first country, in which the French regulations of 1819 regarding justification in libel cases brought by private persons were adopted, was Peru. According to the press law of 1823, 'the penalty shall be imposed on the author or publisher of the defamatory libel, even if he is prepared to prove the truth of the offensive imputation' (art. 7). Similarly in Egypt and Syria such provisions are in force. The Japanese law (1909, art. 45) allows the defendant to submit the actual facts in evidence, if 'the court is of the opinion that the said item was inserted not out of malice, but for the public advantage,' and if the case does not concern the private conduct of the plaintiff.

In Yugoslavia, too, the truth of alleged facts may not be supported by evidence, if they 'concern the family life of private persons or public servants, or the private occupation of either, should such occupation have no relation to their public occupation or position, or with any industrial, commercial, or financial undertaking, which is dependent on public confidence' (art. 34).

The Czechoslovak law for the Protection of the Honour (1933) admits justification and circumstantial evidence regarding facts which concern private life in the following cases only:

(1) If there were reasons for such allegations and for the form in which they were produced; and

(2) If the facts were the subject of a trial in open court.

Permitted Justification Regarding Private-Life

In departure from these regulations, justification is the rule in Portugal. Whoever commits a libel by means of a publication must prove the truth of the facts he alleges, 'whoever the person may be against whom he has made allegations.' Only if the offence is directed against persons in their private capacity, the defendant must restrict himself to an explanation of the grounds on which the offending statement is based (art. 17). If the defendant is unable or unwilling to justify his allegations, he is punished with imprisonment from three months to two years and must pay compensation (art. 18).

In Finland, if 'the person who is summoned for libel substantiates the truth of his allegations, but if it is clear from the form of these allegations or the circumstances under which they are made, that he has intended to cause injury, he shall nevertheless be punished' (Penal Code, art. 6).

In Uruguay the defendant is allowed to justify his statements on the condition that this evidence is not unfavourable to the 'private life of individuals' (Criminal Code, art. 343).

In Italy, in order to avoid the unpleasant consequences which may arise for the defamed person if the defendant is permitted to plead justification, it is left to the plaintiff to decide whether he wishes the evidence to be heard. Justification is admitted only at the plaintiff's request, particularly in those cases where criminal proceedings are in progress against him in the same matter, or if he occupies a public office and the defamation refers to it. Finally, the request of the plaintiff to admit justification will always be granted, if he asks the court for a statement that the charges made against him are unfounded.

Practice in the Anglo-Saxon Countries

In the English-speaking world justification is always admitted in cases of civil libel. As the defamed demands compensation for the damage inflicted on him by the libel, it must be proved in court that he is entitled to bring such a claim. Therefore, in Anglo-Saxon countries detailed evidence involving private affairs is frequently given in civil libel cases and discussed in court.

In proceedings for criminal libel the position is different. Courts in Great Britain and in France, too, hold the view that the truth of the defamatory statement is no defence. On the contrary, 'the greater the truth, the greater the libel.' In fact, untrue offending words can easily be refuted, while it is the unpleasant truth that may drive a person to despair, and thus provoke an assault upon the offender, i.e. a breach of peace, which in the Anglo-Saxon countries is considered a possible consequence of a very serious defamation. Therefore, according to Lord Campbell's Act (1843, s. 6), the plea of justification in the case of a criminal libel is restricted in Great Britain; the accused must not only prove that his allegations are true, but also that he has made them in the public interest. In the case of statements of a blasphemous, obscene or seditious character the plea of justification is excluded altogether.

In the United States, however, justification in criminal libel cases is admitted in a rather liberal manner. 'The truth of the charge made may always be proved in justification of the libel,' runs, for example, the provision concerned in the statutes of the State of Georgia (s. 4435). There is hardly a state in the American Union, the statutes of which do not contain one or two articles about this right. If restrictions exist, they constitute an exception. The French model, according to which the accused person may prove the truth of his charges against public officials regarding their official conduct, is followed in Alabama (s. 7355), Kentucky (Const. s. 9), and Maine (Const. art. 1, s. 4). In the two last-mentioned states it is demanded that the published matter must be proper for general information.

On the whole, it may be said that fair comment will be regarded as a sufficient justification in the Anglo-Saxon countries, if the subject is suitable for public discussion, if the publication was made without malice or gross negligence, and if, as early as possible, a full apology was published. Sometimes also proof that the allegations are true may lead to an acquittal.

Justification of Libels on Public Officials

Two views diamentrically opposed to each other exist regarding the question, whether in the case of defamations of public officials the defendant may prove that the defamatory statement is true. In some countries of Central and Southern Europe, where the parliamentary constitution has not yet wiped out the traces of an absolutist time, the defamation of a public servant, particularly of an organ of the executive, is an offence which is always punished, even if the charges are true. A justification is unthinkable. As long as the official is in office, he may be reprimanded or criticised by his superiors only. In serious cases he will be called to account by the competent disciplinary tribunal or by the ordinary court, but no other person is allowed to comment on his actions.

In the Anglo-Saxon and other demoncratic countries, however, criticism of a public official, unless it affects his private life, is a matter of public concern, and, therefore, the plea of justification is admitted. In a classic manner the author of the French press law of 1819, M. de Serres, put this idea as follows: 'The private life of public servants belongs to them only; their public life belongs to everyone. It is the right, it is often the obligation of every citizen to reproach them publicly for the faults they commit when exercising their duties. Therefore justification is a matter of course in these cases.

Thus a provision to this effect was introduced into the French press law of 1819. It referred to public servants only, but was extended in the course of time to all persons who act in a public capacity. In the press law of 1881 (art. 35) this provision was reproduced in the version that justification must only relate to the official activities of the defamed person. But in the most recent amendment of the French press law (1944) mentioned above justification regarding private matters is not admitted at all. Thus also official persons must not be treated differently from private persons if the defamation concerns matters relating to their private life.

The idea that public officials cannot object to the plea of justification, if comment has been made on their public activities, recurs with various deviations in many press laws. Peru was again the first country which followed the French example. The Peruvian press law of 1823 provides that the author or publisher of a publication 'in which an official or corporation is charged with committing offences in the discharge of their functions... shall not be liable to any penality, if he is able to prove the truth of his allegations' (art. 8). Similar regulations are in force in Egypt (art. 261). In Roumania, too, the truth of defamatory statements may be proved in libel actions brought by public officials or by persons who have been employed in a public position (art. 62), but an intrusion into their private sphere is prevented by the following provision of the Roumanian Constitution (art. 26): '...calumnies, abuse and libels directed against individuals or public officials of whatever category, whose private life or personal honour are affected,' will be judged in the ordinary court in conformity with the ordinary criminal law and not by a jury, which is otherwise competent regarding delinquencies of the press.

In the Anglo-Saxon countries justification in cases of defamation regarding public officials is admitted according to an old-established practice, if public interests are in question. In the American States of New Mexico (s. 35-3522) and of Texas (art. 1290) the truth of any statement charged as libel may be shown in justification of the defendant in the following cases:

'(1) Where the publication purports to be an investigation of the official conduct of officers or men in a public capacity.

'(2) Where it is stated in the libel that a person has been guilty of some penal offence, and the time, place and nature of the offence are specified in the publication.

'(3) Where it is stated in the libel that a person is of a notoriously bad or infamous character.

'(4) Where the publication charges any person in office, or a candidate therefor, with a want of honesty, or having been guilty of some malfeasance in office, rendering him unworthy of the place.

'In other cases the truth of the facts stated in the libel cannot be inquired to.'

Managers of Economic Undertakings as Public Men

According to the French press law (art. 35(2)), the directors and managers of commercial, industrial and financial undertakings which are financed by public bodies range also among the officials, who must accept justification if they sue for libel. The law of 1881 had already been passed by the French Chamber when the Committee of the Senate moved the regulation mentioned above which was then carried. The reason given was that persons by administering public funds in banks or by managing public enterprises like railways, occupy a position not less responsible than that of officials. It is necessary, it was stated, to control such companies, and if required, to reveal their weak points. For this purpose newspaper-men were to be relieved of the fear of being convicted without having the possibility of pleading justification.

Press laws which closely follow the French pattern, e.g. that of Syria (art. 35), have adopted this provision.

The Boundary between Official and Private Conduct

Certain difficulties arise' in practice, if the plea of justification is restricted to the conduct of persons only in so far as they act in the exercise of a public office. Some activities of private life may be incompatible with public functions. A clergyman, a pedagogue, a judge must refrain from habits, which are treated with indulgence when other professions are concerned. A decision of the Swiss Federal Court of 1934 states that the liberty of the press guaranteed by Article 55 of the Federal Constitution (of 1874), confers upon newspapers the right to criticise persons who occupy a position in public life, even in respect of their private conduct, if it affects their public situation. But the criticism must contain facts or, at least, statements which the author has examined and which he could assume to be true.

In cases where a public official is attacked in his official capacity and also in respect of his private life, the defamations are inseparably intermingled. French courts usually transmit such actions to the criminal court and protect the plaintiff from the danger involved in proceedings before a jury.

Formalities Preceding Justification

The French press law enumerates with great minuteness of detail the formalities which must precede justification in libel cases, and indicates the importance, which French legislation attributes to this part of the proceedings. Above all, the offender must not produce unexpected evidence. Within ten days after a summons has been served, the accused must communicate to the public prosecutor, if he has instituted the prosecution, or to the plaintiff, if it is a civil action, all facts which he wants to prove, the witnesses he wants to call, and finally copies of all documents which he wants to put in evidence. Otherwise he would lose the right of justification. Similarly, within a further five days the prosecutor or plaintiff must give the offender the same data referring to the evidence which they wish to submit in reply (1881, articles 52 and 53, and 1944, art. 12).

The idea reflected in the regulations and judgments concerned shows that in democratic countries newspapers are not to be prevented from discussing affairs which may claim public interest. It is one of the foremost tasks of the press to inform the public objectively about everything worth knowing. If it seems that in performing this duty a newspaper, by a vehement attack, exceeds the limits of what is admissible, it must be given an opportunity of proving that it felt entitled to the criticism. In the Netherlands, for example, the law expressly provides that a prosecution for defamation leads to an acquittal, if the accused person 'manifestly acted in the public interest or in necessary defence' and produces such evidence (articles 261 and 262).

Justification of Libels on Women

Regulations in some states of the American Union show a remarkable deviation from the general rule of not allowing painful intrusions into private life in court. In the State of Utah, for example, where the imputation of unchastity is an offence, 'the defendant may in justification show the truth of the imputation, and the general reputation for chastity of the female alleged to have been slandered may be inquired into' (s. 103-38-10).

Other laws of American states lay down that 'the false imputation to a woman of a want of chastity' can be made the subject of a criminal or civil libel action. The expression 'false' indicates that an imputation based upon facts is not unlawful with the result that plea of justification is admissible. Regulations of this kind are to be found in the laws of Alabama (s.4923), Georgia (s. 343), and others.

Failure of Justification

An unsuccessful plea of justification is mostly regarded as an aggravating circumstance, in order to deter the offender from pleading justification lightly and from thus causing hardship to the plaintiff.

In the Netherlands if, in a case of libel, the accused has made the imputation contrary to his better knowledge, and after having been permitted to prove the truth of his statements does not produce such evidence, he shall be punished more seriously (imprisonment up to three years or 300 florins) than in a libel action in which no evidence is given (up to one year or 300 florins). Deprivation of some civic rights may also be pronounced (art. 262).

An Austrian responsible editor who pleads justification but fails may be sentenced, in addition to the penalty he would have incurred otherwise, to the payment of damages to the plaintiff at his request up to 10,000 Austrian shillings (1929, art. 30(6)).

In the United States various regulations facilitate justification. The law of Indiana provides: 'The rule requiring that an answer of justification in cases of libel.... shall be proven beyond a reasonable doubt be and the same is hereby abrogated; and after the taking effect of this Act, the proof of such answer shall be controlled by the rule now applying to the proof of issues in other civil cases' (s. 400). A rule frequently to be found in American statutes provides that in all trials for libel, both civil and criminal, the truth when 'published with good motives and for justifiable ends, shall be a sufficient defence.' (Illinois, Const. art. II, s. 4; Mississippi, s. 1037, and others.) The law of Kansas is satisfied with 'justifiable ends' only (Const. s. 11). The statute of the State of Washington adds to the requirements of 'good motives and justifiable ends': 'It (the publication) is excused when honestly made in belief of its truth and fairness and upon reasonable grounds for such belief, and consists of fair comments upon the conduct of any person in respect of public affairs, made after a fair and impartial investigation' (s. 2425).

Proof of Probability

In many countries the accused person need not prove the truth of the defamation in order to be acquitted. It suffices if he can show that he had good cause to believe his allegations or that they were, if not true, at least probable. Such a proof that the defendant had reasonable grounds for believing that the allegation in question was true, leads to an acquittal and is admitted by the laws of many countries of Europe. The recent press law of Czechoslovakia (art. 4(8)) states: 'If the law demands proof that a statement is true in substance and in fact, then the accused person is not liable to punishment, if it is proved that he had good cause to believe the statement, and if it is clear that the object of the publication was to serve the public interest.' The question 'what serves the public interest?' is answered in detail. In particular, it includes 'compliance with the laws and decrees, endeavours to abolish malpractices in public administration, safeguarding of matters of common interests to certain classes and spheres of society, nationalities and recognised religious organisations' (art. 4(b)).

MEASURES TO DISCOURAGE LIBEL ACTIONS

Among the various lawsuits which come before the courts slander and libel cases have always been regarded as the most unpleasant waste of time. Those who have to deal with them dislike these actions, which, rarely offering an interesting legal point of view, are usually a more or less tiresome display of personal affairs. Defendants who are called to account for a defamation rarely regret and repent; they adhere to their statements and, by trying to prove their truth, add to the offence they have committed. Thus the proceedings in libel cases lead to a highly undesirable end. In order to strengthen their position, the litigant parties are at pains to blacken the reputation of the adversary and to magnify human weaknesses. The result is that the public receives and, unfortunately, retains a distorted and contemptuous picture of person and events.

Add to this that in such cases the decision of the court, however it may prove, is accepted by the party who has lost as a triumph of his adversary and not of justice. Hatred on the one side and malignant satisfaction on the other will thus for years smoulder in the hearts of the opponents.

In view of this deplorable effect, the settlement of actions for slander and libel must appear as an almost ethical achievement. By withdrawing a defamatory statement and by offering an appropriate apology the reputation of the plaintiff is restored, while the defendant is not humiliated; both are spared the painful public interest in details of their private life and other consequences resulting from this kind of litigation.

For these reasons courts and judges in many countries of Europe do their utmost to promote every attempt towards a reconciliation of the litigants. In Central European states, before legal proceedings are instituted, every slander and libel case comes before a committee which must try to bring about a settlement. This summons the parties in order to persuade the plaintiff that a trial would not be satisfactory, and to bring home to the defendant the wisdom of offering an apology to extricate himself from the affair. Moreover, both are told that by a settlement they would save money, time and trouble, since judicial proceedings take sometimes an unexpected course.

Intervention of the Courts in the Settlement of Libel Cases

In many countries the courts consider it an important duty to support and even to co-operate in a settlement before or during the trial. If in the course of the proceedings, the defendant or his counsel shows an inclination to withdraw the defamatory statements, or expresses his regret that they have been made, the judge usually adjourns the trial for an hour or so to give the parties an opportunity of reconsidering their affairs from the new angle. If the negotiations do not make progress, the judge himself often takes part in them and, by his intervention, helps the litigants to overcome the difficult point. Prompted by their dislike of slander and libel cases, the judges often acquit themselves of this task with some energy.

Two recent Czechoslovak laws have stressed very strongly this tendency to settle libel cases by providing that no punishment must be imposed upon the offender, if he is prepared to give adequate satisfaction to the plaintiff. Such a regulation is contained in the Czechoslovak press law of 1924 (art. 18(a)):

'If, during the endeavours to settle the matter with the sanction of the court, the accused person has offered in vain to give the offended party such satisfaction as the court deems to be adequate, for instance publication of a correction, withdrawal of the offending passage, and an expression of regret, then the court, in finding the accused guilty, may abstain from passing sentence. In this case, however, the court must order the accused and the publisher to print the findings of the court.'

This provision stood its test so well that, nine years later, the Czechoslovak law for the Protection of the Honour (1933) provided no punishment for libel in the following three cases:

(1) It is left to the plaintiff to demand that the offender should be found guilty, but not be punished. Thereby the public has no opportunity of drawing from an insignificant penalty conclusions which might be unfavourable to the plaintiff. Such a declaration, however, which the plaintiff cannot withdraw, will not lie in his interest, if it should appear during the trial that the defamation was committed against better knowledge, and a severe punishment would have been passed.

(2) No punishment is to be imposed if the defendant offers satisfaction which the judge considers adequate; and

(3) If the accused has committed the defamation in a state of thoughtlessness or excitement, which has been caused by a provocative or impudent behaviour on the part of the defamed (par. 9).

Apart from these three cases, the court may abstain from punishment if the accused has rendered an adequate satisfaction to the defamed at the latest before the beginning of the trial. This provision modifies and mitigates the Article 18 of the law mentioned above, as the satisfaction may also be given after the first attempt to settle the matter has failed.

Restraining of Defamatory Statements by Injunctions

If a person has reason to believe that a periodical, which has published a defamatory statement against him, will continue these publications, he is in many countries entitled to apply for an injunction ordering the responsible person of the periodical to abstain from such statements. Also if proceedings for libel have been instituted against the journal, applications for so-called interim or interlocutory injunctions restraining publications of this kind pending trial may be made.

In Great Britain the courts do not easily grant injunctions in libel actions and still less interlocutory ones. Only when an alleged statement is so manifestly defamatory that any jury would find it so, and also if the libel is so atrocious that serious injury may be inflicted on the plaintiff, the courts use their right to allow an interim injunction. On the other hand, a libel which is on the face of it too gross and absurd to do the plaintiff any material harm, will not cause an interim injunction, but may, according to the view held by the courts, be more fitly dealt with by criminal proceedings.

Also if no immediate injury is to be expected from the further publication of the libel, the court will not interfere by interlocutory injunctions nor in a case 'where the mischief, if any, has been done, and there is no intention on the part of the defendant to issue any more libellous statements.' Equally, in libel cases being not actionable unless express malice is proved, the courts are reluctant to grant an interlocutory injunction and leave the decision to the jury.

However, an exception is made when the defamation is committed against candidates in times of elections. In such a case an interim injunction can be obtained from the court on the same day and thus the further circulation of the offending statement will be prevented (Corrupt and Illegal Practices Prevention Act, 1895, s. 3).

In the United States the courts also abstain from restraining a mere libel by an injunction, even if the existence of malice is evident. They use their right chiefly in cases where a breach of a trust or of a contract is shown. After a libel action, however, in which a verdict finds the statements published to be false, the plaintiff may have an injunction which restrains any further publication of expressions regarded by the jury as libellous.

Injunction in Trade Libels

Most applications for injunctions are made in trade libels. Businessmen who fear a publication or repetition of statements, which may injure the reputation of their goods or trade, are anxious to see it prevented by the courts. If an interim injunction is sought with regard to an imminent publication, the view is held by courts of the Anglo-Saxon countries that the verdict of juries should not be anticipated by a previous decision of the court. When a trading company claimed an interim injunction to restrain 'the publication in a newspaper of letters and statements in the future similar to those which had been already inserted in the same newspaper, reflecting on the solvency and financial condition of the company, the court would not interfere, on the ground that it would be almost, if not entirely, impracticable so to frame the injunction as not possibly to include in its terms something that might not be libellous.'

Also if the defendant pleads justification, the courts are reluctant to anticipate the verdict of the jury by an interim injunction. In refusing the application a British court stated: 'We cannot feel sure that the defence of justification is one which, on the facts which may be before them, the jury may find to be wholly unfounded' (*Bonnard v. Perryman* (1891)).

In a case which arose from a newspaper article commenting on alleged irregularities in the ordnance department of the British War Office and which caused considerable sensation, the defamations were very serious indeed. All the same, the court refused the application for an interim injunction, because 'the subject matter of the article was clearly one of great public interest,' which will be more adequately determined by a jury (*Armstrong and Others v. Armit and Others* (1886)).

Similar views are held by the courts of the United States, which refuse applications for interim injunctions, if 'the party wronged has an adequate remedy at law by an action for damages or criminal prosecution.' But they will grant an injunction if the utterances 'complained of are not only libellous but are of such a nature as to threaten, intimidate, or coerce customers of the complainant into discontinuing business relations. This principle has perhaps found its most frequent application in boycott cases.'

Among the measures provided by the laws against unfair competition the interim injunction is mentioned first; then follows the grant of damages to the injured party, and finally the passing of the sentence. The plaintiffs make ample use of this opportunity by asking for an interim injunction, and the courts issue the order restraining the defendant from further publications of the libellous statements, even if nothing more than the mere probability can be foreseen that the unfair competition may be repeated.

Penal laws sometimes allow the seizure of a publication at the request and responsibility of an individual or juridical person, who has been defamed by this printed matter. Thus not the libel, but its distribution, will not be prevented or restricted which, in the end, may prove to be an extenuating circumstance for the defendant.

Obligations to Abstain from Libel

An unusual provision contained in the Constitution of the American State of Texas (art. 88) aims at the prevention of the intended publication of libels: 'If any person,' the law states, 'shall make oath, and shall convince the magistrate that he has good reason to believe that another is about to publish... any libel against him... the person accused of such intended publication may be required to enter into bond with security not to... publish... such libellous publication....'

Protection of Valuable Newspaper Contributions

A reduction of libel actions is also attained by the almost general practice of the courts not to regard every libellous criticism as a defamation. Newspaper comments on contemporary statesmen, who are supposed to have committed a political blunder or otherwise not to be equal to their tasks, go often, without interference by the courts, beyond the limits which are admitted when private persons are attacked. The authors of such contributions may claim that their criticism will survive the day. But the decision whether a comment reaches this level lies, of course, with the court, which, apart from considering the contributions's literary and historic value, will also take into account whether the article has been written without hatred and malice and without the intention of inflicting damage upon the persons criticised.

Following this line, French courts have repeatedly held that to accuse men acting in public capacity of having incurred moral guilt of far reaching consequence does not constitute a defamation. However, it will not always be easy to decide when journalistic work has reached the level of a historical contribution.

The idea that valuable newspaper articles are to be protected has been adopted by the press law of Chile, which provides that 'scientific or literary articles are not deemed to be abusive when their object is to investigate scientific, literary or judicial truth' (1872, art. 6).

It is a general rule which helps to discourage many people from instituting libel suits to consider provoked and mutual defamations an extenuating circumstance, sometimes even not punishable at all. The French press law, for example, provides that an insult to a private person, if provoked by him, leads to acquittal (art. 33). Other laws have followed this line. But also when such regulations do not exist, the courts take an offending attitude of the plaintiff into consideration and pass judgments, which rather deter from such suits.

One of the best English books on libel states under the heading 'Legitimate Self-Defence': 'Where an attack has been made on the defendant, he is entitled to answer it and to communicate his answer to all who heard the attack.' And: 'A man, who himself commences a newspaper war, cannot subsequently complain, because he has the worst of the fray. But, in rebutting an accusation, the defendant must not intrude unnecessarily into the private life of his assailant, or make counter-charges against his character, unconnected with his original charge against the defendant.'

Similarly, no punishment is imposed in France when the defamatory statements were published in order to protect certain interests which seemed to be threatened. French courts even allow the argument of defendant newspaper-men that the journal, by writing libellous matter, has satisfied a justifiable curiosity of the public.

Lenient Definitions of the Notion 'Libel'

Some press laws define the notion 'libel' in a way which does not facilitate actions against newspapers. According to the Greek law (6th January, 1919, art. 3 (1, 2, 3)), it is supposed to be the wilful imputation of an act which, if committed by the defamed person, 'would expose him to a judicial inquiry,' while the Finnish penal law (1889, arts. 1 and 2) makes liable to punishment 'any person who against his better knowledge falsely accuses another of a definite offence or other such act as can bring contempt upon him' or 'who intentionally, but not against his better knowledge,' blames another for offence or such acts as mentioned above, 'if the ostensible grounds for the imputation or rumour cannot be produced.' The press law of Persia mentions as punishable libels 'articles dishonouring a family' (art. 33) and 'statements dishonouring or affecting the credit of an individual or society' (art. 34). Thus the incriminating passages must contain serious defamations to become the subject of libel actions.

Still more difficult is the prosecution of press libels rendered in Uruguay where the Criminal Code mentions only the following kinds of defamations committed by newspapers as an abuse of the press, which will cause a prosecution:

'(1) When private vices or defects are attributed to an individual;

'(2) When family secrets are revealed or matters are denounced that affect the honour of the family, provided that they do not affect public order;

'(3) When publication is made of proceedings, documents, or sentences relating to cases of illegitimate offspring, impugning the civil status of fathers to sons and vice versa, adultery, disagreement and actions relating to offence against decency;

'(4) When crimes or offences are calumniously attributed to an individual' (art. 407).

Two provisions of the Portuguese press law serve also the purpose to restrict libel actions committed by newspapers. The first one, which will hardly lie in the interest of the defamed person, provides (1910, art. 15) that in the case of several defamations committed against the same person by the publication 'prosecution can only be made on the ground of all of them.' This provision may involve a hardship, for if various severe attacks are combined with an unimportant defamation, and the plaintiff does not wish to revive just this case, which may have happened many years ago, he will be unable to achieve satisfaction at all. But on the other hand, persons who have rightly been denounced by the newspaper will not be in a position to make an unimportant mistake in the article the subject of an action and to score on a minor point, while disregarding the other statements in respect of which action would have failed.

Also the other regulation of the Portuguese law protects the offender from an action. 'When matter is published,' the law states, 'which might be construed to the detriment of any person, that person may notify the author or editor... and ask whether they intend to refer to him. If the author or editor states that it was not intended for the person in question, he may not be sued; but if he gives no answer, or an unsatisfactory one, he may be sued' (art. 33).

Leniency toward Caricatures

Since the tone of political discussions is usually harsh, the courts, when judging libels against political adversaries, take the atmosphere of the platform into consideration. They also show tolerance towards political cartoons. This leniency is expressly confirmed in the law of the State of New Mexico, which declares that whenever a defendant is accused of libel by means of... caricature, it must clearly appear therefrom that the person said to be defamed was in fact intended to be represented by such... caricature' (s. 35-3508). This provision, too, leads to a restriction of libel cases.

The most efficient measure to prevent actions for libel committed by newspapers is the Right of Reply.

THE RIGHT OF REPLY TO LIBELS

Many months may pass before the court pronounces judgment in a libel case provoked by the press, and the readers come to know about the decision. Meanwhile, the public remains under the impression which the offending contribution has caused. If the statement made by the journal is not defamatory and merely contains untrue facts which cannot become the object of an action, the person or institution affected by the statement has no opportunity whatever to enlighten the readers.

For these reasons the press laws of most countries allow the insertion of an immediate reply in the paper. According to the regulations, persons or corporations which have been attacked or which have been the object of an incorrect statement in a journal have the right to a prompt rectification or explanation. Thus they are able to use the same weapon as that which had been aimed at them and, in the struggle for the judgment of the public, hold no worse position than the newspaper.

The first law of this kind was introduced in France more than a century ago. The need for a right of reply had been felt in the years of the French Revolution. The newspapers made great use of the new freedom of the press and indulged in violent and offensive language. Complicated proceedings were the sole defence; their result came seldom to the knowledge of the readers. Therefore in 1796 the deputy Dulaure brought a motion in the Council of the Five Hundred to impose upon newspaper the duty of accepting a reply to articles injurious to the reputation of a citizen. But the penalties proposed by Dulaure against papers which would not publish such replies were regarded as too severe, and the Bill was rejected. It was not until 1822 that a right of reply was established. Though altered in 1881 and 1919, this law is still in force in France.

1. 'Reply' and 'Rectification'

The rule which is contained in Article 13 of the law is based on the principle that any person mentioned in a newspaper or in a periodical either by name or indirectly, has a right of reply limited only as to extent, but not as to arguments. Slowly this right, after undergoing various changes, influenced the legislation of most countries of Western and Southern Europe, and also of overseas. However, the laws introduced in Central European countries in the middle of the nineteenth century were quite different. Such laws still apply in Germany, Poland, Czechoslovakia, Austria, Hungary, and Yugoslavia, and also in four Swiss cantons (Bern, Grisons, Schaffhausen and Vaud).

According to these laws, the newspaper is only bound to publish a reply limited to the rectification of facts. This 'rectification' (in German *Berichtigung*) is opposed to the free polemics known in France as *reponse*. The difference between them is great. In France the injured person is entitled to lay open his point of view, even if the contentions of the paper do not contain facts, but opinions or conclusions, while in the Central European countries the reply must be motivated by a genuine interest in a correction of untrue statements. The press laws belonging to this group show, more or less distinctly, that the rectification is a defence against a wrong, whereas the French group recognise in the reply the right to an explanation.

In the present century the institution of reply restricted to a correction of facts was adopted by Norway (1902), Finland (1919), Latvia (1924), Egypt (1931), Denmark (1938) and Estonia (1938). Also the press laws of Japan (1909) and of Guatemala (1894) show a greater affinity to the provisions of the Central European than to those of the French group. But between the two groups there are graduations, reflecting in the various names given to this right. Besides 'reply' and 'rectification,' expressions such as notice, elucidation, explanation, declaration, answer, explanatory statement, correction refutation, defence, denial, contradiction, *replique* can be found in press laws.

These expressions go far to explain the nature of the insertion. A correction must be briefer than an explanation, a refutation will not be as detailed as a reply or a defence. It is obvious that the regulations concerning the right of reply must differ in various countries. This is not the place to examine how far political circumstances and the extent of political freedom, the tone of the press and national character have co-operated to form the structure of the right of reply. It is certainly not by chance that the vivid Latin nations decided in favour of the free reply, while Germany and some adjacent countries adopted the rectification of facts.

Length of the Reply

According to most press laws, the reply may be longer than the corresponding article. The person mentioned is allowed to say more than the aggressor. But this idea is not always carried out in practice. On the one hand, the laws endeavour to give injured persons the opportunity to explain their point of view with the necessary minuteness of the detail on the other hand, newspapers must be protected from replies which are intentionally prolix. The result is a compromise. Most press laws fix a certain length for the replies, and any excess must be paid for. This may indeed lead to brevity.

As for the press laws of the French group, this limitation is understandable, since the reply may contain reflections or conclusions, and, therefore, may become very long. Most regulations allow a reply twice the length of the article; if it occupies more space, the surplus is charged for at advertisement rates. We find such provisions in the press laws of Italy, Belgium, Luxemburg, Portugal, Roumania, Greece, Syria, Colombia and Haiti. Formerly French law also contained such regulations, but, owing to frequent abuses, they were altered by an Act of 1919. Since it often happened that payment was made for a reply of extraordinary length to the embarrassment of the newspapers, the French law of 1919 orders that the reply must be free of charge, and the option of exceeding the limit by way of offering payment for the excess no longer exists. The reply must not exceed the length of the article exclusive of the forms of courtesy and request, and also of the signature. At any rate, the reply may comprise fifty lines, even if the article is shorter, and not more than two hundred lines, even if the article is longer. These regulations apply also to *repliques,* i.e. replies to a comment which a newspaper coupled with a reply.

A very unfriendly attitude towards newspapers was shown by the Egyptian press law (1881), which admitted a reply even five times as long as the article. The laws of other countries advocate that replies should be brief. According to the Greek (1914), Japanese (1909) and Estonian (1938) laws, the reply must be only as long as the article; the excess must be paid for.

The press laws of the Central European group regulate the matter differently. As the rectification, according to these laws, is to be restricted to the correction of facts, it cannot be longer than is necessary to correct them. Otherwise it is not a rectification according to the law, and the newspaper may reject it. Therefore the Austrian law (1922) does not limit the length of the rectification, and, of course, does not impose any charge for it. The Hungarian law (1914), restricting the rectification to a statement of facts or to a simple denial of assertions, adopts a similar view. The rectification must not be longer than the article, but it is provided that 'the facts necessary for ratification can be stated in a communication of greater length.' In short, the rectification should be as short as possible and as long as necessary. As in Austria, it must be inserted gratuitously.

The German attitude is quite different: the rectification may not be longer than the article which it corrects, apparently on the ground that the same space must suffice for the correction of facts as was needed for the false statement. If, for instance, a newspaper asserts that Mr. Smith is about to resign as chairman of the X. Bank, the denial of his resignation must not be longer. If it exceeds the length, 'the usual cost for the insertion of advertisements' must be paid for each line in excess.

The reply to a series of articles published in the same newspaper and concerning the same person is dealt with in the press law of the Canton of Vaud (1898). It provides that such a reply may be made by means of one contribution only, at most twice the length of the longest article of the series. In other countries a series of articles is regarded as a single article, with the result that a reply may amount to twice the combined length of the articles. This solution has met with widespread criticism.

A layman will hardly be able to calculate how much space of a newspaper a written text will occupy. For this reason the press laws of Belgium, Luxemburg and Portugal relieve him of the trouble of calculation, and state: The reply should not exceed one thousand letters or twice the space occupied by the article.

Payment for the Excess

The question of payment, if the reply exceeds a certain limit, represented a difficult task for legislators. The expense should prevent too much valuable space being taken up; therefore it should not be too low. The writer of the reply will be compelled to be brief. But, on the other hand, he should not be deterred by a high charge from saying what is necessary; therefore, the insertion should not be too expensive.

Accordingly, the press laws do not leave it to the newspaper or to the writer of the reply to fix the cost of the insertion, but decide it themselves. In a few countries they are fixed at the rate of the usual cost for the insertion of advertisement, e.g. in Germany, Italy, Norway and Estonia. As a rule, the same charges are demanded as for legal notices; in Czechoslovakia and Portugal the average charge for advertisements in the newspaper concerned is the basis, but it may not be higher than the tariff for official publications in the official gazette of the country. The Finnish law demands a calculation 'at the lowest' advertisement rate.' In Haiti a price of 50 centimes a line is fixed by the law. It is obviously the intention of the law to keep the cost of the reply at a low level.

There are only two regulations regarding the mode of payment. The Portuguese law (1926) orders that payment must be made within forty-eight hours of the insertion, the Czechoslovak law (1933) demands payment in advance. But this does not mean that payment in advance may not be asked for in other countries. If this mode of payment is usual, the newspaper is entitled to reject the reply in case payment is not made at the same time. At any rate, payment in advance does not encourage long replies. In France before 1919, when a reply could be twice as long as the article, and when the excess was charged according to the tariff for legal notices, it was said that this low rate and also the payment after publication, at no fixed time, were responsible for the extraordinary length of replies. Another consequence was that replies were sometimes sent by insolvent persons, who never paid for them at all. For these reasons the French regulations were altered.

In this connection it may be pointed out that some press laws apportion the length of the reply in lines or fix the cost of the insertion according to the price of a line. This may cause some confusion, since such a regulation assumes that all newspapers of the country concerned have and also will have in the future uniform columns of the same width. As this is not so, newspapers which have wider columns are at a disadvantage. The line is, therefore, not an apt measure. In order to meet these difficulties, the Polish press law (1938) provides that a newspaper line is considered to comprise six words (art. 30).

Prescription

It is in keeping with the character of the reply as a reparation, which is the more effective the quicker it takes place, that the press laws of some countries fix a relatively short prescription of the right to reply. The contents of a newspaper are soon forgotten; if months elapse before a reply appears, not many readers will remember the libel. Therefore, the press laws of Denmark, Hungary, Yugoslavia, Greece and of the Canton Vaud state that the right to publish a reply expires after a month; but if the author of the reply is abroad when the article is published, prescription is extended to three months according to Greek law. In Austria, Czechoslovakia and Egypt, prescription extends to two months, in Portugal to six months, in Norway to one year.

The French right of reply was made subject to a prescription of one year in 1919. Until then it was held that, according to

Article 2262 of the Code Civil, the prescription of thirty years must apply. But the possibility of publishing a reply almost a generation later, when the contents of the article which caused the reply had slipped out of memory, induced the French legislator to fix a prescription of one year.

Some press laws, e.g. that of Germany, do not provide for prescription, but since the writer of the reply must be 'concerned' and this 'concern' ceases, of course, after a time, a kind of prescription will be assumed by the courts in such cases.

Position and Lettering of the Reply

The reply should be published in such a manner as to enable all those who have read the article to find the reply. The fact that casual readers may have read the attack but not the reply must be ignored. In order to draw the attention of the regular reader to the reply, most press laws, particularly of France and of other countries based on the French law, demand that the reply should be printed 'in the same place' and 'in the same type' as the original article. That is sometimes hardly practicable for technical reasons. A newspaper cannot always arrange for articles to end just where the reply should be placed, nor is it always in the interest of the reply to print it just in the same position as the article. Besides, a newspaper has not every day the same number of pages, nor do the same pages contain always the same sections. It may happen that the part occupied one day by financial news is, two days later, reserved for reviews of films and books, and, consequently, the reply to a paragraph on financial matters would appear on a page, in which, on that day, book lovers and film friends, but not businessmen, are interested.

Proceedings have been instituted repeatedly because replies were not published in the same place as the original article. But the courts have referred to the intention and not to the wording of the law, especially if the mischievous motive of the action was obvious. They have examined whether it will come to the notice to the circle of readers for whom the reply is meant. As a rule, the expression 'place' is not interpreted as meaning the same position in the paper, but the corresponding section.

In consequence, other press laws demand the publication in the same 'part' of the paper, or in the same section, e.g. in Germany, Austria, Czechoslovakia and Latvia. The page is irrelevant. The Yugoslav law paraphrases this thought and says that the reply is to be printed 'in the part of the paper corresponding to that occupied by the relevant article or statement.'

But not all papers divide their contents into various sections. The Finnish law is satisfied with the printing of replies 'in the text,' i.e. it must not be put in a page filled with advertisements. In Guatemala 'a similar page and column' is demanded, in Japan the position is not mentioned. in Czarist Russia position in the same section and the use of the same types were only granted if it was expressly demanded.

While the regulations concerning the position of replies admit of different interpretations, the direction contained in most press laws that the reply must be printed in the same type has but one meaning: The importance of the reply should not be diminished by the use of a smaller print. Moreover the Yugoslav and Greek laws are indulgent on this point and merely demand a 'similar type.'

The press law of Italy does not contain any rules regarding the manner of printing and placing the reply, nor do the courts demand publication in the same place and in the same type. But the duty of the newspaper is not considered as fulfilled if the publication is particularly inconspicuous.

Delivery of the Reply

Press laws do not usually contain special regulations as to the manner in which replies should be delivered to newspapers. It is usual not to address them to the newspaper but to the person legally responsible for the insertion of the reply.

The most effective method is delivery by registered letter, because in case of dispute the sender can show the postal receipt. Cautious people will use an advice of delivery (*avis de reception*). If no time must be lost, the reply will be delivered by a messenger, and a receipt must be given in acknowledgement. The Portuguese law of 1926 (art. 53 (6)) deals expressly with delivery by way of registered letter. Yugoslav law declares that it is permissible to send the reply by post; apparently this statement was found necessary because there was once a spirited discussion about this question, when a French court had declared that the sending of a reply by a registered letter was not sufficient evidence of a reliable delivery. The same law also indicates another way for sending replies: It is permitted to deliver the reply through the intermediary of the Court of First Instance of the district where the paper appears; the court has to forward the reply to the paper on the same day. Thus the reply is under the protection of the court from the outset, and comes into the possession of the newspaper in the manner of an official document.

Austrian law provides a method which excludes every doubt that the reply has reached its destination. Upon demand, the responsible editor is bound to give the sender of the reply a confirmation that publication of a reply was requested.

Other facilities in favour of the persons or institutions requesting the acceptance of a reply are provided by Czechoslovak law. According to it, the reply is to be delivered to the responsible editor. If he does not accept it or if the delivery is impossible for some other reason, it must be presumed that the publication was refused. In addition, the law states that it is sufficient if the reply is delivered to the editor or to the printer.

Reasons for Rejection

Not every press law enumerates the reasons which entitle a paper to reject a reply. But, according to the law as interpreted by the courts, it can be said that a paper is entitled to refuse a reply if the publication would be punishable or injurious to third parties owing to its offensive content or for other reasons. In the press law of Norway this rule is expressed in these words: '... provided the contradiction contains nothing of a penal nature and does not confer a right of contradiction upon any third party.'

Some laws, demand that the reply must be signed by the persons concerned; the reply can be rejected if the name and address of the signatory are not clear. The press laws of Germany, Austria and Hungary make it a condition that the reply must be written in the language of the country or of the paper. This regulation owes its origin to a time of violent national strife. In Czechoslovakia replies can also be sent in a language other than that of the article to which the exception is taken. It is not to be considered a change if the reply is translated into the language of the article, but it must be made clear that it is a translation.

Expiration of the time limit by prescription or a reply that exceeds the allotted length may also furnish a just cause for not accepting a reply.

Besides these external reasons for refusing a reply, there are various internal deficiencies, not always recognisable at first sight. The tone of the reply must be considered. Is a polemical note allowed? If according to the law rectification serves merely to correct facts, there is no occasion for polemics; a quiet, sober tone is an absolute requirement. Every word which exceeds the statement that the allegation of the paper is untrue would deprive the rectification of its character and would justify rejection. But in many countries replies are not restricted to a correction of facts, and as they express opinions and judgments in opposition to those stated in the paper, they become polemical. The courts concede to the replies a tone proportionate to the violence of the attack by the paper. The object of the attack may not only use the same weapon, but should also be allowed to retaliate with equal strength.

Press laws abstain from special regulations on this matter.

But the Yugoslav law demands that the reply should be polite, and the laws of Latvia and Estonia lay down that it must not be of a polemical character. According to the Czechoslovak press law, the newspaper is entitled to reject the rectification if its contents are 'grossly indecent.'

The reply may be refused at once, of course, if the sender is not entitled to write it, i.e. if he is not named or designated in the article as required by the law, and also if the reply does not refer to the article. In Austria, according to the new regulation of 1934, a rectification need not be published if the paper was legally bound to print the notice complained of, or if it can prove the correctness of its communication by a decision or a decree of an Austrian authority.

The writer of the reply learns from the paper within a limit of one or two days, as a rule, whether a reply is refused or accepted. Only the press law of the Canton of Vaud orders that the editor must inform the writer of the reply if he refuses to print the rectification.

Comment on the Reply

Since the publication of a reply involves the admission of some error or mis-statement, newspapers are inclined to add some face-saving comment. The French and the Czechoslovak laws expressly allow it the first-mentioned orders that the *repliques* to comments of the newspaper should be subjected to the same regulations as replies; the latter demands that a comment to a reply should be distinctly recognisable as a remark of the paper. This provision shows that it is not commonly used. But, as a rule, the separation between reply and comment is announced by a change of type, or by printing the reply in quotation marks.

The Hungarian press law prohibits a comment in the same number, but the editor is entitled to state briefly whether or not he maintains the statement to which the rectification refers. Equally, the Polish press law does not permit a comment on the rectification in the same issue or changes of its sense by a heading which does not convey the proper meaning of the letter (art. 28).

In general, the history of the press laws shows that comment to replies was repeatedly a stumbling-block, and some attempts were made — for example, in France and in Germany — to hamper or even to forbid it.

A particularly disagreeable though rare manner of comment consists in interrupting the reply by editorial remarks. The writer of the reply is thus unable 'to finish speaking.' The press law of Latvia does not allow such remarks 'in the text' of the reply; the courts have often declared this manner of comment to be inadmissible.

Contents of the Letter

With one exception, the press laws do not contain provisions regarding the heading of replies. Few writers of replies think of it; they write a letter to the editor, not an article, and leave the form to him. It would seem most convenient if the reply was given the same heading as the article. Indeed, this is the rule but sometimes even a heading contains a falsehood. If, for instance, an article is headed: 'Chairman of the X. Bank resigns,' the reply stating that the Chairman will not resign cannot be published under the 'former title'. It was not for this reason, however, that press laws did not lay down a rule about it. The fact was decisive that, when the first provisions about the right to reply were issued, headings were not so usual as to-day.

In consequence of this, and in order to divert the attention of the readers, some papers to-day print the reply without a heading if they feel it to be vexatious or disagreeable. Moreover, should it be published following a long and probably uninteresting article, separated from it by a thin line, the reply will be noticed only by the few people who were patient enough to read the article to the end. The other readers would at best assume that it is the last part of the preceding article. It is not unusual to place the reply immediately after a striking advertisement, with the result that the unwelcome contribution becomes almost imperceptible. Only a trained eye can notice such replies. When in cases of this kind proceedings are taken by the disappointed writers of replies, the courts dismiss the action, as the law does not contain provisions regarding headings.

Therefore the Czechoslovak law of 1933 demands (in art. 2(4)) that the rectification should bear the title 'Press Rectification.' But as the law does not order the heading to be set up in a type usual for articles of corresponding length, a nettled editor is given the opportunity of having the title composed in so small a type that it will not be easy to find the reply, especially if it is badly placed. For this reason the Polish press law of 1938 provides that the rectification must be published under a heading of the same size as that of the article (art. 28).

The wording of a reply results from its nature. It is usual and expedient to begin with a reference to the provisions concerned, in order to make it clear that the request does not appeal to the kindness of the editor, but is based on the force of the law. It is also advisable to remind the editor of the time limit for publication, of certain placement and type. For example:

Dear Sir,

With reference to Article... of the Press Law of... I request you to publish in the next issue, in the same section, and in the same type, the following rectification of your article (title) which appeared in your paper.... of.... No....., p.....

(Contents of the rectification.)

Yours faithfully,

(Writer's signature)

If a legal representative signs, a power of attorney may be added.

The only press law which contains some instructions about the requirements of a rectification is the above-mentioned Czechoslovak law of 1933. 'In its introduction,' it says, 'the rectification must refer to the title and number of the paper in which the communication was published, and possibly to the heading of the article; at the end, the name of the person who requests the rectification must be given.'

All these provisions have one meaning; rectification must strictly avoid opposing assertions to assertions; it serves only to correct facts, and nothing but facts.

But there are rectifications which also purport to be replies. The most significant example is given by the press law of Colombia. On the one hand, the law speaks of 'corrections or explanatory statements concerning... actions of persons,' but, on the other hand, replies to attacks are allowed. Other press laws also try to combine the advantages of rectifications and replies, for instance the law of Guatemala, which calls the reply 'elucidation, correction and explanation.'

Naturally most press laws demand that the reply must be published without any changes. Indeed, a small alteration can bring about an entirely different meaning. Therefore the conscientious sub-editor, accustomed to finish off the manuscripts and to eliminate stylistic mistakes, must lay down the blue pencil if he is handed a reply, although his collaboration may be sometimes of use to the writer of the reply. He may console himself by remembering that in this case the writer of the reply alone is responsible. No addition or omission or alteration is allowed. The reply is to be published in full or, if found to contravene the law, not at all. Some press laws paraphrase this rule by stating that publication must take place 'without additions and omissions'.

Accuracy

The purpose of the reply is to oppose to the contentions of a newspaper those of the person concerned or attacked. The reader may form his own judgment. As the paper need not produce evidence that its contentions are correct, the reply is not bound to state the truth. It is not a deposition of a witness, but rather a defence, just as the attack of the paper is not always a sober statement, but often a spirited accusation. Both accused and prosecutor incline to exaggerations which are of little help in finding the truth. On the other hand, as the assertions are made in public and can be proved, both sides should, as a rule, be interested in the truth. The court is less concerned about it. If a complaint is made against a paper because it refuses the publication of a reply, the court is only called on to examine, whether the reply conforms to the formal provisions of the law. The truth of the reply is not under consideration.

An important development took place some years ago. The Hungarian press law of 1914 (art. 20 (4)) provides that the editor must publish the rectification, provided that its 'falsity cannot be proved at once decisively.' For the first time the question of the correctness of a reply was raised by a press law. But it was only a small improvement, for it is not easy to demonstrate the falsity of assertions 'at once' and 'decisively.' Two press laws issued in 1933 and 1934 provided the means to prevent the frequent abuse of the right of rectification.

The Czechoslovak press law (1933) states (art. 17): 'When a rectification is published, and the writer knows it to be untrue, the proprietor of the paper can demand payment of the cost of the insertion and of damages caused by the publication.'

The Austrian law (1934) accepted this idea and formulated it more clearly. The proprietor is entitled to demand payment at advertisement rates if the rectification is untrue. With regard to the proceedings to be instituted in the courts, the law (art. 24 (7)) orders: 'If an incorrect rectification is submitted for mischievous motives, the proprietor of the paper may claim a reasonable compensation up to 1,000 Austrian shillings for injuries suffered. If the claim is allowed, the proprietor may publish the judgment in his paper within a certain time limit at the accused's cost.'

This new provision is very important. An untrue rectification creates a great risk for the writer, for not only does he become liable for the subsequent costs, but he may be declared by the court to have stated a falsehood, which, in turn, may prompt a corresponding comment by the paper. Moreover, if such a false statement is wilfully made, the writer commits an offence (art. 24 (7)).

Refusal to Accept Reply

Press laws demand that the reply should be published as soon as possible. If a newspaper refuses publication without good reason, it should be compelled to do so by speedy proceedings. They form the backbone of the laws of reply, for their most important purpose is to furnish persons or institutions with an opportunity for immediate reparation. The Yugoslav law emphasises this purpose by stating (art. 14)'... a speedy decision is desirable in the circumstances... a case concerned with the refusal to publish a correction differs essentially from all other legal proceedings.'

Generally, the reply must be published in the first or second number of the newspaper after the reply has been received. The pertinent regulation reads as a rule: '...within three days' including the day of delivery and the day of publication. If, therefore, the reply arrives on Monday, the publication must take place in Wednesday's issue at the latest. The Portuguese law of 1918 states that the reply must be printed at once, but the law in force since 1926, following the French regulations, demands publication within three days after its receipt. In Roumania the reply must appear 'in the second number.' The Yugoslav law contains the shortest time limit: '... in the first number to appear after the correction has been received by the editor, but if on that date the office of the paper is already closed, the reply must be published in the first number to appear after that date.'

In Germany a similar exception is provided: '... in the number immediately following upon its reception, provided that such number is not already set up in type.' The press law of Haiti allows the extraordinarily long term of a fortnight for the publication of a reply.

In France a special rule applies during the time of general elections. In those days of high tension the reply must be published within twenty four hours. The text must be in the editor's office at least six hours before the paper is printed. For this purpose the editor at election time must announce in the courts at what time he will start to print his paper. The bad impression, which might be created among the electors by an attack on a candidate, should be corrected as soon as possible. The proceedings are also highly accelerated at times of election.

Unless the reply is published in accordance with the law, the injured person may sue the responsible newspaper-man. In Greece the defamed party is relieved of this task. The law of 1918 states: 'In any case of refusal to insert the correction or answer, the editor, proprietor or director is bound to deposit it within the time-limit of three days, together with a statement setting out the grounds on which his refusal is based, with the Public Prosecutor of the Court of First Instance, who is entitled to order any modification of the publication he may deem right.' Accordingly, proceedings take place automatically. It is clear that newspapers will examine the replies thoroughly, as they are under the obligation to show in a written statement the reasons for the refusal and know that the Public Prosecutor will deal with their arguments.

Speedy Proceedings against the Responsible Newspaper-man

Press laws agree that the trial should take place with the greatest possible speed. According to French law, judgment should be given within ten days. In order to prevent delay in consequence of an appeal, the law of 29th September, 1919, ordered that the reply should be published as soon as judgment has been delivered. An appeal against the judgment, which must be decided within ten days, cannot delay the publication.

In time of elections the proceedings are still simpler: judgment must be given within twenty-four hours, and the summons may be delivered at any hour by a special order of the President of the Tribunal.

In Austria the court must give judgment without delay, 'if possible, within twenty-four hours'; an appeal must not delay the publication of the reply. In Czechoslovakia the judgment has to take place 'in the shortest possible time.' The first hearing must be fixed for the third day at the latest; an adjournment is only admissible for three days. The Hungarian press law demands that the case must be tried within three days. The trial is held in camera, but both sides or their representatives may attend and make objections. The exclusion of publicity is intended to prevent the appearance of reports which deal less with the real case than with the attacks by the paper and their background.

In Hungary an appeal must be heard within three days. In Yugoslavia it is not permitted at all.

In Guatemala the reply, the publication of which has been ordered by a judgment, must be printed on the first page and in the first column, regarded as the most favourable place.

Fines for Refusal of Publication

According to some press laws, the courts may not only order the publication of the reply, but may also impose fines which are fixed in France at 50 to 500 francs and in Italy at 100 to 1,000 lire. In fact, however, the courts frequently apply an even lower scale on the ground of extenuating circumstances.

In Belgium, where the Code Penal of 1867 upheld the right of reply created in 1831, this fine amounts to 20 florins, in Roumania to 120 lei for every day of delay; the money is paid to the person mentioned in the article as compensation for the injury he suffered. There are no detailed provisions concerning the conduct of the legal proceedings, save that: 'The authorities may force an editor to publish such a reply.'

In Guatemala the court does not inflict the fine as a matter of course, but the writer of the rectification is entitled to demand a payment of 50 pesos, for the benefit of the municipal funds, if the rectification is not published as the law demands. The Portuguese law of 1926 is particularly severe. The court, which has to make its decision within twenty-four hours, must order the insertion and pass a fine of 500 escudos — not up to 500 escudos! No appeal against this judgment is admitted. Further, the Portuguese law, unique in this respect to my knowledge, provides a particular procedure in matters of publications which do not comply with the provisions. Should, for instance, the rectification be changed by the editor and the sense misrepresented, or should it be inserted in the wrong place or printed in another type, the rectification must appear again on the next day, corrected in due form and in the right place. Should the same or another change, falsifying the sense, take place again, the director of the paper will be condemned to a fine of 1,000 escudos and the paper will be suspended for two months.

The Austrian press law of 1922, as amended in 1934, containing very modern regulations and utilising fully the experience of the courts, establishes the following types of offences:

(1) The publication did not take place within the prescribed period. Fine up to 250 Austrian shillings.

(2) The publication did not take place in the manner laid down by the law, i.e. not in the same part of the paper or not in the same type. Fine up to 250 Austrian shillings and an order for publication.

(3) The publication was refused without good reason. Fine up to 250 Austrian shillings and order for publication.

(4) The publication was only refused because the responsible editor, owing to an excusable mistake, did not consider the rectification to be a correction of

the original statement. The court must order publication and remit the fine.

(5) The refusal of the correction in the form demanded was admissible on the ground that it was not confined to a correction of the original statement. The court will acquit the responsible editor and determine what portion of the correction is to be published.

Adaptation of the Reply by the Court

The latter provision opens a new way in legislation. It is not an easy task to draw up a rectification restricted to a communication of facts, particularly if the original article does not state facts alone, but reproduces opinions and draws conclusions. The new regulation is meant to prevent a rectification being rejected owing to a small mistake, thus depriving the offended person of his right; but on the other hand, the newspaper-man should not be sentenced if he believes that the rectification does not meet the requirements of the law. Therefore the court itself will adapt the rectification to meet the requirements of the law. The plaintiff's interests are satisfied without considerable delay, although the rectification is defective, and the newspaper-man who acts in good faith is not called to account.

The Czechoslovak law has adopted this idea, and provides for a more distinct co-operation in the drawing-up of the rectification. If the draft does not comply with the regulations, the court will draw it up with the consent of the replying person, in order to make it correspond to the law, and then order the responsible editor to publish the revised statement. But the writer of the reply has to pay the costs of the proceedings. Only if the responsible editor intentionally omitted to publish the rectification as a whole in the prescribed form, he will be fined.

In order to stress the mild character of the penalty, it is expressly described as a fine for a minor offence and is limited to 1,000 crowns (about £8) at the most.

Equally, the Egyptian press law (1931) contains a provision to the effect that the court can acquit the editor and order the publication of the reply in the form in which it has been submitted or in a similar one (art. 18).

The Hungarian law deals with the possibility that the rectification may be refused by the paper because it does not comply with the requirements of the law. If in this case the injured party produces at the hearing another statement conforming with the requirements referred to above, the court orders the editor to publish this last-mentioned statement. But the co-operation of the court in drawing up the reply as provided by Austrian law is not envisaged in this case. The assistance of the court in correcting the rectification is implicitly admitted by the Yugoslav law of 1904, as modified in 1921. If publication is refused and the writer of the reply complains, the court frees the editor from responsibility, or decides that the rectification should be printed either 'as originally submitted or subject to any corrections which are necessary,' or it may condemn the editor to the payment of a fine between 300 and 600 dinars, or to a term of imprisonment of between one and two months.

These new provisions which are only to be found in the press laws of the Central European group, save rectifications from the waste paper basket, their inevitable destination if they do not exactly meet the requirements of the law. A very small mistake can give the editor an opportunity of refusing a rectification.

Publication Ordered by the Court

When the court decides that the reply must be printed, publication should take place with the greatest dispatch. The press laws provide various measures directed towards this purpose. In Austria the courts order that the rectification must be inserted in the edition of the periodical immediately following the pronouncement of such order, or in the subsequent issue; or, if such pronouncement is made in the absence of the accused editor, the rectification must be inserted in the issue of the periodical immediately following the service of the order upon him, or in the subsequent edition. Whenever the court pronounces that a rectification must be published, it must order at the same time, that in case of non-compliance with the provisions mentioned above, further publication of the periodical shall cease. Each issue of the periodical published in contravention of this order constitutes an offence, for which the responsible editor shall, at the instance of the person concerned, be fined up to 250 Austrian shillings.

A running fine, in addition to the fine on refusal of publication, is also provided by the press law of Norway. In Finland, too, the court may, besides inflicting a penalty up to a maximum of 500 marks, order the editor-in-chief to fulfil his obligation 'under pain of an additional fine.'

In this regard the Portuguese law of 1926 is very severe. Should the paper refuse to publish the rectification, it will be suspended for three months and its director punished for disobedience. In Guatemala the responsible newspaper-man will be condemned to two months' minor arrest, without the option of commutation, if he does not publish the rectification, although he was sentenced to do so. Besides this, judgment is to be published in another periodical at the expense of the accused.

A remarkable punishment is provided by the Hungarian law, if the editor fails to publish the rectification following an order by the court. The court 'may order him to publish it as the court deems necessary; the court may also order the rectification to be published at the expense of the negligent editor in one periodical or more, appearing either at the same place or else where. If the court's decision has been disregarded by order of the publisher, the latter must bear the expenses incurred by publication.'

An interesting provision regarding the case of a correction not being published in the manner ordered by the court is to be found in Czechoslovak law. Upon application by the person demanding rectification, the court may order that all numbers of the periodical issued after the time limit for publication has passed should be confiscated provisionally until it is proved to the satisfaction of the authorities that the rectification has been published correctly. An appeal against such a decree cannot delay the confiscation, but it will be rescinded if the editor proves that the rectification, has been published.

The publication may not be delayed by an appeal, unless the appeal to the next instance is directed against the wording as drawn up by the court (art. 14(6) of the Czechoslovak law of 1933). But suppose the Court of Second Instance reverses the judgment ordering publication because the rectification does not comply with the regulations? In this case the responsible editor is entitled to publish the decision ordering the cancellation and is thus enabled to inform the readers that he was compelled by the court to print a rectification which was not in compliance with the law. Two press laws, the Austrian (1922) and the Czechoslovak (1933), do not rest satisfied with this theoretical victory. According to the Austrian law, the responsible editor is entitled to publish the judgment of the Court of Second Instance at the plaintiff's cost. In Czechoslovakia also the Court of First Instance must charge the rectifying person, at the demand of the responsible editor, with the cost for the insertion at the average rate for advertisements in the paper.

We find the same idea expressed in the new press law of Egypt (1931). There, too, an appeal does not delay the publication of the reply. If the judgment of the Court of First Instance is overruled, the editor is entitled to publish the decision of the Court of Appeal at the cost of the party (art. 11). The judgment may contain an order suspending the newspaper for a period of not less than two weeks and not more than three months, unless the rectification is published.

The Japanese law provides two possibilities for correcting a false statement: a spontaneous correction by the paper or the insertion of a letter of correction. On the whole, this law is very polite in its tendency. For instance, it does not suppose that anyone can be injured by a paper, and only admits the possibility of 'errors in items.'

In Bulgaria a right of reply on the French model was introduced in 1887. But vehement political contrasts and violent disputes in the press caused such abuses of this right that it was abolished. Those offended by a newspaper now have the opportunity of suing it and of demanding publication of the judgment. The court names the papers in which the judgment should be published at the cost of the accused editor.

A Special Court in Denmark

In Denmark rectifications are considered so important that, by regulations recently promulgated (1938), a special court, the 'Committee for Rectifications,' was established to deal with them. It consists of three members: one, the chairman, must be a judge of the Supreme Court, another is to be elected by the Association of Danish Journalists, and the third by the publishers of either newspapers or periodicals as the publication may be in which the rectification is to be printed (art. 10 (1)).

If the editor is of the opinion that in view of the contents of the article a rectification is inadmissible, or that the letter in the form in which it has been submitted does not meet the requirements of the law, he must communicate with the writer of the letter as soon as possible, who may approach the Committee mentioned above. In this case the Committee will rule whether the rectification is to be published or may be refused (art. 9 (2)). Whatever the decision will be, the person who considers himself offended by the article will be allowed to insert a communication free of cost stating that he has brought an action as a result of the defamatory publication. The offended person may also publish the result of this action.

If the rejection of a rectification is unfounded, the editor may be fined by the Committee; on the other hand, the writer of a rectification is liable to a fine if there was no reason for submitting a rectification. Should this fine exceed 300 crowns, an appeal may be lodged, which is decided by three judges of the Court of Appeal who sit in camera.

Delayed Publication of the Reply

It may happen that publication is delayed or interrupted owing to external circumstances, e.g. on account of holidays which prevent papers from appearing within the time limit provided by the law, usually three days. Most of the press laws which order publication within three days overlook this difficulty. The Czechoslovak law only states: 'If the periodical does not appear during this time, the rectification must be published in the next number.' But this principle applies implicitly to other press laws, as the non-appearance of a newspaper owing to a holiday amounts to *vis major*. Those press laws which order that the rectification is to be published in the first or second number after its receipt would appear to be clearer in this respect, e.g. the laws of Austria and Hungary.

It may occur that a paper is confiscated or ceases to appear. With regard to the former case, the Czechoslovak law provides that the rectification is to be published in the new issue of the confiscated number, and if no new issue is to be printed, in the first number after confiscation. In the latter case the same law orders that the court upon demand may allow the rectifying person to publish the rectification in one or more papers named by the court at the cost of the editor or proprietor of the offending paper. In France, in the absence of a provision of this kind, the courts decide in a similar sense; if paper which should have published a reply has ceased to appear, insertion in another paper is ordered.

Finally, since it may happen that the rectification could be printed only in a part of the edition, the above-mentioned law provides that the publication must take place in all copies of the paper.

The requirements of the law are fulfilled with the publication of the reply. It is the concern of the injured party, and not of the court, to examine whether the reply is printed according to the law, and to lodge a complaint if this is not so. Nevertheless, the Hungarian law provides that the editor, after having been ordered by the court to publish the reply, must send to the court the number containing the rectification.

Only in Poland the law (1928) demands that the issue of the paper in which the rectification is published must be sent to the writer of the reply, at his own cost.

2. Official Rectification

In some countries, where an opposition press criticised government authorities and officials, the rules in the matter of reply were felt to be too lenient. Therefore the governments created a new institution to discourage critical remarks regarding the activities of the public administration, i.e. the official rectification. The hitherto existing right of reply continued as a private right.

Official rectifications enjoy greater privileges than private replies and are consequently far more burdensome to the press. As a rule, it must occupy the best place, to the disadvantage of the paper. The reader is disappointed when he finds, at the place where he usually reads the most important news or the editorials, a long, boring statement to the effect that the article of the previous day concerning some public authority is incorrect. It is not less annoying if the newspaper, according to some provisions, is not allowed to add any editorial remarks to as official rectification in the same number. The reader, generally not well acquainted with the law, receives the impression that the paper told an untruth and was reluctant to reply. The paper may give a comment on the following day, but for this purpose the matter must be repeated in parts, also the risk of a new official rectification of the comment must be run. Finally, the fines for a refusal or for an incorrect publication are heavy, usually twice the amount fixed for the refusal of private replies.

It is obvious that a strict application of these provisions not only made the critics more cautious, but also aroused an increasing aversion against official rectification. It so happened that when after the First World War the Austrian Republic was established in 1918 and democratic laws were promulgated, the exceptional position of official rectification which had existed in the Austro-Hungarian Monarchy was removed, and authorities and officials were not granted any greater privileges in replying to newspapers than the people. Special regulations about official rectifications are absent in the laws of Hungary, Yugoslavia, Denmark, Norway and some other countries.

Like the private reply, official rectification originated in France where it was first called *'rectification officielle'* (9th June, 1819, art. 8). By a decree of 1852 (17th February, art. 19) it received the name *'communique.'* Both served to correct inexact reports about official institutions and officials; but the authorities, particularly under Napoleon III, also made use of them for other purposes and sent communications to newspapers to be published, if no error had occurred. The first press law to introduce the name 'rectification' was that of 1881 (art. 12).

Official publications, which do not necessarily bear the character of official rectifications in the strict meaning of the word, but are rather rectifications of public opinion, are also known in other countries. In Germany only papers or periodicals which accept advertisements are 'bound to reproduce at the request of public authorities any official notices communicated to them by such authorities in one of the two following numbers of the paper, at the usual rates for the insertion of advertisements' (art. 10). A similar regulation exists in Finland.

Austria, in order to counter the violent Nazi propaganda, issued in 1933 an order about the publication of certain official communications. They were often polemical replies to articles published in Austrian papers and abroad, and had to be printed 'in the political part without interpolations, omissions, additions and contrary remarks, also without charge, and as to the headlines and the text, in such a manner that they did not seem inferior to other important news or reports of the paper.'

Equally, in Poland exists an obligation to publish official communications. They must appear in the next issue, in the place and in letters used for important communications, and must not exceed 250 lines. No alterations or comments are allowed.

French law orders that the publication must be placed at the top of the paper, i.e. in the first column of the first page. This is the most prominent place in French papers. It must appear in the next number, and may occupy twice the length of the article which it corrects. Contraventions are punished by fines varying between 100 and 1,000 francs, while the regulations on private replies only provide for fines from 50 to 500 francs. In Italy, Roumania, Turkey, Portugal and in other countries the press laws of which are adapted to the French example, provisions regarding official rectifications are drawn up in accordance with that model and do not differ much from each other.

While most laws demand insertion free of charge, the Italian law orders official rectification to be paid for. In Haiti a charge of 50 centimes per line is provided. In Turkey the publication may be placed in the same column as the article, and in Greece the law refrains from demanding the insertion at the top or in the same place. The law of Haiti requires governmental approval of the official rectification before it is sent to the paper; the last regulations of Greece (1938) demands approval by the competent member of the cabinet, other laws are satisfied with the formal official signature of the injured person. On the whole, the provisions concerning proceedings, responsibility, delivery, prescription and so on are almost the same as those concerning private replies.

Publication Reserved for Privileged Bodies and Persons

In Bulgaria rectifications or denials submitted by the National Assembly, the Government, the Cabinet, or by one of its members must be published at once (1922). The penalties for a violation of these provisions are severe and amount to one month's imprisonment or a fine up to 20,000 levas.

The Czechoslovak law (1933) contains a similar provision: If the President of the Republic, the chairman of a Legislative Assembly or a member of the Cabinet have reason to correct a paper, they need not do it themselves. The authorities entrusted with the management of their affairs can demand the acceptance of the rectification. Therefore these high personalities are not compelled to enter into polemics with opposition papers or with those of doubtful reputation, and thus need not run the risk of impairing their prestige. An additional provision of 1934 (10th July) orders that this rectification may occupy more than treble the space of the article—treble is the usual maximum according to the law—but half a column at most. The rectification is not restricted to facts which are to be corrected, but it can also contain other facts if connected with the matter of the article and if it represents a contribution towards a fuller clarification of the case. Moreover, the authorities, courts and other public institutions may leave it to the public prosecutor to expedite an official rectification, who will do it, of course, with good effect.

Comments on official rectifications were prohibited altogether in some old press laws. At present, they must not be added in the same issue. The Bill of a Czechoslovak law (1932) admits an immediate annotation, if it is made recognisable as such.

9

Free Press and Fair Trial

SIMON E. SOBELOFF

I suppose that all editors would agree as an abstract proposition that the right of a man to a fair trial should be respected and all judges would assent to the proposition that the press should be free. Let us look away from the necessarily imprecise legal boundaries that have been sketched out in various decisions of the courts, and consider more generally the interests of society that are at stake.

The courts and the press both have their responsibilities. The courts have a duty to assure fair trials; the press has a duty, no less vital, to inform the public. Each of these functions is essential in a civilised society. But while the direct burden of ensuring fair trials is on the courts, the press, too, carries a responsibility for the fairness of court trials. It should be equally clear to the judges that while journalists naturally have a primary role in maintaining the freedom of the press, the courts are also concerned to preserve this freedom. Freedom is indivisible.

Fair trials could not be held if newspapers were free without limit to intrude in pending judicial proceedings, and conversely, it is equally certain that trials would not long remain fair if newspapermen were not free to observe and report proceedings in court, and then comment freely upon the court's performance.

In our society both the judge and the editor enjoy special status. Our system has no special consideration for judges and editors either as individuals or as a class, beyond assuring to them independence in the performance of their respective public duties. If special powers and freedom are granted to them, it is not in tribute to their individual merits or to exalt them, but to protect the functions they perform. It is the simple but august task which the Declaration of Independence calls "securing the blessings of liberty." The editor and the judge are set apart from other citizens only that they may act as guardians of other men's liberties.

Both judges and editors sometimes forget this and think only in terms of their previleges and immunities. Both need to be reminded that it is neither the judges' rights nor the editors' rights that are of primary importance; the area is completely filled by the citizens' rights. When editors or judges forget their responsibilities they sink, not to the common level, but below it, for they are recreant to their trust.

I hasten to add that I realize that not all newspapers are alike. With 1700 papers performance is bound to be unequal. So also, not all judges are alike. The profession has a quaint saying that equity varies according to the length of the chancellor's foot. Generalizations are misleading. Most courts operate with dignity and effectiveness while a few cover up under the protective label of "judicial discretion" the most extreme indiscretion and arrogance. It is not flattery but simple truth to say that, by and large, newspapers are mindful of their public responsibility, as are courts. And if there are abuses, we can take comfort from Chief Justice Marshall, who said that we must bear with the inaccuracy of the press as "the calamity incidental to freedom." But newspaper publishers, as businessmen, are not immune from the laws regulating business.

Courts are not exempt from scrutiny and criticism by the press. My illustrious fellow-townsman, Henry I., Mencken, once gave an irreverent definition of a judge. "A judge," he said, "is only a law student who marks his own examination paper." If that were really so, what a happy existence it would be—for him; but it is not so. No judge marks his own examination papers. The examination papers of judges are marked by other judges, at all levels of the judicial hierarchy, even in the rarefied heights of the tribunal from which there is no appeal to any other human tribunal. And their examination papers are constantly being marked by the public. To make this possible is one of the reasons for newspaper reporting and commenting on court cases.

It is a great illusion shared by too many that only the courts are the guardians of our freedom. The courts have on numerous important occasions made historic contributions to freedom's cause; but while I hold the judicial function in reverence, I submit that it is a limited one. It is not the only branch of government that is charged with the preservation of freedom. Nor is the government as a whole the sole custodian of the people's freedom. In a free society each individual has a responsibility, but the press has a unique responsibility.

Free speech and fair trials are two of the most cherished policies of our civilization, and that it would be a trying task to choose between them. The core of difficulty in judging is that there is hardly a question that comes before the Court that does not involve more than one so-called principle. Anybody can decide a question if only a single principle is in controversy. "All rights tend to declare themselves absolute to their logical extreme. Yet all in fact are limited to the neighborhood of principles, of policies which are other than those on which the particular right is founded." The truth is that both principles—the independent judiciary and the free press—have to be made effective. The advocates of one side or another make a mistake when they insist on arrogating to either principle an importance which would ignore or unfairly subordinate the other.

Recently the Court of appeals of New York invalidated the conviction of a socially prominent young man charged with profiting from the immoral activities of young women. The ground of the reversal was that the presiding judge had barred the press from the trial. The law that insists that trials be kept public is not for the benefit of the press; public trial is deemed essential to a fair trial.

The horrors of the Star Chamber were fresh in the minds of those who wrote the First Amendment. The press is given a status here only as it serves a larger public purpose. I think that your profession and mine both welcome the doctrine laid down by the Court of Appeals of New York in the case I mentioned. Courts may not take unto themselves the power to enforce their notions of public decency and morality and suppress the sensational and the vulgar, if in doing so they sacrifice basic rights.

We will all agree that it is better not to have a court sit in judgment over what is good and what is bad for the public to know. Granted, judges are no more competent than other men to act as censors of public information, even information emanating from the courts. But is this an end to the question? Does it, therefore, mean that the press has no further obligation, but should avail itself to the full of its legal right and publish with impunity every sordid detail of a vice trial, or divorce proceeding? One of our greatest newspapers has coined the phrase: "All the news that's fit to print." Lesser journals, I am told, have changed it to "All the news that fits." Does not the press owe an obligation to consider the question of fitness, and ask itself earnestly whether the public's "right to know" really requires the indiscriminate spreading of such matter before them?

In some places interrogation of discharged jurors is not allowed. In others it is legally permissible, but it is a serious question for the press to ask itself how far such inquiries may be pressed without embarrassing former jurors or inhibiting future jurors.

I would like to suggest, in all good spirit, that in the frontier cases, in areas where the law is still in the making, if the press abuses its freedom, restrictive decisions may emerge. In England, as you know, far less latitude is permitted the press than in this country. There proposals were pressed for still further restrictions, and apparently this led to the creation of voluntary committees of journalists to police the profession from within.

There have been, as we know from observation, useful by-products of great public advantage from the full and free reporting of public proceedings, judicial and other. Fraud, corruption and dishonesty, in and out of government, would in many instances go undiscovered but for the vigilance of the press. Many social evils would go uncorrected, because unnoticed, if it were not for the activity of the newspapers.

The turbulence which surrounds this question of the freedom of the press in relation to judicial proceedings and elsewhere is not something to be deplored. It proves the vitality of the idea of freedom. Much more to be feared would be a condition in which the question did not arise, for quiescence on the part of the press would be the surest sign that freedom was on the wane.

In all walks of life there is an unfortunate disposition to treat legality as synonymous with propriety. Not everything which is lawful is wise: not everything which is permissible is decent and just. The thesis which I respectfully submit is that even if a publication is within legal limits, a newspaper has an obligation to weigh the propriety and fairness of what it publishes. Indeed, in this area, where it is so largely free from control, it is the newspaper rather than the judge that bears the greater responsibility. It is interesting to point out that judges operate within a framework of law which cabins them; we are fond of speaking of a government of laws rather than men. But what of the editor? If he is to a large degree exempt from judicial or other government control, what is to guide him? Has he not a heavy responsibility?

Three times in recent years (since 1941) the Supreme Court has considered the validity under the First Amendment of convictions of newspapers and editorial writers for contempt for editorial comment on pending cases. In each case, a majority of the Court concluded that on the facts before them they could not find a sufficiently serious threat to the administration of justice to warrant abridgment of the freedom of the press to comment on the trials in question. But it would be a disservice to journalism to suggest that the scope of the freedom to report and to comment on pending trials that the Supreme Court has recognized is a license to abandon self-restraint. Such reserve is frequently desirable, if not absolutely essential, to the attainment of impartial justice.

So, may I, in this spirit, and without presumption, suggest that even where there is no legally enforceable obligation there is a high moral duty to act with as great a measure of discriminating judgment as is possible under admittedly difficult circumstances. It is your high ethical obligation to avoid injuring the good name of an innocent person or to prejudice one accused of crime or a litigant in an ordinary civil case.

Headliners have a facile formula—action verbs and few qualifiers. It is an answer to plead the limitations of space in the headline? Many do not read beyond the headline, and sometimes people are injured by this kind of hit-and-run treatment.

I am not even remotely intimating that there should be legislation to restrict reporting any time in any way. I raise no question as to whether you are within your rights to publish. What is more, in most cases you may not even be answerable in a libel suit. But is the indiscriminate megaphoning of abuse consistent with sound and wholesome journalism? It seems to me that though you are free, you are not discharged of responsibility. Rather, because you are free, you are the more responsible. What I have been saying is so general that it may offer little help in specific instances. I have purposely avoided here all pretense of particularity. You will know better than I the precise application of what I am saying. What is important is the spirit in which these matters are approached in the day to day decisions you make.

And let us never forget that one of the reasons for press freedom is to enable it better to pursue the task, so indispensable in a democracy, of educating the people to enable them to perform their civic duties intelligently. May I raise the question whether newspapers, in selecting what to report of court proceedings, and how, are acting with due regard for their educative function. If a Sadie Zilch is haled before the police court for entertaining strangers in her home, there is likely to be adequate press coverage of every detail. If the Supreme Court hears a case involving the constitutional powers of the president to make agreements with foreign nations, not much is likely to be said about it, even in good papers. I can assure you that there is good, interesting news, and real drama in the higher courts. It isn't all technical by long odds, but these sources are often neglected on the assumption that the public is not interested. Are readers really on such a low level of taste and intelligence? Are you sure that what you give them is really what they want? And how far is it legitimate to think when there is a market for it? I speak merely for better coverage of more important court proceedings in the sharp competition for limited space, and I am thinking of the newspaper's role to educate, as well as titillate, its readers.

EDITORIAL WRITING MADE EASY

Louis M. Lyons

The tradition of the newspaper editorial is that it presents the view of the newspaper editor. In the editorial his readers expect to find the editor's considered judgment on the news. That is what they have been led to expect.

THE IMPOSSIBLE ROLE OF THE PRESS

Robert Lasseter

No institution of our society is assigned a task more nearly impossible of complete attainment than the press. Essentially it is to furnish the people with information upon which they can base their decisions in governing themselves and conducting their daily relationships. The newspaper that perfectly performed this function would mirror the world aloft, for all to see, with no other regard than the fidelity of the image. With this as a criterion, the short comings of American newspapers today are apparent.

There is nothing innately wrong with the American system of newspaper publication—that is, nothing that cannot feasibly be corrected or in large part meliorated by public influence within the present limits of the constitution. The founders of our nation, who had a closer and more personal acquaintance with the evil of restraint on expression than is possible for us today, held a considered belief that, if the people were left free to print whatever they wished, the chemistry of popular democracy would provide a compensatory reaction to any abuse of the privilege. They saw newspapers operating by a rule of democratic principle: just as the government would be kept in line with the popular will by the votes of the citizens, so newspapers, legally unrestrained, would be persuaded to keep a position within the limits of public sanction by their need of the support and patronage of the people to survive. But the men who made our constitution, although they did detect an inherent danger in the growing commercialism of their young new land, did not foresee modern advertising, the connective by which newspapers would come to depend for their existence more upon the support of commercial interests than upon the people at large. Nevertheless, the logic upon which our forefathers reasoned, that newspapers can be expected generally to show an allegiance to that group upon which they are most dependent, was valid. It is reaffirmed in today's situation where newspapers tend to reflect the way of thinking of business, of property and privilege, rather than the viewpoint of the democratic community as a whole.

Briefly stated, the major defect of our American press system today is this: as a result of changes, economic, social, and technological, the base of support of our machinery of public information has shifted until today most of its burden bears upon one segment of our society instead of upon society as a whole. Business today pays three fourths of the cost of maintaining our newspapers; the public pays, directly, one fourth. It is inevitable, in this situation, that newspapers should tend to see from the business viewpoint. And the evil of this is that too often the public welfare, looked at from the privileged position of profit and property, does not have quite the same shape as when seen from the common level.

It is a serious error to assume that the peccancies of American newspapers are in any large sense the result of the deliberate intent of the men who control the press to misemploy their powers for their own personal interests. There are publishers, of course, who do not hesitate to deceive, conceal and otherwise manipulate the news, even to lie, for their own purposes. And there could be cited many instances of the prostitution of newspapers to mercenary ends. But, projected against the broad general background of the American press, these instances are exceptional. For every newspaper that deliberately abuses its moral responsibility to the public, scores can be named that have consistently shown their consciousness of a public trust.

The main valid general criticism that can be made of American newspaper publishers today is, not that they are morally irresponsible, but that they are primarily profit-seekers, and newspapermen only incidentally and secondarily. They think first of survival, and then of their public responsibilities, and too often the terms are not synonymous. Yet, it is pointless to sort out newspaper publishers by this criticism, which can just as correctly be laid against every other class of business or professional men in American life. What they do, most other men would do in their places. It is no mere accident that newspaper publishers tend to be liberal crusaders, exponents of democracy's need for dynamic forward change, while they are struggling for a start, and tend to acquire a conservative laissez-faire attitude when they become established and secure. It is no accident; it is human nature.

The second sound indictment that can be returned against the newspapers of America is their low intellectual level. The truth of this charge cannot be denied; yet, studied in the panorama of all its causes, this criticism, too, is largely a criticism of our whole American society. The rule that any publication seeking general distribution must adapt itself to general standards needs no exposition, and newspapers, by nature and practical definition, are publications seeking general distribution. People read things that they understand, that deal with what they are interested in; newspapers, needing readers to survive, attract them with whatever experience shows them the people respond to the most. The said consequence of this, of course, is that readers above the average intellectual level must take the common fare.

Yet the more intelligent persons are not wholly ignored. An increasing number of American newspapers do publish editorials and features of fairly high content. And there are publications other than general newspapers edited especially for the more literate readers; they fill the demand, and the extent of their circulations may be taken as the measure of the demand.

But some critics see newspapers as the source spring of all culture, and, assuming that it is a primary function of democracy's newspaper to lead the people into the paths of intellectual and social righteousness, proceed to the easy fallacy of blaming national imperfections on the newspapers. The premise is wrong, and the whole idea fallacious, for two reasons. One, we cannot charge the press with the responsibility of making public opinion without granting someone—and who but the newspaper publishers?—the right of deciding what public opinion should be, a right which the democratic idea inherently denies to any one. And two, the assumption credits the press with more power over public opinion than it, functioning legitimately and ethically, possesses.

There can be no doubt that broad thought patterns, what Philosopher Alfred North Whitehead has called the public's "tone of mind," are established largely on a basis of what the people read in the newspapers. But this influence is in the news itself, in the event, rather than the newspaper; the newspaper is merely the reporting agency, the mode of communication. Broadly, a newspaper's influence is like a law's influence; in a democracy like ours, as prohibition has shown, a law is effective in the degree that it is understood and its essential purpose approved by the mass of the people. A newspaper can crystallize, consolidate existing public opinion, can bring dormant opinion into life, but it cannot autocratically *make* or *mold* public opinion as desired, except as it interrupts the stream of news, distorts the image, by concealment, falsification, calculated selection or misinterpretation. It is only in the unanimity of newspaper publishers in their attitudes towards business—they are all necessarily businessmen, no matter how they disagree otherwise—that they have been able to impose their attitudes on the public mind.

Also contributing to the desultory texture of America's newspapers, their dullness, their shallowness, their incoherence, is the low state of journalism as a means of livelihood. News is a nebulous, tricky, elusive material; handling it with precision and probity is one of the most difficult of all modern jobs, requiring instant acute perceptions and immediate decisions, and also a great resource of general knowledge. Yet journalism, the reporting and editing of the news, has been one of the least rewarding endeavours of American life.

By the measure of the importance to the public welfare of competent and trustworthy news reporting and editing, the wage standard is low. It is low because it is not sufficient to justify the education and training necessary to proper execution of the job, not sufficient to attract the men who by talent and discipline are best fitted for the work. As a result, newspapermen have been too generally men striving beyond their capabilities. Every newspaper office knows the boy who practices typing in his spare time, learns the word formula and a few other tricks of the trade, and eventually becomes a fairly proficient reporter, able to do a slick job on any assignment. But despite the sympathetic appeal of this Horatio Alger picture, more than native intelligence and a slick way with words are required to do a proper job of reporting; it needs also a background of knowledge, of liberal enlightenment, to interpret events and analyze their significance in the broad lights of wisdom. There are too many miniature Westbrooks in the newspaper offices of the land: keen, eager youngsters and men, sincere and honest perhaps, but doing a job simply beyond the scope of their knowledge.

There is little criticism that can be cast at the social viewpoint of working newspapermen as a class. They probably tend more than any other occupational group in the country to be democrats at heart. News judgment requires constant thinking in terms of the many, and this is certainly an attribute of all good democrats. And the duties of reporting tend to expose them to all strata of our society, an experience which is usually conducive to the development of a sense of man's human dignity and of a realization, no matter how cynical, of the broad reaches into which our society has yet failed to carry the blessings of the community.

But perhaps the clearest and most present danger to the public welfare in the American press today is in the unmistakable trend towards newspaper monopoly. For the rule of democratic principle to apply to newspapers, it is necessary that there be competitive newspapers. The court of public opinion, rendering daily judgments on the press, can enforce its decrees only if there is a choice of newspapers.

It is astonishing to find these familiar names among the cities of the United States today where daily newspaper monopolies exist: Mobile, San Bernardino, Peoria, Evansville, South Bend, Des Moines, Topeka, Louisville, Springfield (Mass.), Worcester, Lansing, Duluth, Minneapolis, St. Paul, Jackson (Miss.), Kansas City, Butte, Omaha, Reno, Manchester (N.H.), Camden, Rochester, Utica, Asheville, Winston-Salem, Akron, Springfield (Ohio), Youngstown, Oklahoma City, Tulsa, Allentown, Reading, Wilkes Barre, Charleston, Chattanooga, Nashville, Memphis, Wichita Falls, Norfolk, Richmond, Spokane, Huntington, Wheeling, Waterbury, Pensacola, El Paso, and Providence.

In 170-odd cities one firm publishes both morning and evening papers, and in all but a handful of cases these papers appear under different names and in different makeup. And in 49 of these cities the morning and evening papers, although having the same owners, brazenly claim to espouse different political beliefs.

Ownership of radio stations contributes to the monopoly hold on the news of daily newspapers in many cities. A recent report of the federal Communications Commission showed that 285 newspapers owned interests in radio stations, over 200 of them holding majority and controlling interests.

The current tragedy of American journalism, however, is not the warped vision of a business-dominated press, nor the venality of a few newspaper publishers, nor the tightening news control, nor the low state of the Fourth Estate. Instead it is the sad example of New York's *PM*, which now has failed its design to build a mold for the adless newspaper.

Here, in PM, it appeared that the dream of all good newspapermen, for a paper free to practice the art of pure reporting, with no axes to grind, no cows to nurse, was to come true. Here, by a rich man's indulgence, newspapermen, who have always salved their professional frustrations with boasts of what they could do if unrestrained, were to get their chance. Here America, growing testy at a press that paid first deference to business, was to be shown that advertising is not essential to a newspaper, that a newspaper wholly dependent upon its readers could justify its existence. Here, in PM, was to be cut the pattern of a new American journalism.

But the art of pure reporting found no place of expression in PM. Instead of to calm, unbiased, dispassionate reporting, PM was dedicated to a type of dogmatic, bigoted, intolerant journalism. It was the colossal arrogance of opinionated journalism that was *PM*'s weakness. Everyday PM undertook to answer the question that wise men have ever posed as unanswerable. What is truth? The adless PM failed for the simple reason that it performed the democratic function of a newspaper even less efficiently than its worst ad-carrying competitors. Readers could get at least a hint of both sides from the standard press; PM let not a drop leak through of the opposite view.

But although PM muffed its unique chance—unique in that Marshall Fields come only once—nevertheless adless newspapers still seem theoretically to offer an avenue towards the responsible and responsive journalism that democracy demands.' And there are substantial reasons for hope that an ad-free press may yet develop in America.

Newspaper endowments may be one product of the growing national interest in the press and its functions as a democratic institution, as evidenced in the debates, polls, symposiums, and surveys of recent years. And an endowed press quite logically could be adless. The trend towards cooperative ownership and control of enterprises with public and semipublic functions has not yet reached the press, but possibly it will; it may be that the form of America's future journalism is an adless press owned cooperatively by its readers. Newspaper subscription prices have been rising steadily; the public now is becoming seasoned to a subscription price level that can support newspapers depending wholly upon circulation for their income. The government has a great potential weapon for encouraging ad-free newspapers in its control of the mailing privilege, a power already upheld by the Supreme Court; with public sanction, however tacit, this power might be put to use.

With even a small start, a trend towards adless newspapers could be expected to gather momentum. Special news and feature services would be likely to appear, once there was sufficient demand, and with their availability establishing adless papers would be still easier. A general access to the standard big news services, now that the government antimonopoly suits have been finally won, should be an encouragement. And ad-free newspapers have certain natural advantages, anyway, making them easier to establish than conventional advertising papers: they need only half the shop and press capacity to carry the same amount of news, use only half the paper and ink, require no advertising sales staff, and are a much less complex managerial problem all around.

What is needed now is a practical demonstration that a standard, serviceable, workaday ad-free newspaper can make its way in an average community; with that once shown, other ad-free papers will appear. And even though it is unlikely that the advertising press of America ever will disappear—advertising performs a valuable economic function—it is certain that an ad-free press, scattered over America, would be a valuable gauge and guardian of the responsibility of the advertising press.

And public pressure upon the government for legal reforms touching the press undoubtedly would have great effect. Laws respecting newspapers that now seem both feasible and advisable include one requiring newspapers to accept advertisements, within certain limits: this would at least guarantee minority groups their chance to be heard. A law requiring equal space and position to correct libels would seem only fair. While they would be difficult of enactment under present conditions, it is conceivable that laws establishing some professional licensing standards for newspapermen could be constitutionally upheld; if compulsory Guild membership is constitutional certainly professional licensing standards should be. Government competitive scholarships for newsmen, administered by educational authorities and with a free choice of institution, would elevate journalistic standards, as would the inauguration of a custom of sabbatical leaves for study for newsmen.

A proposal that the government could constitutionally place some limitations on newspaper ownership at least deserves consideration. A law prohibiting any individual from having an ownership interest in more than one newspaper could possibly be construed as not abridging freedom of the press, as long as no restrictions were put upon what a man could say in whatever newspaper he did own. There seem at least some grounds for a belief that newspaper ownership of radio stations is not in the public interest. Laws prohibiting newspaper ownership by individuals holding public office would certainly seem ethically advisable. And there could be legal restrictions tending to discourage absentee ownership, and to encourage local proprietorship and control.

The most immediately practical way of making American newspapers better is by improving the status of journalists, and thereby the standards of journalism. Ideally, newspapermen should be a group set part, free from all influences except that of broad public opinion as expressed upon and through the newspaper. Short of this, however, there are quite definite things that can be done. Newspapering has made some strides as a means of livelihood in the past decade; newsmen are better paid today, more secure, and generally more capable, than they were before 1930. Much of this advance can be credited to the influence of the Newspaper Guild, and it is difficult to deny that the Guild has been, and is, in general, an influence tending to make better newspapers. But from the standpoint of broad democratic policy, there are questions as to the extent and type of union organisation of newspapermen that would be most compatible with the best interests of the public.

Since newspapermen should be, ideally, a group set apart, it follows that a newspapermen's union should be an editorial craft union, and independent of any national union group other than its own. General laws and policies cannot always be applied, with full reason, to newspapers and newspapermen; what an ironworker thinks affects only himself, but what a newspaperman thinks is extended to all who read his newspaper. And it is the legitimate concern of the community to see that there is a minimum of unequable pressure upon a newspaperman's way of thinking, and also that newspapermen are not generally committed to any one viewpoint.

Schools of journalism are, increasingly, stocking newsrooms with men who have at least some degree of formal preparation for their calling. But there perhaps is a just complaint that too generally courses of journalism, by training men pointedly for practical ends, tend to perpetuate the existing pattern of journalism rather than to improve it. Journalism perhaps should be a graduate study, based on a liberal education; of the two, the liberal education is certainly more important, judged by the interests of democracy itself. Specialization in preparation for careers of journalism probably should be encouraged; master's degrees in journalism, after bachelor's degrees in concentrated liberal fields, should produce newspapermen well qualified to serve as the eyes and ears of the public, at least in respect to their subjects.

Whatever the practical possibilities of inaugurating changes in our newspaper system such as have been considered above, certain it is that widespread discussion of possible reforms, legal and otherwise, should have a salutary effect in itself. As newspaper publishers detect a possibility that the public is taking seriously suggestions for such reforms, the result probably will be critical self-examination by the press itself.

There must be a clear and stressed differentiation between Freedom of the Press, the individual's right, and State of the Press, the qualitative condition of our journalism. Blending of the two concepts dilutes the strength and clear significance of each. Unless the line between the two ideas is kept plain and unmistakable there is danger that we may, in our efforts to improve our newspapers, undermine a basic right. We would be stupid to deprive the people of the right to free expression, or to abridge this right, merely because of the failure of the press to be perfect, or the sins of a few publishers.

Our ideal must be a press that, while unrestrained in its expression, is both responsible and responsive to the people. In an important sense, America does not want a free press: it does not want a press free *from* the people, which is the sort of press that Germany had. America wants a press bound to the people, bound so tightly that the people cannot stir, however slightly, without that movement becoming visible in the newspapers. America wants a press that owes no other allegiance than to the whole community, and so established that any digression from the true course of that allegiance will bring its immediate corrective penalty. A press so situated that the public interest is not only the moral course, but also the only profitable course. Such a press, it is true, would not be absolved of all the sins of today's press; indeed, such a press possibly would be more bound to the common level, more susceptible to public ailments. Press that is limited by the common quality than it can risk a press independent of the people's touch.

And to obtain a truly responsive and responsible press, there are two requisites: one, its burden must be distributed generally, and not borne unequally by any class or group; and two, the people must have a choice of competitive papers.

Lastly, if we are to have better newspapers, we must have better newspapermen. The rewards of journalism must be such that the calling will attract to it the men best suited to perform its vital functions. And newspapermen must be, insofar as possible, free of any influences that may tend to distort the news image which they pass along to the public.

RESPONSIBILITY OF THE REPORTER AND EDITOR

Clifton Daniel

To be brief it could simply be said that the responsibility of reporters is to get the facts straight and spell the names right. And the responsibility of editors is to fire them if they don't. That is really not a bad creed for newspapermen, but there is more to it than that.

Let us begin with the basic assumption that journalism is not a trade, not a profession, but a calling—that is not necessarily above politics, but should certainly be apart from politics. This may sound very austere and self-denying, but I mean it to sound that way. The man who embraces journalism as a career should be no less dedicated than the parson or the doctor. Like them, he should have his own standards—standards that are not subject to change by the shifting winds of public taste or political expediency.

My colleague Anthony Lewis of the *New York Times* said in a recent talk at Harvard: "There is no sure guide for all situations, but I think it is clear that the reporter must not become entirely committed—an obvious special pleader. His instinct should be all the other way. If he has a concern for the public good... he must reconcile himself to satisfying that urge by uncommitted reporting. Justice Frankfurter has put it that the reporter *is an educator, not a reformer*. I accept that definition, with the proviso that the educator must be allowed to harbor within him just a little of the spirit of reform."

The reporter, must satisfy his concern for the public good by uncommitted reporting. To translate that into practical terms, a reporter may belong to worthy organizations, he may contribute to good causes, he may campaign for civic virtue and public betterment, but he should never commit himself irretrievably to one cause, one organization, one course of action. In the words of the Code of Ethics of editors. "Freedom from all obligations except that of fidelity to the public interest is vital." Actually, the reporter who understands his mission has a higher destiny than mere dedication to a single cause. His function is to create and preserve an atmosphere in which all noble causes may flourish.

These facts impose a peculiar responsibility on the journalist. It is a responsibility, not to his employer, not to a particular paper, not to a particular point of view, but to the public and to his own conception of the obligations of his profession. The publisher, the man who meets the payroll, is not alone responsible for the conscience of the profession. Each reporter and editor is the keeper of his own conscience.

"The modern journalist," "is an employee. But his responsibility remains to serve the reader as his client. That describes the responsibility and the whole of it. He departs from it or compromises with it at the peril of his soul."

Mr. Lyons' conception of the responsibility of the journalist is based on the premise that information is essential to people who propose to govern themselves, and that those who supply the information must be above partisanship and self-interest. In other words, the duty of the reporter and editor, is to do "what every sovereign citizen is supposed to do, but has not the time or interest to do for himself"—that is, to gather information, pick out what is important, digest it thoroughly, and without partisanship or prejudice relate it to the problems of the day.

If the press is going to discharge this function fully, it must be among the bravest and boldest. It must say what no one else dares say, what no one else can afford to say. It must tell the people what they need to know, not what they would like to hear. If you ask me who decides what the people need to know, I can only say, "The editor," If he can't do that, he has no right to the title. If he allows someone else to do it for him—the government or some special interest—he forfeits his freedom.

There was a time when newspapermen seemed to be more outspoken than they are today, more contemptuous of authority, more defiant of restraints on their freedom. Nowadays, when we are engaged in a desperate competition with world communism, it is sometimes suggested that the newspapers should voluntarily restrict themselves.

This issue arose not long ago when it was proposed that the press limit its coverage of President Eisenhower's trip to the Soviet Union (the one that was canceled in May) and of similar visits by Soviet leaders to this country. A number of editors were questioned by the Associated Press Managing Editors Association. Nobody voted in favour of the press limiting its own freedom. One editor wrote: "If anybody proposes to limit the number of newsmen accredited to cover important international stories, let him do it if he dares. If such restrictions are imposed and found to be disadvantageous, let the enterprising newspaperman evade and defy them if he dares. If these opposite interests clash—and what is 'the American life' but a cacophony of colliding interests under the law?—then let the courts and the Congress draw the line, if they dare. But let's not circumscribe ourselves with our own pencils."

I like that fellow's spirit. It is the spirit with which I think we should meet the problem of official restrictions on news.

Somehow, I feel we newspapermen complain too much about the concealment of news by official quarters—"top secret" labels on inane documents, closed meetings of city councils, secret sessions of legislative committees, and so on. And we rely too much on the politicians to open these doors for us. The classic function of the aggressive reporter and editor—a part of the responsibility they owe to the public—is to open doors with the power of the press—pry them open, blow them open.

Of course, the issue of responsibility arises sometimes in matter more serious than a local political fight. It sometimes involves national security. Obviously, newspapermen must not be irresponsible in the reporting of news that might affect the safety and security of our own country, our own homes. But the primary responsibility for safeguarding our national interests must rest always with our government.

When Nikita Khrushchev arrived in the United States, newspapers around the country received thousands of letters, telegrams and telephone calls urging them to boycott the visit, to ban Khrushchev from their news columns. So far as I know, there was not a single daily paper in the country that ignored Khrushchev entirely. However, there was one that gave him only six paragraphs on his arrival in New York. The *New York Times* printed 27 columns, and a very angry woman in New York called me up and demanded to know why we published a picture of that "Russian pig" on page I. She said we should have printed pictures of President Eisenhower and the American flag instead.

While I appreciated her patriotism, I tried to explain—although she was too angry to listen—what I felt the responsibility of the press to be. Restricting news of Khrushchev's visit presupposes that it is more important for the press to show its disapproval of him than to inform the public of what he is and what he is doing. Perhaps the Russians would not have us so much on the defensive today if we had not, journalistically speaking, turned our backs on them for a whole generation and ignored what they were achieving in education, industry, and science.

There are still people who think it is unpatriotic to call attention to the Soviet challenge or to publish news that is in conflict with the opinions and policies of our government. What is the responsibility of the reporter and editor in *that* area? The answer is not simple, but it seems to me that, up until the time we are actually at war or on the verge of war, it is not only permissible but it is our duty as journalists and citizens to be constantly questioning our leaders and our policy.

Some people argue that newspapers should not print facts that might embarrass our government in its relations with other governments. But it may be that those very facts are the ones our people need to know in order to come to a clear decision about our policy. In our democracy, the purposes of the press and the government are not necessarily always identical.

Although our government does not recognize Communist China and prevents the Chinese government from being seated in the United Nations, there is no doubt in my mind that American newspapers should have correspondents on the Chinese mainland. We need to know what the Chinese Communists are doing because some day they may be doing it to us. It is nothing less than folly to let this great power grow up in the Pacific without our having any first hand knowledge of its aims and accomplishments and its potential. Here is the most populous country on earth, and we have not a single diplomatic or journalistic representative there to tell us what is going on.

Looking back and second-guessing, I would say that we made a mistake in not sending our correspondents to China in 1956 when we had the chance. The Chinese government offered to admit a long list of newspapermen. But we declined. We did not want to embarrass our government. We did not wish to offend the sensibilities of those whose sons had died in Korea or were imprisoned in China. I think we were wrong. I think we overlooked our primary loyalty which is, as I have tried to suggest, to the American public—to give the public the information it needs to make intelligent decisions on our national policy with regard to China.

Our government has since changed its mind. A certain number of correspondents are now free to go to China. But Peiping has also changed. The Chinese are not prepared to admit our correspondents except on terms that Washington is unwilling to meet.

Without going into the diplomatic intricacies of this question, let me say only that any effort by journalism or government to break this impasse and see that the American people are informed about China would be a contribution to our national security.

In election years there are inevitably proposals, from inside the profession and outside, that the newspapers should guarantee equal space and equal billing to the two candidates for President. Of course, we should give them an even break. But the principle should not be carried to ridiculous extremes. Newspapers should be edited not with a tape measure but on the basis of the best news judgment of competent, serious, responsible reporters and editors. A reporter knows pretty well when he is leaning toward one side or the other, and so does his editor. The only answer to that is: Don't do it.

Again and again these days we hear that factual reporting is not enough, that objectivity is out of date, that the news has become so complex that it must be explained, that interpretation is now necessary. A good deal of this talk is nonsense. Of course the news should be explained. There is nothing new about that. The news has always required interpretation, but interpreting the news does not exclude the possibility of objectivity in reporting it. As I have said, a reporter knows pretty well when he is being objective, and so does his editor. The important thing is that they should appreciate the need for objectivity, and its relationship to the role they play in our democracy.

Stripped to essentials, the responsibility of the reporter and editor is simply to serve the public—not the profession of journalism, not a particular newspaper, not a political party, not the government, but the public.

10

Review of Press and Journalism in England

Politically the press was now free. Wilkes, 'Junius,' and Woodfull and others less able and less remembered but by no means always their inferiors in courage had won for it the right to report and the right to criticise—to criticise, if they were so minded, even the King's Ministers and the King himself. But between the right to report and comment and the independence to use it there is a wide gap.

The ruling class deeply suspicious, as was to be expected, of the potential challenge of this new power had been forced to retreat a little. But its hostility was unimpaired. For the next seventy years the history of newspapers was to be largely the history of this hostility, and of the various means tried by Governments and party rulers to prevent newspapers from seizing the opportunities for greater circulation and public influence given by victory in the battle for the right to report Parliament.

Men like Wilkes and 'Junius' might, as guerrilla fighters do, disrupt the settled order of things for a time and even score a few major victories but the press as a whole was still subservient. To keep it so, to prevent the development of independent and, above all, of popular newspapers, was from now on one of the primary objectives of the ruling class whether Whig or Tory.

That this should be so is no matter for surprise. Established powers, as has been said earlier, cannot be expected to welcome the advent of new ones. Nor need resistence to the development of an independent press be regarded as evidence of an especial malevolence on the part of those who feared and hated it, any more than is the current Parliamentary dislike of television and radio discussion. Their view was shared by many of the most able and disinterested men in public life as well as some of the worst, for it threatened to call in judgment against them those whom the whole context of the age made them regard as ignorant, licentious and low and to place in the hands of classes they regarded as altogether ignorant of the necessities of statemenship the power to criticise and perhaps to shape it. To Burke the press appeared as the grand instrument for the subversion of order, morals, religion and the social system; to Windham as the distributor of a poison that spread its venom every twenty-four hours to the extremity of the kingdom. Southey complained that newspapers 'inflamed the turbulent temper of the manufacturer and disturbed the quiet attachment of the peasant,' and even as late as 1829 Sir Walter Scott could write to Lockhart: 'Your connection with any newspaper would be a disgrace and degradation. I would rather sell gin to poor people and poison them that way.'

To many of the best minds of the age as well as to those opposed to all reform the great need of the time came to be the restriction of newspaper circulations to limit the harm they could do. But a counter-interest was also at work, that of political groups anxious to use newspapers as instruments of propaganda. From their point of view independence not circulation was the danger. Kept in control newspapers could have their uses, merit employment in much the same way as a paid bully or a hired informer—and be held in the same contempt.

From both these points of view the newspaper stamp duties were peculiarly valuable. They ensured that those attracted to the dubious trade of journalism would be in no financial position to ignore their betters. And they made it impossible for them to offer their wares at a price the lower classes could pay. For any who kicked against the pricks the Government had other weapons to hand in the Post Office, which was the sole agent for distribution at home and abroad and controlled the entry of all newspapers into the country. Distribution of those papers regarded as dangerous could be held up, as Cobbett alleged the distribution of his daily paper the *Porcupine* and his famous weekly the *Political Register* frequently was; the foreign journals upon which newspapers relied for most of their foreign news could be delayed or lost—as *The Times* repeatedly declared to happen to those addressed to it.

Heavily taxed, hampered in distribution, his supply of foreign news interrupted, cut off from the official intelligence made available to those acceptable to the Treasury and the Foreign Office, denied the regular payments from secret service funds that went to his rivals, the journalist who dreamed of independence had little to encourage him in his fantasy. Nor were such secret or overt means of bringing him to his senses as these all he had to contend with. The law was a sword waiting to strike. Until Fox's Libel Act of 1792 restored to juries the right to decide upon every indictment for libel whether the defendant was guilty or not guilty newspapers were at the mercy of judges who often scarcely bothered to conceal their readiness to act as agents of Ministers. Nor, even after the Act of 1792, was the journalist's position much better in those matters which the Government regarded as affecting its interest. The Attorney-General had the right to require that any press prosecution he conducted be tried by a special jury. Such juries, composed for the most part of civil servants and magistrates, commonly did what he asked them.

This weapon of prosecution was not allowed to grow rusty with disuse: there were seventy press prosecutions in the first thirty-one years of George III's reign. Sentences were savage. For publishing a paragraph that annoyed the Russian Ambassador one printer was sentenced to imprisonment for a year and sent to the pillory. For the same offence another was sent to gaol for eighteen months and fined £200, and two others imprisoned for a year and fined £100 each. One, but only because she was a woman, was let off with six months' imprisonment and a fine of £50. Moreover the Attorney-General had a further privilege well adapted to the intimidation of newspapers of too independent a spirit. He had the right to file ex-officio information for libel and dispense with a preliminary hearing before a Grand Jury: an instrument of coercion as Professor Aspinall remarks in *Politics and the Press 1780-1850* well suited to terrify journalists into 'compromise, compliance and servility,' for by its means the threat of proceedings could be kept hanging over the heads of recalcitrant newspapers for months or even years. At one time more than half the newspapers published in London had such threats of prosecution hanging over their heads—although not one of the charges was ever brought to court. Moreover the mere filing of such ex-officio information involved newspapers in heavy costs so that the Attorney-General could in effect inflict a large fine on any journalist or newspaper proprietor he did not like. No wonder John Almon, publisher of the *London Magazine*, declared: 'A man had better make his son a tinker than a printer. The laws of tin he can understand but the law of libel is unwritten, uncertain and undefinable. It is one thing today and another tomorrow. No man can tell what it is. It is sometimes what the King or Queen pleases, sometimes what the Minister pleases, sometimes what the Attorney-General pleases.'

Yet even so there were forces at work too strong for any deterrent to be effective. Public opinion with its need for information was on the move.

'Give me the liberty of the Press,' declared Sheridan in the House of Commons in 1810, 'and I will give the Minister a venal House of Peers, I will give him a corrupt and servile House of Commons, I will give him the full swing of the patronage of office, I will give him the whole host of ministerial influence, I will give him all the power that place can confer upon him to purchase submission and overawe resistance and yet, armed with the liberty of the Press, I will go forth to meet him undismayed....'

And there was still another force at work no less important—commercial development. It was this that was in the end to give the press the means to freedom for as commerce developed and became more profitable it brought with it not only the demand for reliable information but the possibility of economic independence through advertising revenue despite the penal advertisement taxes. It is not accidental that of the nine newspapers published daily in London twelve years after Wilkes's victory five were primarily advertisement sheets: the *Daily Advertiser, Public Advertiser, General Advertiser, Public Ledger,* and *Public Gazetteer,* while of the remaining four the *Morning Post* carried the sub-title of *Cheap Daily Advertiser,* and the *Morning Chronicle,* the *Morning Herald* and *Citizens' Morning Post* devoted at least half and usually more of their space to advertisements.

The dangerous dependence of newspapers upon advertisements has often been the theme of newspaper reformers—usually from outside its professional ranks. But the daily press would never have come to existence as a force in public and social life if it had not been for the need of men of commerce to advertise. Only through the growth of advertising did the press achieve independence.

What were they concerned with, these daily papers launched for the most part to satisfy the advertising needs of the syndicates of businessmen who founded them? By the very nature of the news-gatherer's trade and the political and social compulsions of the time, they could not avoid becoming something much more than instruments of commercial exchange. The editor as such hardly yet existed although he was soon to become an increasingly important figure. Nor did the leader-writer. Those newspapers that concerned themselves with politics and public questions commonly employed for their hazardous excursions into criticism and comment the medium of a letter 'To the Printer.' It was thus that 'Junius's' letters appeared.

Apart from the morning papers there were some ten tri-weekly papers published in London on Tuesday, Thursday and Saturday in time to catch the mail to the provinces. These carried more news and fewer advertisements than the dailies. And although it was still illegal to sell anything but milk and mackerel on a Sunday and those found hawking newspapers were subject to a fine, Sunday papers had already begun to make their appearance. They appealed to a more popular and less educated public than did the dailies and were peculiarly the subject of official anxiety as 'vehicles of treason.' Over and above these daily, tri-weekly and Sunday newspapers there was a varied, shifting and steadily expanding concourse of political, literary and social journals and periodicals which—if only because they could exist on smaller resources than could the dailies or tri-weeklies—were responsible for some of the most vigorous and critical journalism of the time. It is thus a lively enough picture that the press presents in the closing years of the eighteenth century, despite all the efforts of the ruling classes to cage the dangerous animal.

Sales were, of course, still small. This was so not only because of the difficulties of distribution, the primitive communications, the illiteracy of large masses of the population and the obstacles placed in the way by Ministers but also because the technological conditions necessary to the development of a mature newspaper industry were still lacking. Until 1814 when *The Times* short ahead of its rivals with the introduction of steam-driven machinery capable of printing 1,100 sheets an hour all newspapers were printed by hand. The maximum number of sheets they could run off in an hour was no more than 250 and often in practice considerably less. Even a daily print of 2,000 or 3,000 was a long-drawn-out and difficult operation.

In every aspect, political, legal, economic, the trade of journalism was a hazardous one. But it was also a lively and expanding one responding to the deep compulsions of the time and it did not fail to attract to itself men of diverse character with motives as varied as their personalities.

Among them four stand out as making a particular impact upon the journalism of their time: John Bell, James Perry, David Stuart, John Walter. These are the ancestors of the men who produce the 30,000,000 newspapers of today.

Bell brought to the journalism of the second half of the eighteenth century gifts that it badly needed: lightness and entertainment, appeal to the eye as well as to the intellect, ranging curiosity about a great many things. He had already established himself as a successful bookseller and a publisher with a flair for hitting fashionable taste before ever he turned to journalism: one of his books was the famous *Apology for the Life of George Anne Bellamy* whose dazzling career as mistress of half the aristocracy had set the town talking. This work he advertised in a manner to fill the circulation manager of a modern Sunday paper with envy. It would, he promised, disclose the hitherto unsuspected secrets of every well-known man about town in London. As a publisher he had made it his ambition to be recognised as the finest typographer of his age. He brought the same interest in good appearance to journalism and exercised upon the make-up of the newspapers of his time somewhat the same effect as the *Daily Express* has exercised on ours. He was one of the syndicate of twelve that, along with the founders of Christie's and Tattersall's, launched the *Morning Post* in 1772. But it is not on the *Morning Post,* in which he was never more than a minority shareholder, that his reputation rests but on the *World and Fashionable Advertiser*, started fifteen years later, and on a host of subsequent papers and periodicals to which he brought an energy and a flair that give him the right to be regarded as one of the great innovators and impresarios of the press, the Northcliffe of his day.

His partner in the *World* was Captain Edward Topham, a gentleman of means who wished to promote the career of a Drury Lane actress, Mrs. Wells, who had shown her affection for him by bearing him four children. But it was Bell who made the paper. The *World* was something new in journalism. Light-hearted, sophisticated, knowing, concerned with the gossip of the fashionable world rather than with great principles, and vastly superior in type and lay-out to anything that had been seen before, it permanently altered the conception both of what a newspaper should look like and what it should write about—the first swallow that presaged the summer of popular journalism.

It was not the first specifically woman's magazine. That had appeared nearly a hundred years before in 1693 in the form of a broadsheet called the *Ladies Mercury* which contained excellent advice on a range of matters from whitening the teeth to the moral dilemma of a young lady of quality who having earlier suffered the calamity of being 'so seduced as to give up the very Soul of Beauty, My Honour, to a lewd and infamous rifler' had since married a rich and worthy man and wanted to know whether she should tell him. The *Ladies Mercury* said 'No.' But although Bell's magazine was far from being the first to appeal exclusively to women it set, as the *World* had in daily journalism, a new standard in presentation, offering excellent coloured fashion plates and drawings along with a great variety of reading matter. Six years later Bell hit on an even more successful idea, a Sunday magazine called *Bell's Weekly Messenger* for those wanting to be 'informed or amused at the Sunday Breakfast table.'

Again Bell was the adapter, not the inventor. The first Sunday newspaper had been published sixteen years before by a woman, Mrs. E. Johnson. It had evoked a fine crop of imitators, among them the *Observer* which was already five years old when Bell came along with his *Messenger*. But whereas these earlier Sunday papers were primarily weekly newspapers he invented a formula that still draws the millions to popular Sunday newspapers more than a century and a half later. His *Messenger* gave a summary of the news of the week but its real appeal lay in feature articles catering for every sort of taste from sport, politics and scandal to the latest theatrical and literary events. It had an immediate and enormous public success and became one of the most emulated periodicals in the history of journalism.

Bell was not much concerned with principles. He was an entertainer and populariser, not a prophet: a pathfinder for the popular journalism of the future. But he has a place in the struggle for the freedom of the press larger than that of some more serious-minded men because he showed the way to that popular appeal upon which such freedom rests. 'He possessed,' says Leigh Hunt of him in his autobiography, 'no acquirements, perhaps not even grammar; but his taste in putting forth a publication and getting the best artists to adorn it was new in these times, and may be admired in any....' Bell's son, with whom he quarrelled, founded the *News of the World*.

If Bell may be described as the first of the popular press proprietors, Perry, 'a pleasant man with a dash, no slight one either, of the Courtier' according to Charles Lamb, was the first of the great editors in the modern mode—or rather in a mode now passing. It is, indeed, from him that the idea of the importance of the editor first comes.

Wilkes's victory was twelve years old when, at the age of twenty-seven, Perry was invited to manage the *Gazetteer*, an unimportant advertisement sheet just turned into a general newspaper. Earlier as a reporter on the *General Advertiser* he had made a name for himself by his vivid account of the court-martial of Admiral Keppel and it was to an improvement in the news reporting of the *Gazetteer* that he first applied himself. The most influential and widely read paper in the country was the *Morning Chronicle*. This position it held largely because of the excellence of its Parliamentary reports and Perry made up his mind to surpass them. The *Chronicle's* leadership in Parliamentary reporting depended primarily upon one man: its editor, William Woodfull, younger brother of that Henry Sampson Woodfull of the *Public Advertiser*, who had published the 'Letters of Junius.' Woodfull was possessed of a phenomenal memory, far exceeding even that of that earlier Parliamentary reporter, Guthrie of the *Gentleman's Magazine.* He regularly produced from memory reports of debates up to seven columns or more in length. It was these reports, unequalled elsewhere, that sold the paper.

Perry could not hope to emulate Woodfull's feat as a memory man. Instead he organised a corps of Parliamentary reporters—the first in newspaper history. Each of them was instructed to follow the debate for a short stretch and then with memory still fresh write out his report while another took over, to be succeeded in his turn by a third, a system still in operation among Parliamentary shorthand reporters. By the standards of the time it was a very expensive method of getting a Parliamentary report. But it paid. The *Gazetteer* was able to come out with a much longer report than the *Chronicle* and one produced at greater speed and with more accuracy.

The moment was propitious. Lord North's Government had fallen, crushed by Cornwallis's surrender to Washington's forces at York Town and by the loss of the North American colonies. George III was forced to accept what he had so long resisted, a Whig administration determined not only to stop the war but to end the royal domination of Parliament. An era of the liveliest public interest in Parliamentary affairs was opening. Moreover a new star of the first magnitude was rising in the Parliamentary sky—the younger Pitt. When Perry had been managing the *Gazetteer* for a year the elections of 1784 brought Pitt to the premiership in a House of Commons which if not in any full sense representative, for that was not possible without reform, was yet for almost the first time since the Commonwealth the result of a genuine uprising of public feeling. The issues with which this Parliament had to deal, including as they did the impeachment and trial of Warren Hastings, were of a nature to keep popular interest at fever point.

In his determination to have the best Parliamentary reports in the country Perry was therefore guided by one of the basic maxims of successful journalism in any time and place—that it is virtually impossible to give your readers too much of a really big story. His policy paid. Indeed it paid so much that it almost put the *Chronicle* out of business. That paper suffered the penalty that lies in wait for all newspapers that fall behind in the sheer technique of their trade, it lost circulation rapidly to its more enterprising rival. Woodfull was not prepared to adopt Perry's methods. He could not bring himself to believe that his wonderful memory had had its day. When his partners demanded that he do as Perry did he left the paper in a huff. Within six years of Perry's innovation the *Chronicle,* fallen in circulation and prestige, came on the market. Perry bought it with a loan of £500 from his bank, an investment of a similar amount from a schoolmaster friend at Charterhouse with journalistic ambitions, and the promise of financial backing from Bellamy, the doorkeeper of the House of Commons who was also a prosperous wine merchant—the eighteenth century was favourable to dual roles.

He revived it by the same methods as had enabled the *Gazetteer* to ruin it, spending what was for the time the extraordinary sum of between £2,000 and £3,000 a year on what he wryly described as 'these disgusting though necessary reports of Parliamentary chattering.' At the same time he greatly improved its news coverage in other directions: he spent a year in Paris during the French Revolution organising reports of what had become the greatest news of the day. But he did not confine himself to improving the paper's news service only. He also attracted to his service as contributors the most eminent writers he could find: Sheridan, Coleridge, Lamb, Thomas Moore, Ricardo, all wrote regularly for him and Hazlitt became his dramatic critic. He remained editor of the *Chronicle* for twenty-eight years, its principal owner until his death in 1821, and to a degree that had not formerly been the case even in its greatest days he made it far and away the most influential and widely read paper in the country, one that, as that stern critic Cobbett said, 'discovered a spirit of independence rarely to be met with and a degree of talent that does great honour to the Press of this country.'

Perry, taking over the *Morning Chronicle* when it had become a shadow of its former self, raised it to a new level of authority and esteem by recognising and catering for the public demand for news. Although he was succeeded as editor by a journalist of parts who had served under him—John Black who gave Dickens his first chance as a reporter—the independence he had won for it soon disappeared after his death. When its circulation fell to less than a third of that in his day it lost its economic freedom and became a Government mouthpiece—'What the heads of the party desire to be inserted is immediately published,' said Roebuck; 'the Treasury sends its missives and they must be obeyed.'

What Perry did for the *Morning Chronicle* Stuart did for the *Morning Post*—only for it also to follow the same path to party subservience after he left it: striking evidence of a truth uncongenial to some newspaper proprietors who change their editors more frequently than they do their cooks, that great newspapers are made by great editors.

The *Morning Post* had been founded, some twenty-three years before Stuart acquired it, to catch the raffish taste of fashionable and would-be fashionable London. It was at first remarkably successful in doing so under the editorship of a dissolute young clergyman, Henry Bute, whose penchant for public brawling made him popularly known as 'The Fighting Parson.' Its first number included the offer for sale of a complete, up-to-the minute list of the names and addresses of 'those ladies of the town to be found at home in or near Piccadilly' and until Bute landed himself in prison for libelling the Duke of Richmond it was the favoured reading of most of the young bloods of the town. After that it hired itself to the Treasury as a whip to beat the Prince Regent with but switched sides when the Prince offered its manager a thousand guineas and £350 a year to keep quiet about Mrs. Fitzherbert.

In 1795, when Stuart bought it, it had lost the last shreds of its reputation in a sensational libel action and was known only as an insignificant and wholly contemptible mouthpiece of Carlton House. Its circulation was down to 350 copies a day. This derelict and disreputable publication, Stuart, then twenty-nine, bought for £600 and turned within little more than a year into one of the most admired and successful journals in the country with a circulation of over 4,500: evidence, said Coleridge, 'that genuine impartiality with a respectable portion of literary talent will secure the success of a newspaper without the aid of party or Ministerial patronage.'

His success was built on a combination of editorial talent and shrewd business sense. It was rooted in the belief (some modern editors seem to imagine that it was they who invented it) that although public affairs are important to be successful a newspaper must be 'cheerfully entertaining, not entirely filled with ferocious politics'; a dictum that the Victorian age was almost entirely to forget. One part of his formula for success, a formula that echoes like a familiar Fleet Street story across the centuries, has been agreeably described by Charles Lamb, who was one of Stuart's regular writers at sixpence a paragraph:

'The chat of the day—scandal, but, above all, dress—furnished the material.... A fashion of flesh, or rather pink-coloured hose for the ladies, luckily coming up at the juncture when we were on our probation for the place of Chief Jester to S's Paper established our reputation in that line. Then there was the collateral topic of ankles. What an occasion to a truly chaste writer like myself, of touching that nice brink, and yet never tumbling over it, of seemingly every approximating to something "not quite proper"; while, like a skilful posture-master, balancing betwixt decorums and their opposites, he keeps the line, from which a hair's breadth deviation is destruction.....'

Journalistically Stuart's great achievement and the true basis of his success was to show the world that a readiness to entertain was not incompatible with literary quality or responsible reporting or serious political purpose. He made the *Morning Post* sell by giving its readers plenty of variety and by providing a paper that men and women of many differing tastes could both enjoy and respect. He learned a good deal from Bell, as did every other journalist of the time, but he turned Bell's technique to more public-spirited purposes and he kept a constant eye on advertising revenue.

He was one of the first to see that in addition to being essential to economic and political independence advertisements were also highly attractive to readers in their own right.

'Advertisements act and re-act,' he said. 'They attract readers, promote circulation and circulation attracts advertisements.' He would have found wholly incomprehensible the lordly contempt of the editorial staff for the advertisement department that characterised Victorian journalism. Not only as a proprietor but as editor he regarded advertisement revenue as a matter of his most intimate concern. It was what gave him freedom from the party managers and he set himself to encourage it by every means in his power, holding small advertisements (classified advertisements as we should now call them) to be particularly valuable to a paper because 'the more numerous the customers, the more permanent and independent the custom.'

Bell, Perry, Stuart, each in their several ways, planted signposts for other newspapers to follow and demonstrated that even in an era when the press was continually subject to threat or bribe independence could be won by producing a paper that satisfied the public taste. Yet oddly enough the credit for making independence not merely the luxury of an outstanding editor but a settled principle of newspaper organisation must go to a journalistic dynasty founded by a man infinitely smaller in journalistic stature than any one of these three—John Walter I of *The Times*.

John Walter was not a great journalist, nor even a particularly high-minded or honest one. Nor did he embark on newspaper publication out of any natural feeling for news. He did so merely because, having failed as an underwriter at Lloyd's and being disappointed in his expectation of some post under the Government, he found himself at the age of forty-five compelled to look around for something new to do, his 'business sunk by hasty strides, and the world to begin afresh, with the daily introduction to my view of a wife and six children unprovided for and depending on me for support.' In the course of thus looking for something new he became interested in a patent for an improved system of typography invented by a London printer, Henry Johnson. With the assistance of two City friends, a merchant and a solicitor, he bought the rights in it and acquired a disused printing works in Printing House Yard, Blackfriars, formerly belonging to the King's Printer. This done he set forth with energy and fortitude to rebuild his fortunes.

A daily newspaper was no part of his original plans. His modest ambition was to print books and pamphlets and set himself up in business as a bookseller. Only as an afterthought did he add to these activities those of a daily newspaper and for the first seven years of his new career it was the effort to establish himself as a publisher and bookseller that occupied most of his energies.

The strange heresy of press freedom stirred no such response in John Walter's businesslike breast as it did in those of Perry and Stuart as he embarked upon newspaper proprietorship. He supported the Government and expected to be paid for it like anyone else, contracting for a fee of £300 a year to publish any paragraphs that came to him with the private mark of Thomas Steele, the Joint Secretary of the Treasury. As it turned out this was an unfortunate bargain. Within three years two of the paragraphs thus sent to him were held by the Court of King's Bench to be criminal libels on the Prince of Wales and the Duke of York, and poor Walter, after refusing very honourably, to divulge the source of his information, found himself sentenced to two years in Newgate. He got no particular credit from his paymasters for his reticence, receiving, as he complained to Lord Hawkesbury, 'no tidings to relieve my anxious moments nor the least comfort oı any other nature but am abandoned to ruin, disgrace and infamy as far as the Sentence of the Law can convey the Idea, torn from my Family, my business left to mercenaries, my Health suffering from Confinement in a noxious Prison where I am lock'd in every night at 8 o'clock.' 'And all,' as he declared with understandable bitterness, 'without a sixpence for the extraordinary Expenses I am at.' But though he complained he did not quarrel with his paymasters. He had too sharp an understanding of their power for that. He continued to draw his £300 a year and do as he was bid until they, not he, decided to end the bargain eight years later.

Nor was a secret Treasury subsidy the only means embraced by Walter to cushion himself against the financial perils of newspaper publishing. He adopted a practice still followed very profitably in many parts of the Middle East and among the less reputable scandal sheets of Hollywood of offering to those in the public eye the privilege of paying him not to blacken their reputations. It was a rewarding sideline. Mrs. Wells, Topham's former mistress, records in her memoirs that after her second marriage she and her husband both found *The Times's* interest in her disconcerting. Thereupon her husband invited Finney, the 'editorial conductor' of *The Times* under Walter, to call upon him and 'pulling out from his escritoire a large parcel of notes handed over a packet to him saying "Will that be enough?" To this Finney devoutly replied: 'Give me a few more and by St. Patrick I'll knock out the brains of anyone in an office who dare even whisper your name.

'Suppression fees,' 'contradiction fees,' payments for puffs, all were grist to the mill of the first John Walter as he set about his unintended task of establishing the greatest newspaper in the world and the first to become wholly and permanently independent. He was, said Crabbe Robinson who served him and was for a time editor under his son, 'as dishonest, worthless a man as I have ever known, at least among those who preserved appearance.' And william Combe, author of the *Tour of Dr. Syntax,* whom he employed for a time as a writer on *The Times,* declared of him that 'he never did an honest act in his life' but established his fortune by 'the vilest arts—extortion of money through calumny etc.'

All this no doubt is true. With one or two exceptions like Perry and Stuart the same could be said of most of those who practised the same profession at the same time. This was the soil in which the journalism of the eighteenth century was nurtured: a soil natural to the age and no more sour than that in which most of the century's politics and a good deal of its social life were rooted.

But John Walter I had one quality more important in the perspective of time than any of these defects. And he had one remarkable piece of good fortune. The quality was tenacity. With it went good sense. Starting as the producer of a mediocre commercial sheet he recognised more quickly than most the implications of the revolution in newspaper production brought about by Bell's innovations and reorganised his paper accordingly. Under its new and handier title of *The Times,* the *Daily Universal Register* brightened both its appearance and style, taking on new writers for the purpose. Nor did it hesitate to outstrip even the *World* in the provision of scandal and innuendo. But Walter had the wit quickly to recognise the changing public taste brought by the French Revolution. Gossip and scandal had served well. Now, as at all times of great crisis, what newspaper readers wanted was hard news. With every new day interest in public affairs mounted, touching every level of society. The era of journalistic flippancy that Bell had inaugurated and that Walter had been delighted to exploit was over.

Although deeply involved in his own personal difficulties, for he was in the midst of preparing his unsuccessful reply to the charge of libelling the Royal Dukes, John Walter bent all his energy to the task of organising a news service from the Continent, laying in the process the foundations of that pre-eminence in the field of foreign reporting that was later to give *The Times* its great authority. Moreover he was quick to recognise that events of such magnitude required wholly new treatment in space and typographical display and on the very eve of his imprisonment completely reorganised the make-up of the paper, bringing out—odd though it now seems to think of *The Times* in this guise—paper with headlines larger and more sensational than had ever been seen in any newspaper before: the *Mirror* of its time. Nor even in prison did he allow his own misery to interfere with his awareness of the needs of his paper. During the whole of his enforced stay in Newgate he continued to exhort his staff to fresh efforts in securing news sources abroad.

It is doubtful whether, even so, *The Times* would have survived all the other journals of the time or John Walter I be remembered except as a minor name in the history of eighteenth-century journalism had not good fortune come to his aid. He was a business man, not a journalist. His luck lay in the fact that although his eldest son was neither, his second son, John Walter II, was not only a better business man than his father but possessed, what he did not, a burning integrity and a passion for independence. It was to this second son that John Walter I passed the management of the paper when he himself returned to his real interest, the printing business. Yet even so the father scarcely deserved the luck that made him the founder of the most famous newspaper dynasty in history. He quarrelled with his son and cut him off in his will with only a tiny minority interest in *The Times*, a mere three-sixteenths of the shares instead of the full possession his son had been led to expect. However, even in anger he was at least enough of a newspaper-man to realise that 'the conduct and interest of a newspaper concern requires the most absolute power in the persons carrying on the same in making allowance and payment at their discretion.' Although he refused to leave to his second son the financial control he hoped for he made it a condition of his other bequests that 'my son John continue to have the sole management.'

By these means the future of *The Times* was secured. John Walter I founded it. But it was John Walter II and the remarkable editor, Thomas Barnes, whom he had the good fortune to discover and to whom he gave an editorial freedom such as no other employee of a newspaper had ever possessed, who made it great. In so doing they won independence not only for *The Times* but for the whole of the British press.